PENGUIN  CLASSICS

JOHN CLARE: SELECTED POEMS

JOHN CLARE was born in Helpstone, Northamptonshire, in 1793. The son of a labourer, he worked variously as a ploughboy, reaper and thresher. Although his mother was illiterate and his father barely literate, Clare himself early became an avid reader and began to write verse at the age of thirteen. As a youth, he fell in love with Mary Joyce, a local farmer's daughter, but their relationship ended around 1816, seemingly at the insistence of her father. Her memory, however, was to haunt him for the rest of his life.

It was in 1820 that his first book, *Poems Descriptive of Rural Life*, was published. He went to London, met many literary figures and in the same year married Patty (Martha) Turner. His second volume of poems, *The Village Minstrel*, appeared in 1821 and, two years later, he began to plan a long ambitious poem, *The Shepherd's Calendar*, which appeared, severely edited, in 1827.

Meanwhile, however, his health was showing signs of serious trouble. He had bouts of severe melancholy, doubt and hopelessness, brought on perhaps by his disassociation from all that was familiar to him and a sense of not having securely arrived somewhere else. In 1821, at the instigation of well-meaning friends, he left his native cottage for Northborough, but the move was disturbing and served only to reinforce the theme of loss in his work.

In June 1837, little improved by the publication of *The Rural Muse* (1835), he was admitted to an asylum at High Beech, Epping. He escaped in 1841, walking home to Northamptonshire in the delusion that he would be reunited with Mary, to whom he thought himself married. She had died, a spinster, in 1838, and after five months with his family, he was again taken away, this time to Northampton General Lunatic Asylum. He died there in 1864.

JOHN CLARE
SELECTED POEMS

Edited with an introduction and notes by
GEOFFREY SUMMERFIELD

PENGUIN BOOKS

PENGUIN BOOKS

Published by the Penguin Group
Penguin Books Ltd, 80 Strand, London WC2R 0RL, England
Penguin Putnam Inc., 375 Hudson Street, New York, New York 10014, USA
Penguin Books Australia Ltd, 250 Camberwell Road, Camberwell, Victoria 3124, Australia
Penguin Books Canada Ltd, 10 Alcorn Avenue, Toronto, Ontario, Canada M4V 3B2
Penguin Books India (P) Ltd, 11 Community Centre, Panchsheel Park, New Delhi – 110 017, India
Penguin Books (NZ) Ltd, Cnr Rosedale and Airborne Roads, Albany, Auckland, New Zealand
Penguin Books (South Africa) (Pty) Ltd, 24 Sturdee Avenue, Rosebank 2196, South Africa

Penguin Books Ltd, Registered Offices: 80 Strand, London WC2R 0RL, England

www.penguin.com

This selection first published in Penguin Books 1990
Reprinted with first line and title indexes 2000

5

Selection, Introduction and Notes copyright ©
Geoffrey Summerfield, 1990
All rights reserved

Copyright in the unpublished and in much of the published work of John Clare
is owned by Professor Eric Robinson who has together with Oxford University
Press authorized this publication. Requests for permission to reproduce any of
the poems in this anthology should be addressed to Curtis Brown Group Ltd,
162–168 Regent Street, London WIR 5TB. The editor and the publishers thank
Professor Robinson, the Oxford University Press and Curtis Brown Ltd,
London, for particular permission to reproduce the following poems: 'Summer
Evening', 'Crows in Spring', 'Sunday with Shepherds and Herdboys', 'Snow
Storm', 'To the Snipe', 'The Martin', 'The Hedgehog', 'The Fox', 'The
Badger', 'Dedication to Mary', 'I've ran the furlong', 'The Mores' (from *Selected
Poems and Prose of John Clare*, Oxford University Press, copyright © Eric
Robinson 1967), and 'The Lament of Swordy Well' (from Oxford Authors *John
Clare*, Oxford University Press, copyright © Eric Robinson 1984).

Printed in England by Clays Ltd, St Ives plc
Filmset in Linotron Bembo

CONTENTS

ACKNOWLEDGEMENTS

My most immediate debt is to friends who have offered generous encouragement: David Erdman, Marilyn Gaull, Hugh Haughton, Seamus Heaney, John Holloway and Adam Phillips. I am indebted also to the perceptive critical commentaries of Tim Chilcott and Tom Frosch; to Mark Storey's splendid edition of Clare's letters; to Kelsey Thornton for perceptive advice; to John Maynard for his magnanimity; and to Eileen Joyce, Eleanor Nicholes and Jean Paira-Pemberton for their acute observations on Clare's mind.

I am pleased to acknowledge the generous cooperation of the librarians at Northampton, Peterborough, the Bodleian Library and New York University Library; also of Microform Academic of Wakefield, especially of Michelle Mortimer. My work was supported in part by a grant from New York University's Research Challenge Fund, and for this I am grateful.

My thanks are due also to Paul Keegan for the invitation, to Peter Sharpe for the loan of his eyes, and to my wife, Judith, for she-knows-what.

I wish to dedicate this book to: Jerome Bruner, David Hammond and Ted Hughes.

Geoffrey Summerfield
New York, 1988

INTRODUCTION

John Clare's poetry is primarily a celebration and affirmation of life: of human life and of all forms of natural life – of animals, birds, insects; of the dawn and dusk and of the seasons; of the soil and of weather; of trees, rivers, sunlight and cloud. But it is also, inescapably, a song of sorrow and mourning, of loss, deracination and disenchantment. Delight and sorrow co-exist and interact, each rendering the other more intensely poignant.

When Clare was young, he enjoyed the common illusion that the natural order, the world as given, was eternal, a safe stronghold, a protected space: his early poetry is an unexceptionable expression of such confidence: secure verse presenting a secure world. As he began, however, to know the sharper vicissitudes of human intention and hope, his poetry, in order to continue to be true, learned to register and incorporate all those contingencies that threaten to make of any life, of any mind, a diminished thing: time, circumstance, mutability, loss, defeat and the less benign aspects of human culture.

The compliant naivety of childhood that leads us to accept our early environment without question as 'natural', was in Clare's case well justified, for he grew up in a world that seemed to a considerable degree unmarked by human hands. It was in his youth and early manhood that 'improvements' began to dismember what had been a relatively unspoilt, organic-seeming landscape: pastures were put to the plough; trees and shrubs uprooted; streams re-routed and tidied up; fens drained; common land enclosed. Dikes, ditches, drains, embankments, new or improved roads reshaped the landscape irrevocably, just as the railways were to do again in mid-century.

The delicate and harmonious balance of nature and culture, manifest in the richness of wildlife cheek by jowl with village paths and stiles – this was disrupted with a determination, a mania for improvement, that struck Clare's snail-horn sensitivity as a calamity, a destruction of Eden, an act of monstrous sacrilege. It is, then, hardly surprising that Clare's poetry takes on a clamatory and elegiac note, a note of urgency, protest and grief, so that he both compassionates with wild things turned out of their homes and comminates the more systematized and efficient agriculture that imposed on his fellow-villagers a new and demeaned economic status and a raw despoliation of their hitherto stable landscape. For Clare, poetry became his best way of registering such dreadful loss and of crying out against it: and his subtext from henceforth was to be the resonant and inclusive myth of the loss of Eden. Thus, willy-nilly, he found his theme, his theme found him.

Such was the general predicament – a breaking of old ties, the felling of sacred trees, an obliteration of preconscious rhythms, the mortal damage to old unquestioned ways – but Clare's individual plight intensified his perceptions of such change; for his trauma was not a matter merely of a general plight, a deleterious change in the culture of the rural poor, further exacerbated by the economic consequences of the Napoleonic wars; it was also the peculiar tragedy of a man, an individual, in limbo. As a spectator, he inhabited the role of a literary onlooker, re-reading his society and his landscape from points of view, through perspectives and lenses, derived from his readings in eighteenth-century topographical and philosophical poetry and botany. Once having tasted of the fruit of such trees of knowledge, how could he ever again feel himself to be at home with illiterate and even brutalized tillers of the soil? At the same time, how could he hope effectively to become, to be, a poet? How find an economically viable life's work as a poet? He remained, to all intents and purposes, a day-labourer, counting his pennies, following the plough, a muddy rustic with straw in his hair and a non-standard dialect on his lips.

Economic necessity, the daily burden of feeding a family and keeping a roof over their heads, pressed down hard on him, even as he felt confusingly alienated from his unquestioning illiterate neighbours. He ended, thus, in a no man's land, where he was neither spectator nor participant, exiled by his dreams of metropolitan literary recognition, and yet tugged back in to local dailiness by his need to earn a shilling and by his dependence on the more primal, oral, local roots of the village and its landscape.

In his maturity as a poet, in his middle years, 1820–35, we see him achieving a precarious balancing act, holding in suspense these conflicting elements, both achieving a coherent literariness and also finding the confidence, the resourcefulness, the integrity, to acknowledge and in-corporate in his poetry the gifts of his oral tradition, both of story and song.

But his moments of individuation, of reconcilement, of achieved coherence, were snatched from the long and severe turmoil of a total distress: social, intellectual, vocational and emotional. There is, even yet, no clinical consensus about Clare's mind and its wounds,* and no categorical endorsement or denial of the judgements of those who nudged Clare into the confinement of a lunatic asylum. But it is clear from his manuscripts, both his poems and his letters, that under emotional, vocational and economic stress, his fantasies, both positive and negative, slipped over into periodic delusion, and poetic fictions lurched crazily into bouts of hallucination. The tensions that possessed and wracked him – tensions between an irretrievable Edenic past and a pressing, bleak prospect of loss and confinement – these tensions drove him sporadically into something close to schizophrenia or paranoia. Yet, even so, his spiritual strength, his peasant resilience, were such that at times he could transform these tensions into the penetrating eloquence and achieved, stabilizing form of song, of lyric, of elegy, making resonant harmony out of radical discord. And his more extended later poems, written by or through a Byronic persona – such poems derive considerable energy and power from an often savage dialogue between hope and despair, memory and desire, what might have been and what was.

Salient moments in his life's wretched chronology include: 1820 and 1821, the publication of his first two volumes; 1820, 1822, 1824, his visits to London to meet the literary lions and to be both honoured and patronized as a 'green man'; 1824–7, his struggles with Taylor, his publisher, to agree on publishing his *Shepherd's Calendar*; 1832, his enforced move from Helpstone, his birthplace, to Northborough; 1835, publication of his *Rural Muse*; 1837–41, his term in High Beech Lunatic Asylum, Epping Forest; 1841, his escape, followed by his removal to Northampton Asylum; 1841–64, his confinement at Northampton.

Clare was born in Helpstone, midway between Peterborough and Stamford, near Peterborough Great Fen. His mother was illiterate; his father, barely literate, had a good repertoire of folk-songs. According to the law of averages, Clare should have become an agricultural labourer, earning a bare subsistence wage, and in possession, at best, of a merely functional literacy.

Aroused, however, by oral tales and chapbook romances, he early became an avid reader; and when he was thirteen, his reading of Thompson's *Seasons* excited him so intensely that he began to write verse. When he had learned to read and write, he had become something of an exception: when he committed himself to writing poetry, he became an anomaly.

Still a boy, he set to earn his living by selling the labour of his hands: he worked variously as a ploughboy, as a reaper and thresher, a jobbing-gardener, and at lime-burning. And while still a young man, he fell in love with Mary Joyce, a local farmer's daughter. Their relationship ended around 1816, seemingly at the insistence of her father. Clare was to be haunted by her 'presence' almost to his dying day.

In 1820, as a result of some fortunate contacts, his first book, *Poems Descriptive of Rural Life and Scenery*, was published; he visited London and, through his publisher, John Taylor, met many literary figures; and he married Patty Turner, who was already six months pregnant with their child. His book quickly went into four editions, and he became a nine-days' wonder.

His second volume, *The Village Minstrel*, appeared in 1821, and two years later he began to plan a long, ambitious poem, *The Shepherd's Calendar*, which appeared after many frustrations and delays in 1827. His health first showed signs of serious trouble in 1823, and from then on he was visited by bouts of severe melancholy, severe doubt and hopelessness. His emotional/ nervous afflictions have been posthumously subjected to various analyses; the most plausible diagnosis seems to be a manic-depressive condition in which he became periodically psychotic.

In 1828, he paid his fourth visit to London; in 1830, a sixth child was born; and in 1830 and 1831 he again suffered a severe and prolonged illness. Friends and patrons joined in a well-meaning scheme for his relief, which involved moving him and his family to a more commodious cottage, with a modest smallholding, in the village of Northborough, about two and a half miles – as the crow flies – from Helpstone, and about three and a half miles by road.

His work up to about 1825 is predominately a prolific series of celebrations of delight in perceiving and representing natural life, and an exploration of the relationships of a hardworking lowly human society to its rural environment and the cycle of the year, with its swing between benign summer and bleak winter.

'What are days for?' asked Philip Larkin in a celebrated poem. 'Days are where we live . . . They are to be happy in . . .' Clare's representations of his days and seasons, times and places, appear to endorse Larkin's conclusion. The microcosm of the moment, like the macrocosm of the season – each is celebrated as offering its own distinctive satisfactions, and in his earlier poetry Clare seems to be possessed by the particular vividness of moments and of local places. As Tim Chilcott has remarked, these poems construct and mediate a vivid sense of presentness and of simultaneity. Their achievements, their numbers and their effects can be summed up in one word: plenitude. Given his acutely responsive – and appreciative – sensibility, there was always something worthy of his keenest attention.

Structurally, most of his earlier poems are relatively simple, especially in their syntax, which lies closer to the rhythms of a speaking voice than to those of prose: their subtlety and richness are to be found, not in a sophisticated syntax, but in an intimately absorbed attentiveness to commonplaces – the ordinary is embraced and transformed by the intensity of attention into the extraordinary – and in a stubborn belief in the mimetic sufficiency of ordinary local language, a dialect which registered a special acuity of perception in the realm of elemental sensation. The relationships between word and world appear to be perfectly harmonious and unstrained, as if that which Clare perceived could speak with its own voice.

For over twenty-six years, the constraints of the sonnet and of the rhyming couplet provided Clare with two of his most congenial and elastic frames; and as he became well-versed in the seventeenth-century poets, on some of whom he fathered some of his own poems, and drew more deeply and more surely on English folk-song, so he developed his own distinctive lyricism, and reaffirmed spoken song as one of the distinctive gifts of the English-speaking poetic genius.

By 1832, some difficult truths had shaken Clare's delicate and vulnerable sensibility: very early he had made the crucial and irreversible shift from a primarily oral culture to a literate and literary culture. But even as his work was in fact published, meeting with a confusing variety of responses from his readers, the integrity of his vision and of his native language was challenged and compromised by well-meaning friends, patrons and editors, and he continued inescapably to live among people to whom poetry was a closed book. His own wife could not share his life as a poet, and Mary Joyce had been absent from his life for over ten years but continued obsessively to engage his deepest and most intense feelings, an emblem of what might have been.

All aspects of his experience, all his social and literary relationships, served to enforce his sense of having left familiar ground yet of not having securely arrived somewhere else; he discovered himself to be adrift, in limbo, an anomalous and wrong-footed misfit: liminal man, in no man's land, stuck at some kind of threshold, unable to go either back or forward. Even his sacral landscape had proved impermanent, despoiled often beyond recognition by the 'improvements' of enclosure.

Such was Clare's predicament, in which the move to Northborough proved to be the last straw: an intended amelioration of his plight merely served to exacerbate his sense of alienation. In June 1837, little improved by the appearance of *The Rural Muse* (1835), he was taken to Dr Matthew Allen's private asylum at High Beech in Epping Forest. He spent just over four years there; his physical health improved considerably, but his mental condition showed little change. He resolved the matter for himself by running away – escaping – in July 1841, and walked all the way to Northborough in search of 'home' and in the hope of being reunited with his 'first wife', Mary Joyce. She had died, a spinster, in 1838: when his family told him of this, he did not believe them.

After five months with his family, 'homeless at home', he was removed in December 1841 – he was allowed to wait until after Christmas but was taken before he could say, or hear, 'A Happy New Year' – to Northampton General Lunatic Asylum. There he was treated humanely and allowed generous freedom of movement until his misbehaviour resulted in confinement to the asylum grounds. He died there, 20 May 1864, and was buried at Helpstone five days later.

In 1832, Clare was midway in his life as a poet; under the various stresses and limits of his circumstances, his poetry was undergoing a deep change. No longer could he find a seemingly inexhaustible delight in the 'eternal recurrence of common order'; no longer did he find himself 'rapt with satisfied attention . . . to the mere spectacle of the world's presence – one way, and the most fundamental way, of confessing one's sense of its unfathomable significance'; no longer was he able to believe that 'life is always worth living if one have . . . responsive sensibilities'. * On the contrary, a deepening sense of disenchantment, of loss and alienation, of having lost his way, threatened to overwhelm the impulse to celebrate the affirmation of joy and delight.

How, then, to resolve the tensions, the collisions and contradictions of the positive and the negative charges? Was any kind of integration, of resolution, possible? His earlier answer – corresponding presumably to his manic-depressive swings of mood – had been to keep them separate, to channel them into two different kinds of poetry, affirmative and elegiac. But from about 1830 on, he was increasingly disposed to let them fight it out within the same, one, text; as a result his poetry realizes a richer and more complex tension, in poems that enact the often savage interplay of his inner dialectic. So his poetry continued, but also modulated: on occasions it reverted, even to the end of his life, to a spare melodic lyricism, close to folk-song: on the other hand, and increasingly so, it unravelled as an endless, seamless interwoven sequence of meditations, reflections, speculations, arguments, self-communings, appeals, accusations, rejoinders, speaking out of the unresolvable quarrel between the claims of the heaven and of the hell which pressed in on his purgatorial soul. In one sense, he evolved a less rich poetry, less rich in terms of sheer sensuous registration – 'a few weathered images/on the bottom of the burned-out eye' (Z. Herbert); in another, he came to make a richer poetry, richer for realizing the energies of a mind in conflict with itself.

Clare's reputation during his lifetime flared briefly like a shooting star, waned and disappeared into a limbo of neglect. Posthumously, it has progressed in fits and starts; but in every generation since his death he has been briefly rediscovered, most conspicuously by Edmund Blunden and Alan Porter after World War I; by Anne Tibble and her husband in the 1930s; and by Geoffrey

Grigson during World War II. His critical reputation has always been problematical; academics have tended to cling to received opinion: romantic poetry had achieved a kind of definition by the mid-nineteenth century, and was known to comprise Wordsworth, Coleridge, Keats, Byron and Shelley. This constellation has persisted, like holy writ, consigning Clare to the outer ditches and hedgerows. The poets, however, have known better: Edward Thomas, Robert Graves, Blunden, James Reeves, Dylan Thomas, John Hewitt, Theodore Roethke, Charles Causley, John Fowles, Ted Hughes and Seamus Heaney have all borne witness to his fructifying presence in their lives as readers and writers. In so doing, they have taught us that to ask, 'Is John Clare a major poet?' is to ask the wrong (pecking-order) question; they have, conversely, taught us to recognize what he, distinctively, can continue to give us: what it is that, variously, we can discover and rediscover; how we can be animated and reanimated through listening to him: a joyful, even ecstatic, obliteration of self in the act of attending; responsiveness to all forms of life; how to speak of vicissitude and loss; how to love local truths, and how to treasure our parochial blessings, and all that our infatuation with Progress would destroy. As Seamus Heaney has written, 'it was the unique achievement of John Clare to make vocal the regional and particular, to achieve a buoyant and authentic lyrical utterance at the meeting-point between social realism and conventional romanticism.' And, again, Heaney has helped us to recognize how John Clare 'lived near the abyss but resolved extreme experience into something infinitely gentle'. *

A NOTE ON THE TEXT

The texts of John Clare's poems are particularly vulnerable, in a variety of ways.

Texts published during his lifetime were the result of an unsatisfactory compromise between his own intentions and pressures from his patrons and publishers. Differences centred not only on the sentiments expressed, but also on Clare's use of the syntax and lexicon of his own non-standard dialect, which was construed as 'provincial' and lower class or vulgar.

For reasons that are not altogether clear, Clare himself was impatient of the conventions of punctuation and, with few exceptions, his own manuscripts are unpunctuated. Again, his spelling is, to modern eyes with benefit of dictionaries, deviant: he consistently wrote 'hugh' for 'huge', 'loose' for 'lose', 'then' for 'than' and 'childern' for 'children', for example. Many other words he spelled inconsistently. Again, in his own manuscripts, the syntax is that of his local dialect, especially in the vexed matter of subject–verb agreement. Should Clare's poems then be published exactly as they appear in his manuscripts?

In 1961, when Eric Robinson and I began to transcribe Clare's poems from the manuscripts in Northampton Library, we realised at once that the undertaking did indeed require two pairs of eyes. For about four years we worked our way through many of the manuscripts, both at Northampton and at Peterborough; for personal reasons, I then turned to other tasks. Eric Robinson, helped by others, continues the work of transcribing and editing John Clare to this day. Two volumes of the Early Poems (1804–1822) and two volumes of the Later Poems (1837–1864) have thus far been published by the Clarendon Press, Oxford.

Our initial work of transcription was provoked simply by the obvious inaccuracy of published texts, especially by Geoffrey Grigson's *Poems of John Clare's Madness*: we decided, therefore, to aim for an absolutely literal transcription, and that was the policy that Robinson and I employed in our editions of Clare in 1964, 1966 and 1967.

For the purposes of the present volume, my decision has been to respect the spirit of that editorial policy, but to make changes where the idiosyncrasies of Clare's manuscripts would merely distract the reader and do nothing for the peculiar integrity of the text. Clearly, a policy of non-intervention can be said to respect the integrity of Clare's *own* writing: and what else *is* there? Some readers are pleased to know that they are reading a text that is as close as may be to Clare's own hand. Others argue that no writer's text should be published without the benefit of the standard conventions – orthographic, syntactical and punctuation – of published texts.

The question is complicated by the status of the surviving manuscripts. To generalize, these fall into three rough categories: undated fragments of work in progress: parts of texts to be incorporated into a whole text; undated drafts of complete texts; and undated manuscripts that are some kind of fair copy prepared by a publisher or amanuensis, to provide the printer with a manuscript from which to set up printed copy. In the second and third categories, the relationship between Clare's own intentions and any particular text is not clear. There are no annotations to signify that, yes, *this* is the version that Clare himself approved as a 'final', print-ready version. In the Northampton years, the problem is further compounded by a progressive decline in Clare's own control over any text, and by the fact that most of the Northampton poems survive only in the form of Knight's transcripts. But even a cursory reading of Knight's texts demonstrates that many of the poems are *over*-punctuated in ways that sometimes run counter to the structure and sense of the text, and there is also some evidence of bowdlerizing.

Given such a confusing context, a reader is entitled to know exactly what any printed text offers: what editorial policy has been chosen. Let me, therefore, spell out my policy for this volume. In texts which derive from a re-examination of unpunctuated manuscript sources – most of the poetry included in this volume – I have *added* apostrophes to indicate the possessive and abbreviations; a minimum of on-line punctuation in places where the syntax is ambiguous; and, in order to minimize the need to read twice before identifying the intended meaning, some changes of spelling (e.g., breathes/breaths; ne'er/near; where/were). I have added question marks whenever they are needed to clarify the text. I have also given 'and' for the ampersand, and capitalized all names.

In poems which derive from transcripts or from earlier published texts I have removed some of the editorial punctuation to move the text rather closer to Clare's unpunctuated manuscripts.

In those few instances where a word in an unedited manuscript text is clearly an error or oversight, I have made a silent correction.

In general, I have used no convention or spelling which is not to be found somewhere in Clare's own manuscript.

For the sources of all texts in this edition, see pp. 362–3.

SELECTED POETRY

DAYS AND SEASONS

Clare's day is the day of the agricultural labourer – rising with the sunrise and marking the passage of time not with watch or clock but with shifts of light, the passage of the sun, the activities of birds and beasts, the rhythms of manual labour. It is a day of sustained physical labour, more or less exhausting. When he observes the activities of other people's days, he tends to focus on those whose tasks are immemorial – the milkmaid, the shepherd and the ploughboy, working in a rural economy that offered a tolerable level of subsistence, until the effects of enclosure changed the economy of the village for the worse, and the Napoleonic Wars were followed by severe inflation.

Where, then, is Clare in all this? Is he creating a representative scene from a gentlemanly aesthetic distance or is he, so to speak, observing himself at work? Under the influence of the poets of the eighteenth century, he veers toward the former; but as he grows into a recognition of his own social position, he tends toward the latter. It seems to have taken him many years to resolve this contradiction, but when he acquires the confidence to write from a participant's position, his poetry embraces with increasing confidence the expressive idiosyncrasies of his own native dialect and a more nervously vibrant sense of momentariness. Because his early literary models were of the eighteenth century – genteel and cultivated – he swings between a detached kind of visitor's connoisseurship, composing 'typical' vignettes in which the rustics figure as 'clowns' or as pastoral idealizations, and an insider's view, which provides a more authentic sense of rural life.

Clare's year is clearly apprehended as a cycle of seasons, each with its own distinctive tones and emotions; and here again he first inherits, absorbs and gradually abandons many of the conventions of eighteenth-century pastoral poetry, learning to trust both the intensity and the intimacy of his own distinctive sensibility, acute in its perceptions, sensitive in its apprehensions, and finding expression in the 'dialect of his tribe'. In his winter poems he celebrates the modest comforts and oral traditions of his own class: the exigencies of outdoor labour are never far from his mind; conversely his winter-evening vignettes convey a sense of modest contentment, despite the persistence of age-old superstitious fears. Spring and summer both invite him to the evocation and praise of plenitude, of immemorial assurances, of nature's beneficence and a realization of living growth, of an organic burgeoning that is almost erotic in its intensity. Autumn, probably his favorite season, offers both fulfilment and melancholy, harvest fruits and a most vivid sense of transience. His early poetry is mostly innocent of negative tendencies, and only in the more inclusive poetry of his early maturity does he begin to register and explore the pains and contradictions of rural England in a cruel time.

EARLY IMAGES*

Come early morning with thy mealy grey
Moist grass and fitful gales that winnow soft
And frequent – I'll be up with early day
And roam the social way where passing oft
The milking maid who greets the pleasant morn
And shepherd with his hook in folded arm
Rocking along accross the bending corn
And hear the many sounds from distant farm
Of cackling hens and turkeys gobbling loud
And teams just plodding on their way to plough
Down russet tracks that strip the closen green
And hear the mellow low of distant cow
And see the mist up-creeping like a cloud
From hollow places in the early scene

And mark the jerking swallow jerk and fling
Its flight o'er new-mown meadows happily
And cuckoo quivering upon narrow wing
Take sudden flitting from the neighbouring tree
And heron stalking solitary thing
Mount up into high travel far away
And that mild indecision hanging round
Skys holding bland communion with the ground
In gentlest pictures of the infant day
Now picturing rain – while many a pleasing sound
Grows mellower distant in the mealy grey
Of dewy pastures and full many a sight
Seems sweeter in its indistinct array
Than when it glows in morning's stronger light

THE MORNING WIND

There's more then music in this early wind
Awaking like a bird refreshed from sleep
And joy what Adam might in Eden find
When he with angels did communion keep
It breathes all balm and insence from the sky
Blessing the husbandman with freshening powers
Joy's manna from its wings doth fall and lie
Harvests for early wakers with the flowers
The very grass in joy's devotion moves
Cowslaps in adoration and delight
This way and that bow to the breath they love
Of the young winds that with the dew pearls play
Till smoking chimneys sicken the young light
And feeling's fairey visions fade away

THE WHEAT RIPENING*

What time the wheat field tinges rusty brown
And barley bleaches in its mellow grey
'Tis sweet some smooth-mown baulk to wander down
Or cross the fields on footpath's narrow way
Just in the mealy light of waking day
As glittering dewdrops moist the maiden's gown
And sparkling bounces from her nimble feet
Journeying to milking from the neighbouring town
Making life bright with song – and it is sweet
To mark the grazing herds and list' the clown
Urge on his ploughing team with cheering calls
And merry shepherd's whistling toils begun
And hoarse-tongued bird-boy whose unceasing calls
Join the lark's ditty to the rising sun

A MORNING WALK*

Ah sure it is a lovely day
As ever summer's glory yields
And I will put my books away
And wander in the fields
Just risen is the red round sun
Cocks from the roost doth loudly bawl
And house bee busily begun
Hums round the mortered wall

And while I take my staff to start
Birds sing among the eldern leaves
And fighting sparrows glad at heart
Chirp in the cottage eaves
Nor can I help but turn and view
Ere yet I close the creaking door
The sunbeams eager peeping through
Upon the sanded floor

The twilight streaks of lightsome grey
Hath from the Eastern summit gone
And clouds cloathed in the pride of day
Put golden liverys on
The creeping sun large round and red
Yet higher hastens up and higher
Till blazing o'er its cloudy bed
It shines a ball of fire

Cows now their morning meals pursue
The carthorse to its labour's sped
And sheep shake off the nightly dew
Just risen from their bed
The maids are out and many a smile
Are left them by the passing swain
Who as they lightly skip the stile
Will turn and smile again

All nightly things are on the run*
By daylight's burning smiles betrayed
And gnats retreating from the sun
Fly dancing to the shade
The snail is stealing from the light
Where grass a welcome shelter weaves
And white moths shrink in cool delight
Behind the bowering leaves

The hares their fearful morsels eat
Till by a snufling dog descried
Then hastening to their snug retreat
They waited eventide
The rabbit bustled out of sight
Nor longer cropt each thymy hill
But seeks his den where gloomy night
Is kept imprisoned still

The walks that sweetest pleasure yields
When things appear so fresh and fair
Are when we wander round the fields
To breathe the morning air
The fields like spring seem young and gay
The dewy trees and painted sky
And larks as sweetly as in May
Still whistle as they fly

The woods that oft my steps recieves
I cannot search for resting bowers
For when I touch the sleepy leaves
Dews patter down in showers
But I can range the green and share
The charms the pasture scene displays
Crooking down sheep tracks here and there
That lead a thousand ways

Bowing dewdropping by the stream
The flowers glow lively on the sight
Awaking from night's summer dream
As conscious of delight
Nor could I crop them in such hours
Without regret that I'd destroyed
A joy in my companion flowers
As sweet as I enjoyed

The stinking finweed's blushing bloom
Their pea-like flowers appear so fair
That bees will to their bosoms come
And hope for honey there
For bumble bees ere flowers are dry
Will wake and brush the trembling dew
And drone as mellancholy by
When dreams are proved untrue

While waving rushbeds winding through
I idly swing my staff about
To free their tasseled tops from dew
The leveret startles out
And now the lark starts from its nest
But not to sing – on thistle nigh
It perks in fear and prunes its breast
Till I have journeyed bye

The resting cow just turns its head
To stare then chews its cud again
The colt more timid leaves its bed
And shakes its shaggy main
The shoy sheep flye and faster still
The wet grass smoking 'neath their flight
When shepherds urged their whistles shrill
And dogs appear in sight

Still there is joy that will not cease
Calm hovering o'er the face of things
That sweet tranquility and peace
That morning ever brings
The shadows by the sun portrayed
Lye basking in the golden light
E'en little hillocks stretch their shade
As if they loved the sight

The brook seemed purling sweeter by
As freshened from the cooling light
And on its breast the morning sky
Smiles beautiful and bright
The pool's still depth as night was by
Warmed as to life in curling rings
Stirred by the touch of water flye
Or zepher's gentle wings

And cows did on its margin lie
As blest as morn would never cease
And knapping horse grazed slowly by
That added to its peace
No flies disturbed the herding boys
Save flies the summer water breeds
That harmless shared the morning's joys
And hummed among the weeds

Birds fluttered round the water's brink
Then perched their dabbled wings to dry
And swallows often stooped to drink
And twittered gladly bye
And on the brook-bank's rushy ridge
Larks sat the morning sun to share
And doves where ivy hides the bridge
Sing soothing dittys there

The leaves of ash and elms and willows
That skirt the pasture's wildered way
Heaved to the breeze in gentle billows
Of mingled green and grey
The birds the breeze the milker's call
The brook that in the sun did glisten
Told morn's delight that smiled on all
As one that loves to listen

O who can shun the lovely morning
The calms the crowds of beautious things
O where's the soul that treats with scorning
The beauty morning brings
With dewdrops braided round her hair
And opening flowers her breast adorning
O where's the soul that cannot share
The loveliness of morning

By hedgerow side and field and brook
I love to be its partner still
To turn each leaf of nature's book
Where all may read as will
And he who loves it not destroys
His quiet and makes life a slave
His soul is dead to loves and joys
His own heart is their grave

The very boys appear to share
The joy of morning's lovely hours
In rapture running here and there
To stick their hats with flowers
Some loll them by a resting stile
To listen pleasing things around –
Dove lark and bee – and try the while
To imitate the sound

The shepherd muses o'er his hook
And quiet as the morning seems
Or reads some wild mysterious book*
On 'fortunes, moles and dreams'
While by his side as blest as he
His dog in peaceful slumber lies
Unwakened as he used to be
To watch the teazing flies

Rapt in delight I long have stood
Gazing on scenes that seem to smile
And now to view far field and wood
I climb this battered stile
There sails the puddock still and proud
Assailed at first by swopping crows
But soon it meets the morning cloud
And scorns such humble foes

The mist that round the distance bent
By woodland side and slopeing hill
Fled as each minute came and went
More far and further still
And the blue tinge which night renewed
Round the horison's fairey way
More faster than the eye pursued
Shrank unpercieved away

By leaning trees beneath the swail
For pleasing things I love to look
Or loll o'er oak brig's guarding rail
That strideth o'er the brook
To mark above the willow row
The painted windmill's peeping sails
Seeming in its journey slow
Pleased with the easy gentle gales

And oft I sit me on the ground
Musing upon a neighbouring flower
Or list' the church-clock's humming sound*
To count the passing hour
Or mark the brook its journey take
In gentle curves round many a weed
Or hear the soft wind first awake
Among the rustling reed

THE HEAT OF NOON

There lies a sultry lusciousness around
The far-stretched pomp of summer which the eye
Views with a dazzled gaze – and gladly bounds
Its prospects to some pastoral spots that lie
Nestling among the hedge, confining grounds
Where in some nook the haystacks newly made
Scents the smooth level meadow-land around
While underneath the woodland's hazley hedge
The crowding oxen make their swaily beds
And in the dry dyke thronged with rush and sedge
The restless sheep rush in to hide their heads
From the unlost and ever haunting flie
And under every tree's projecting shade
Places as battered as the road is made

SUMMER EVENING

The sinken sun is takin' leave
And sweetly gilds the edge of eve
While purple clouds of deepening dye
Huddling hang the western skye
Crows crowd quaking over head
Hastening to the woods to bed

Cooing sits the lonely dove
Calling home her abscent love
Kirchip kirchip 'mong the wheat
Partridge distant partridge greet
Beckening call to those that roam
Guiding the squandering covey home
Swallows check their rambling flight
And twittering on the chimney light
Round the pond the martins flirt
Their snowy breasts bedawbd in dirt
While the mason 'neath the slates
Each morter-bearing bird awaits
Untaught by art each labouring spouse
Curious daubs his hanging house
Bats flit by in hood and cowl
Thro' the barn hole pops the owl
From the hedge the beetles boom
Heedless buz and drousy hum
Haunting every bushy place
Flopping in the labourer's face
Now the snail has made his ring
And the moth with snowy wing
Fluttring plays from bent to bent
Bending down with dews besprent
Then on resting branches hing
Strength to ferry* o'er the spring
From the haycocks' moistend heaps
Frogs now take their vaunting leaps
And along the shaven mead
Quickly travelling they proceed
Flying from their speckled sides
Dewdrops bounce as grass divides
Now the blue fog creeps along,
And the bird's forgot his song:
Flowrets sleep within their hoods
Daisys button into buds
From soiling dew the buttercup

Shuts his golden jewels up
And the rose and woodbine they
Wait again the smiles of day
'Neath the willow's wavy boughs
Nelly singing milks her cows
While the streamlet bubling bye
Joins in murmuring melody

Now the hedger hides his bill
And with his faggot climbs the hill
Driver Giles wi' rumbling joll
And blind Ball jostles home the roll
Whilom Ralph for Doll to wait
Lolls him o'er the pasture gate
Swains to fold their sheep begin
Dogs bark loud to drive 'em in
Ploughmen from their furrowy seams
Loose the weary fainting teams
Ball, wi' cirging lashes weald
Still so slow to drive afield,
Eager blundering from the plough
Wants no whip to drive him now
At the stable door he stands
Looking round for friendly hands
To loose the door its fastening pin
Ungear him now and let him in
Round the Yard a thousand ways
The beest in expectation gaze
Tugging at the loads of hay
As passing fotherers hugs away
And hogs wi' grumbling deafening noise
Bother round the server boys
And all around a motly troop
Anxious claim their suppering up
From the rest a blest release
Gabbling goes the fighting geese
Waddling homeward to their bed

In their warm straw-litterd shed
Nighted by unseen delay
Poking hens then loose their way
Crafty cats now sit to watch
Sparrows fighting on the thatch
Dogs lick their lips and wag their tails
When Doll brings in the milking pails
With stroaks and pats they're welcomd in
And they with looking thanks begin
She dips the milk pail brimming o'er
And hides the dish behind the door

Prone to mischief boys are met
Gen the eaves the ladder's set
Sly they climb and softly tread
To catch the sparrow on his bed
And kill 'em O in cruel pride
Knocking gen the ladderside
Cursd barbarians pass me by
Come not, turks, my cottage nigh
Sure my sparrows are my own
Let ye then my birds alone
Sparrows, come from foes severe,
Fearless come, ye're welcome here
My heart yearns for fates like thine
A sparrow's life's as sweet as mine
To my cottage then resort
Much I love your chirping note
Wi' my own hands to form a nest
I'll gi' ye shelter peace and rest
Trifling are the deeds ye do
Great the pains ye undergo
Cruel man woud Justice serve
Their crueltys as they deserve
And justest punishment pursue
And do as they to others do
Ye mourning chirpers fluttering here

They woud no doubt be less severe
Foolhardy clown ne'er grudge the wheat
Which hunger forces them to eat
Your blinded eyes, worst foes to you,
Ne'er see the good which sparrows do
Did not the sparrows watching round
Pick up the insect from your grounds
Did not they tend your rising grain
You vain might sow – to reap in vain
Thus providence when understood
Her end and aim is doing good
Sends nothing here without its use
Which Ignorance loads with its abuse
Thus fools despise the blessing sent
And mocks the giver's good intent
O God let me the best pursue
As I'd have other do to me
Let me the same to others do
And learn at least Humanity

    Dark and darker glooms the sky
Sleep 'gins close the labourer's eye
Dobson on his greensward seat
Where neighbours often neighbour meet
Of crops to talk and work in hand
And battle News from foreign land
His last wift he's puffing out
And Judie putting to the rout
Who gossiping takes great delight
To shool her knitting out at night
Jingling newsing 'bout the town
Spite o Dob's disliking frown
Chattering at her neighbour's door
The summons warn her to give o'er
Prepar'd to start, she soodles home,
Her knitting twirling o'er her thumb
As, loth to leave, afraid to stay,

She bawls her story all the way:
The tale so fraught with 'ticing charms,
Her apron folded o'er her arms,
She leaves the unfinished tale, in pain,
To end as evening comes again
And in the cottage gangs with dread,
To meet old Dobson's timely frown,
Who grumbling sits, prepar'd for bed,
While she stands chelping 'bout the town.

Night winds now on sutty wings
In the cotter's chimney sings
Sweet I raise my drowsy head
Thoughtful stretching on my bed
Listning to the ushering charms
That shakes the Elm tree's mossy arms
Till soft slumbers stronger creep
Then rocked by winds I fall to sleep

MIST IN THE MEADOWS

The evening o'er the meadow seems to stoop
More distant lessens the diminished spire
Mist in the hollows reeks and curdles up
Like fallen clouds that spread – and things retire
Less seen and less – the shepherd passes near
And little distant most grotesquely shades
As walking without legs – lost to his knees
As through the rawky creeping smoke he wades
Now, half-way up, the arches dissappear
And small the bits of sky that glimmer through
Then trees loose all but tops – while fields remain
As wont – the indistinctness passes bye
The shepherd all his length is seen again
And further on the village meets the eye

The crib-stock fothered, horses suppered-up
And cows in sheds all littered-down in straw
The threshers gone, the owls are left to whoop
The ducks go waddling with distended craw
Through little hole made in the henroost door
And geese with idle gabble never o'er
Bate careless hog untill he tumbles down
Insult provoking spite to noise the more
While fowl high-perched blink with contemptuous
    frown
On all the noise and bother heard below
Over the stable ridge in crowds the crow
With jackdaws intermixed known by their noise
To the warm woods behind the village go
And whistling home for bed go weary boys

EVENING PASTIME*

Musing beside the crackling fire at night,
While singing kettle merrily prepares
Woman's solacing beverage, I delight
To read a pleasant volume where the cares
Of life are sweetened by the muse's voice –
Thomson or Cowper or the Bard that bears
Life's humblest name though nature's favoured choice
Her pastoral Bloomfield – and as evening wears
Weary with reading list' the little tales
Of laughing childern who edge up their chairs
To tell the past day's sport which never fails
To cheer the spirits – while my fancy shares
Their artless talk man's sturdy reason fails
And memory's joy grows young again with theirs

The winter wind with strange and fearful gust
Stirs the dark wood and in the lengthy night
Howls in the chimney top while fear's mistrust
Listens the noise by the small glimmering light
Of cottage hearth where warm a circle sits
Of happy dwellers telling morts of tales
Where some long memory wakens up by fits
Laughter and fear and over all prevails
Wonder predominant – they sit and hear
The very hours to minutes and the song
Or story, be the subject what it may,
Is ever found too short and never long
While the uprising tempest loudly roars
And boldest hearts fear stirring out of doors

Fear's ignorance their fancy only harms
Doors safely locked fear only entrance wins
While round the fire in every corner warms
Till nearest hitch away and rub their shins
And now the tempest in its plight begins
The shutters jar the woodbine on the wall
Rustles agen the panes and over all
The noisey storm to troublous fancy dins
And pity stirs the stoutest heart to call
'Who's there?' as slow the door latch seemly stirred
But nothing answered so the sounds they heard
Was no benighted traveller – and they fall
To telling pleasant tales to conquor fear
And sing a merry song till bed time creepeth near

SUNSET

Welcome sweet eve thy gently sloping sky
And softly whispering wind that breathes of rest
And clouds unlike what daylight galloped bye
Now stopt as weary huddling in the West
Each by the farewell of day's closing eye
Left with the smiles of heaven on its breast
Meek nurse of weariness how sweet to meet
Thy soothing tenderness to none denied
To hear thy whispering voice – ah heavenly sweet
Musing and listening by thy gentle side
Lost to life's cares thy coloured skies to view
Picturing of pleasant worlds unknown to care
And when our bark the rough sea flounders through
Warming in hopes its end shall harbour there

COTTAGE FEARS

The evening gathers from the gloomy woods
And darkling creeps o'er silent vale and hill
While the snug village in night's happy moods
Is resting calm and beautifully still
The windows gleam with light the yelping curs
That guards the henroost from the thieving fox
Barks now and then as somthing passing stirs
And distant dogs the noises often mocks
While foxes from the woods send dismal cries
Like somthing in distress the cottager
Hears the dread noise and thinks of danger nigh
And locks up door in haste – nor cares to stir
From the snug safety of his humble shed
Then tells strange tales till time to go to bed

NIGHT WIND

Darkness like midnight from the sobbing woods
Clamours with dismal tidings of the rain
Roaring as rivers breaking loose in floods
To spread and foam and deluge all the plain
The cotter listens at his door again
Half doubting whether it be floods or wind
And through the thickening darkness looks affraid
Thinking of roads that travel has to find
Through night's black depths in danger's garb arrayed
And the loud glabber round the flaze soon stops
When hushed to silence by the lifted hand
Of fearing dame who hears the noise in dread
And thinks a deluge comes to drown the land
Nor dares she go to bed untill the tempest drops

FIRST SIGHT OF SPRING

The hazel blooms, in threads of crimson hue,
Peep through the swelling buds and look for spring
Ere yet a whitethorn leaf appears in view
Or March finds throstles pleased enough to sing
On the old touchwood tree woodpeckers cling
A moment and their harsh-toned notes renew.
In happier mood the stockdove claps his wing
The squirrel sputters up the powdered oak
With tail cocked o'er his head and ears errect
Startled to hear the woodman's understroke
And with the courage that his fears collect
He hisses fierce, half malice and half glee,
Leaping from branch to branch about the tree
In winter's foliage moss and lichens drest

Spring cometh in with all her hues and smells
In freshness breathing over hills and dells
O'er woods where May her gorgeous drapery flings
And meads washed fragrant with their laughing springs
Fresh as new-opened flowers untouched and free
From the bold rifling of the amorous bee
The happy time of singing birds is come
And love's lone pilgrimage now finds a home
Among the mossy oaks now coos the dove
And the hoarse crow finds softer notes for love
The foxes play around their dens and bark
In joy's excess mid woodland shadows dark
And flowers join lips below and leaves above
And every sound that meets the ear is love

POESY A-MAYING

Now comes the bonny May dancing and skipping
Accross the stepping stones of meadow streams
Bearing no kin to April showers a-weeping
But constant sunshine as her servant seems
Her heart is up – her sweetness all amaying
Streams in her face like gems on beauty's breast
The swains are sighing all and well-a-daying
Love-sick and gazing on their lovely guest
The Sunday paths to pleasant places leading
Are graced by couples linking arm in arm
Sweet smiles enjoying or some book areading
Where love and beauty are the constant charm
For while the bonny May is dancing by
Beauty delights the ear and beauty fills the eye

The birds they sing and build and nature scorns
On May's young festival to keep a widow
There childern too have pleasures all their own
A-plucking ladysmocks along the meadow
The little brook sings loud among the pebbles
So very loud that water-flowers which lie
Where many a silver curdle boils and dribbles
Dance too with joy as it goes singing bye
Among the pasture-molehills maidens stoop
To pluck the luscious marjoram for their bosoms
The greensward's smothered o'er with buttercups
And whitethorns they are breaking down with
blossoms
'Tis nature's livery for the bonny May
Who keeps her court and all have holiday

Princess of months – so nature's choice ordains
And lady of the summer still she reigns
In spite of April's youth who charms in tears
And rosey June who wins with blushing face
July sweet shepherdess who wreaths the shears
Of shepherds with her flowers of winning grace
And sun-tanned August with her swarthy charms
The beautiful and rich – and pastoral gay
September with her pomp of fields and farms
And wild November's sybilline array
In spite of beauty's calender the year
Garlands with beauty's prize the bonny May
Where e'er she goes fair nature hath no peer
And months do loose their queen when she's away

Up like a princess starts the merry morning
In draperies of many-coloured cloud
And sky larks, minstrels of the early dawning,
Pipe forth their hearty anthems long and loud

The bright enarmoured sunshine goes a-maying
And every flower his laughing eye beguiles
And on the milkmaid's rosey face a-playing
Pays court to beauty in its softest smiles
For May's divinity of joy begun
Adds life and lustre to the golden sun
And all of life beneath its glory straying
Is by May's beauty into worship won
Till golden eve ennobles all the West
And day goes blushing like a bride to rest

CROWS IN SPRING

The crow will tumble up and down
    At the first sight of spring
And in old trees around the town
    Brush winter from its wing

No longer flapping far away
    To naked fen they flye
Chill fare as on a winter's day
    But field and valleys nigh

Where swains are stirring out to plough
    And woods are just at hand
They seek the upland's sunny brow
    And strut from land to land

And often flap their sooty wings
    And sturt to neighboring tree
And seems to try all ways to sing
    And almost speaks in glee

The ploughman hears and turns his head
   Above to wonder why
And there a new nest nearly made
   Proclaims the winter by

The schoolboy, free from winter's frown,
   That rests on every stile
In wonder sets his basket down
   To start his happy toil

SPORT IN THE MEADOWS*

May time is to the meadows coming in
And cowslap peeps have gotten e'er so big
And water blobs and all their golden kin
Crowd round the shallows by the striding brig
Daisys and buttercups and lady smocks
Are all abouten shining here and there
Nodding about their gold and yellow locks
Like morts of folken flocking at a fair
The sheep and cows are crowding for a share
And snatch the blossoms in such eager haste
That basket-bearing childern running there
Do think within their hearts they'll get them all
And hoot and drive them from their graceless waste
As though there wan't a cowslap peep to spare
For they want some for tea and some for wine
And some to maken up a cucka ball
To throw accross the garland's silken line
That reaches o'er the street from wall to wall
Good gracious me how merrily they fare
One sees a fairer cowslap then the rest
And off they shout – the foremost bidding fair
To get the prize – and earnest half and jest
The next one pops her down – and from her hand
Her basket falls and out her cowslaps all

Tumble and litter there – the merry band
In laughing friendship round about her fall
To helpen gather up the littered flowers
That she no loss may mourn – and now the wind
In frolic mood among the merry hours
Wakens with sudden start and tosses off
Some untied bonnet on its dancing wings
Away they follow with a scream and laugh
And aye the youngest ever lags behind
Till on the deep lake's very brink it hings
They shout and catch it and away they start
The chace for cowslaps merry as before
And each one seems so anxious at the heart
As they would even get them all and more
One climbs a molehill for a bunch of may
One stands on tiptoe for a linnet's nest
And pricks her hand and throws her flowers away
And runs for plantain leaves to have it drest
So do they run abouten all the day
And teaze the grass-hid larks from getting rest
– Scarce give they time in their unruley haste
To tie a shoestring that the grass unties
And thus they run the meadow's bloom to waste
Till even comes and dulls their phantasys
When one finds losses out to stifle smiles
Of silken bonnet strings – and others sigh
O'er garments rent in clambering over stiles
Yet in the morning fresh afield they hie
Bidding the last day's troubles a goodbye
When red-pied cow again their coming hears
And ere they clap the gate she tosses up
Her head and hastens from the sport she fears
The old yoe calls her lamb nor cares to stoop
To crop a cowslap in their company
Thus merrily the little noisey troop
Along the grass as rude marauders hie

For ever noisey and forever gay
While keeping in the meadow holiday

WOOD PICTURES IN SPRING

The rich brown umber hue the oaks unfold
When spring's young sunshine bathes their trunks in
     gold
So rich so beautiful so past the power
Of words to paint – my heart aches for the dower
The pencil gives to soften and infuse
This brown luxuriance of unfolding hues
This living lusious tinting woodlands give
Into a landscape that might breathe and live
And this old gate that claps against the tree
The entrance of spring's Paradise should be
Yet paint itself with living nature fails
– The sunshine threading through these broken rails
In mellow shades – no pencil e'er conveys
And mind alone feels, fancies and pourtrays

HOME PICTURES IN MAY

The sunshine bathes in clouds of many hues
And morning's feet are gemmed with early dews
Warm daffodils about the garden beds
Peep through their pale slim leaves their golden heads
Sweet earthly suns of spring – the gosling broods
In coats of sunny green about the road
Waddle in extacy – and in rich moods
The old hen leads her flickering chicks abroad
Oft scuttling 'neath her wings to see the kite
Hang wavering o'er them in the spring's blue light
The sparrows round their new nests chirp with glee

And sweet the robin spring's young luxury shares
Tuteling* its song in feathery gooseberry tree
While watching worms the gardener's spade unbares

SUMMER HAPPINESS

The sun looks down in such a mellow light
I cannot help but ponder in delight
To see the meadows so divinely lye
Beneath the quiet of the evening sky
The flags and rush in lights and shades of green
Look far more rich than I have ever seen
And bunches of white clover bloom again
And plats of lambtoe still in flower remain
In the brown grass that summer scythes have shorn
In every meadow level as a lawn
While peace and quiet in that silent mood
Cheers my lone heart and doth my spirits good
The level grass the sun the mottled sky
Seems waiting round to welcome passers bye

Summer is prodigal of joy, the grass
Swarms with delighted insects as I pass
And crowds of grasshoppers at every stride
Jump out all ways with happiness their guide
And from my brushing feet moths flirt away
In safer places to pursue their play
In crowds they start. I marvel, well I may,
To see such worlds of insects in the way
And more to see each thing however small
Sharing joy's bounty that belongs to all
And here I gather by the world forgot
Harvests of comfort from their happy mood
Feeling God's blessing dwells in every spot
And nothing lives but ows him gratitude

HAYMAKING

'Tis haytime and the red-complexioned sun
Was scarcely up ere blackbirds had begun
Along the meadow hedges here and there
To sing loud songs to the sweet-smelling air
Where breath of flowers and grass and happy cow
Fling o'er one's senses streams of fragrance now
While in some pleasant nook the swain and maid
Lean o'er their rakes and loiter in the shade
Or bend a minute o'er the bridge and throw
Crumbs in their leisure to the fish below
– Hark at that happy shout – and song between
'Tis pleasure's birthday in her meadow scene.
What joy seems half so rich from pleasure won
As the loud laugh of maidens in the sun?

WOOD PICTURES IN SUMMER

The one delicious green that now prevades
The woods and fields in endless lights and shades
And that deep softness of delicious hues
That overhead blends – softens – and subdues
The eye to extacy and fills the mind
With views and visions of enchanting kind
While on the velvet down beneath the swail
I sit on mossy stulp and broken rail
Or lean o'er crippled gate by hugh old tree
Broken by boys disporting there at swee
While sunshine spread from an exaustless sky
Gives all things extacy as well as I
And all wood-swaily places, even they
Are joy's own tennants, keeping holiday

THE HAIL STORM IN JUNE 1831

Darkness came o'er like chaos – and the sun
As startled with the terror seemed to run
With quickened dread behind the beetling cloud
The old wood sung like nature in her shroud
And each old rifted oak-tree's mossy arm
Seemed shrinking from the presence of the storm
And as it nearer came they shook beyond
Their former fears – as if to burst the bond
Of earth that bound them to that ancient place
Where danger seemed to threaten all their race
Who had withstood all tempests since their birth
Yet now seemed bowing to the very earth
Like reeds they bent like drunken men they reeled
Till man from shelter ran and sought the open field

THE SUMMER SHOWER

I love it well, o'ercanopied in leaves
Of crowding woods, to spend a quiet hour
And where the woodbine weaves
To list' the summer shower

Brought by the South-west wind that balm and bland
Breathes luscious coolness loved and felt by all
While on the uplifted hand
The raindrops gently fall

Now quickening on and on the pattering woods
Recieves the coming shower birds trim their wings
And in a joyful mood
The little woodchat sings

And blackbird squatting in her mortared nest
Safe hid in ivy and the pathless wood
Pruneth her sooty breast
And warms her downy brood

And little Pettichap like hurrying mouse
Keeps nimbling near my arbour round and round
Aye there's her oven house
Built nearly on the ground

Of woodbents withered straws and moss and leaves
And lined with downy feathers. Safety's joy
Dwells with the home she weaves
Nor fears the pilfering boy

The busy falling rain increases now
And sopping leaves their dripping moisture pour
And from each loaded bough
Fast falls the double shower

Weed climbing hedges banks and meeds unmown
Where rushy fringed brooklet easy curls
Look joyous while the rain
Strings their green suit with pearls

While from the crouching corn the weeding troop
Run hastily and huddling in a ring
Where the old willows stoop
Their ancient ballads sing

And gabble over wonder's ceaseless tale
Till from the South-west sky showers thicker come
Humming along the vale
And bids them hasten home

With laughing skip they stride the hasty brook
That mutters through the weeds untill it gains
A clear and quiet nook
To greet the dimpling rain

And on they drabble all in mirth not mute
Leaving their footmarks on the elting soil
Where print of sprawling foot
Stirs up a tittering smile

On beauty's lips who slipping mid the crowd
Blushes to have her anckle seen so high
Yet inly feeleth proud
That none a fault can spy

Yet rudely followed by the meddling clown
Who passes vulgar gibes – the bashful maid
Lets go her folded gown
And pauses half afraid

To climb the stile before him till the dame,
To quarrel half-provoked, assails the knave
And laughs him into shame
And makes him well behave

Bird–nesting boys o'ertaken in the rain
Beneath the ivied maple bustling run
And wait in anxious pain
Impatient for the sun

And sigh for home yet at the pasture gate
The molehill-tossing bull with straining eye
Seemeth their steps to wait
Nor dare they pass him bye

Till wearied out high over hedge they scrawl
To shun the road and through the wet grass roam
Till wet and draggled all
They fear to venture home

The plough-team wet and dripping plashes home
And on the horse the ploughboy lolls along
Yet from the wet grounds come
The loud and merry song

Now 'neath the leafy arch of dripping bough
That loaded trees form o'er the narrow lane
The horse released from plough
Naps the moist grass again

Around their blanket camps the gipseys still
Heedless of showers while blackthorns shelter round
Jump o'er the pasture hills
In many an idle bound

From dark green clumps among the dripping grain
The lark with sudden impulse starts and sings
And mid the smoking rain
Quivers her russet wings

A joy-inspiring calmness all around
Breathes a refreshing sense of strengthening power
Like that which toil hath found
In Sunday's leisure hour

When spirits all relaxed heartsick of toil
Seeks out the pleasant woods and shadowy dells
And where the fountain boils
Lye listening distant bells

Amid the yellow furze, the rabbit's bed,
Labour hath hid his tools and o'er the heath
Hies to the milking shed
That stands the oak beneath

And there he wiles the pleasant shower away
Filling his mind with store of happy things
Rich crops of corn and hay
And all that plenty brings

The crampt horison now leans on the ground
Quiet and cool, and labour's hard employ
Ceases while all around
Falls a refreshing joy

BEANS IN BLOSSOM

The South-west wind, how pleasant in the face
It breathes, while sauntering in a musing pace
I roam these new-ploughed fields and by the side
Of this old wood where happy birds abide
And the rich blackbird through his golden bill
Utters wild music when the rest are still
Now luscious comes the scent of blossomed beans
That o'er the path in rich disorder leans
Mid which the bees in busy songs and toils
Load home luxuriantly their yellow spoils
The herd cows toss the molehills in their play
And often stand the stranger's steps at bay
Mid clover blossoms red and tawney white
Strong-scented with the summer's warm delight

SUMMER MOODS

I love at eventide to walk alone
Down narrow lanes o'erhung with dewy thorn
Where, from the long grass underneath, the snail
Jet-black creeps out and sprouts his timid horn
I love to muse o'er meadows newly mown
Where withering grass perfumes the sultry air
Where bees search round with sad and weary drone
In vain for flowers that bloomed but newly there
While in the juicey corn the hidden quail
Cries 'wet my foot' and, hid as thoughts unborn,
The fairy-like and seldom-seen land-rail
Utters 'craik craik' like voices underground
Right glad to meet the evening's dewy veil
And see the light fade into glooms around

SUMMER IMAGES

Now swathy summer by rude health embrowned
Presedence takes of rosey-fingered spring
And laughing joy with wild flowers prankt and
    crowned
  A wild and giddy thing
With health robust from every care unbound
  Comes on the zepher's wing
  And cheers the toiling clown

Happy as holiday-enjoying face
Loud-tongued and 'merry as a marriage-bell'
Thy lightsome step sheds joy in every place
  And where the troubled dwell
Thy 'witching smiles weans them of half their cares
  And from thy sunny spell
  They greet joy unawares

Then with thy sultry locks all loose and rude
And mantle laced with gems of garish light
Come as of wont – for I would fain intrude
   And in the world's despite
Share the rude mirth that thine own heart beguiles
   If haply so I might
   Win pleasure from thy smiles

Me not the noise of brawling pleasures cheer
In nightly revels or in city streets
But joys which soothe and not distract mine ear
   That one at leisure meets
In the green woods and meadows summer-shorn
   Or fields where bee-fly greets
   One's ear with mellow horn

Where green-swathed grasshopper on treble pipe
Singeth and danceth in mad-hearted pranks
And bees go courting every flower that's ripe
   On baulks and sunny banks
And droning dragonflye on rude bassoon
   Striveth to give God thanks
   In no discordant tune

Where speckled thrush by self-delight embued
Singeth unto himself for joy's amends
And drinks the honey dew of solitude
   Where happiness attends
With inbred joy untill his heart oerflows
   Of which the world's rude friends
   Nought heeding nothing knows

Where the gay river laughing as it goes
Plashes with easy wave its flaggy sides
And to the calm of heart in calmness shows

What pleasure there abides
To trace its sedgy banks from trouble free
    Spots solitude provides
    To muse and happy be

Or ruminating 'neath some pleasant bush
On sweet silk grasses stretch me at mine ease
Where I can pillow on the yielding rush
    And acting as I please
Drop into pleasant dreams or musing lye
    Mark the wind-shaken trees
    And cloud-betravelled sky

And think me how some barter joy for care
And waste life's summer health in riot rude
Of nature nor of nature's sweets aware
    Where passions vain intrude
These by calm musings softened are and still
    And the heart's better mood
    Feels sick of doing ill

Here I can live and at my leisure seek
Joys far from cold restraints – not fearing pride
Free as the winds that breathe upon my cheek
    Rude health so long denied
Where poor integrity can sit at ease
    And list' self-satisfied
    The song of honey bees

And green lane traverse heedless where it goes
Naught guessing till some sudden turn espies
Rude battered finger-post that stooping shows
    Where the snug mystery lies
And then a mossy spire with ivy crown
    Clears up the short supprise
    And shows the peeping town

And see the wild flowers in their summer morn
Of beauty feeding on joy's luscious hours
The gay convolvulus wreathing round the thorn
    Agape for honey showers
And slender kingcup burnished with the dew
    Of morning's early hours
    Like gold yminted new

And mark by rustic bridge o'er shallow stream
Cow-tending boy to toil unreconsiled
Absorbed as in some vagrant summer dream
    And now in gestures wild
Starts dancing to his shadow on the wall
    Feeling self-gratified
    Nor fearing human thhrall

Then thread the sunny valley laced with streams
Or forests rude and the o'ershadowed brims
Of simple ponds where idle shepherd dreams
    And streaks his listless limbs
Or trace hay-scented meadow smooth and long
    Where joy's wild impulse swims
    In one continued song

I love at early morn from new-mown swath
To see the startled frog his rout pursue*
And mark while leaping o'er the dripping path
    His bright sides scatter dew
And early lark that from its bustle flyes –
    To hail his mattin new
    And watch him to the skyes

And note on hedgerow-baulks in moisture sprent
The jetty snail creep from the mossy thorn
In earnest heed and tremulous intent

Frail brother of the morn
That from the tiney bents and misted leaves
   Withdraws his timid horn
   And fearful vision weaves

And swallows heed* on smoke-tanned chimney-top
As wont be first unsealing morning's eye
Ere yet the bee hath gleaned one wayward drop
   Of honey on his thigh
And see him seek morn's airy couch to sing
   Untill the golden sky
   Besprents his russet wing

And sawning boy by tanning corn espy
With clapping noise to startle birds away
And hear him bawl to every passer-bye
   To know the hour of day
And see the uncradled breeze refreshed and strong
   With waking blossoms play
   And breathe Eolian song

I love the South-west wind or low or loud
And not the less when sudden drops of rain
Moistens my glowing cheek from ebon cloud
   Threatening soft showers again
That over lands new-ploughed and meadow-grounds
   Summer's sweet breath unchains
   And wakes harmonious sounds

Rich music breathes in summer's every sound
And in her harmony of varied greens
Woods meadows hedgrows cornfields all around
   Much beauty intervenes
Filling with harmony the ear and eye
   While o'er the mingling scenes
   Far spreads the laughing sky

And wind-enarmourd aspin* – mark the leaves
Turn up their silver lining to the sun
And list the brustling noise that oft decieves
    And make the sheep-boy run
The sound so mimics fast-approaching showers
    He thinks the rain begun
    And hastes to sheltering bowers

And mark the evening curdle dank and grey
Changing her watchet hue for sombre weed
And moping owl to close the lids of day
    On drowsy wing proceed
While chickering cricket tremulous and long
    Light's farewell inly heeds
    And gives it parting song

While pranking bat its flighty circlet makes
And gloworm burnisheth its lamp anew
O'er meadows dew-besprent – and beetle wakes
    Enquiries ever new
Teazing each passing ear with murmurs vain
    As wonting* to pursue
    His homeward path again

And catch the melody of distant bells
That on the wind with pleasing hum rebounds
By fitful starts – then musically swells
    O'er the dim stilly grounds
While on the meadow-bridge the pausing boy
    Listens the mellow sounds
    And hums in vacant joy

And now the homebound hedger bundles round
His evening faggot and with every stride
His leathern doublet leaves a rustling sound

Till silly sheep beside
His path start tremulous and once again
   Look back dissatisfied
   And scan the dewy plain

And greet the soothing calm that smoothly stills
O'er the heart's every sense its opiate dews
In meek-eyed moods and ever balmy trills
   That softens and subdues
With gentle quiet's bland and sober train
   Which dreamy eve renews
   In many a mellow strain

I love to walk the fields they are to me
A legacy no evil can destroy
They like a spell set every rapture free
   That cheered me when a boy
Play, pastime – all time's blotting pen conseals –
   Come like a new-born joy
   To greet me in the fields

For nature's objects ever harmonize
With emulous taste that vulgar deed anoys
It loves in quiet moods to sympathise
   And meet vibrating joys
O'er nature's pleasant things – nor slighting deems
   Pastimes the muse employs
   As vain obtrusive themes

The summer she is gone her book is shut
That did my idle leisure so engage
Her pictures were so many – some I put
On memory's scroll – Of some I turned the page
Adown for pleasure's after-heritage
But I have stayed too long – and she is gone.
Decay her stormy strife begins to wage
Scenes flit and change and new scenes hurry on
Till winter's hungry maw shall gorge them every one

The cleanly maiden down the village streets
In pattens clicks o'er causways never dry
While eves drop on her cap – and oft she meets
The laughing urchin with mischevious eye
Who tryes to plash her as she hurrys bye
The swains afield right early seek their ploughs
And to the maids right vulgar speech applies
Yet gentler shepherd pleads and she alows
His proffered aid to help her over sloughs

The hedger soaked with the dull weather chops
On at his toils which scarcely keep him warm
At every stroke he takes, large swarms of drops
Patter about him like an April storm
The sticking dame with cloak upon her arm
To guard against the storm walks the wet leas
Of willow groves or hedges round the farms
Picking up aught her splashy wandering sees
E'en withered kecks – and sticks winds shake from off
    the trees

Boys often clamber up a sweeing tree
To see the scarlet hunter hurry bye
And fain would in their merry uproar be
But sullen labour hath its tethering tie

Crows swop around and some on bushes nigh
Watch for a chance whene'er he turns away
To settle down their hunger to supply
From morn to eve bird-scaring claims his stay
Save now and then an hour which leisure steals for play

Gaunt greyhounds now the coursers' sports impart
With long legs stretched on tiptoe for the chace
And short loose ear and eye upon the start
Swift as the winds their motions they unlace
When bobs the hare up from her hiding place
Who in its furry coat of fallow stain
Squats on the lands or with a dodging pace
Trys its old coverts of wood grass to gain
And oft by cunning ways makes all their speed in vain

The pigeon with its breast of many hues
That spangles to the sun – turns round and round
About his timid paramour and coos
Upon the cottage ridge – while o'er them wews
The puddock and below the clocking hen
Calls loud her chickens out of danger's way
That skulk and scuttle 'neath her wings again
Nor peeps again till danger's far away
And one bye one they peep and hardly dare to stray

So summer went and so the autumn goes
Hedge orchard wood to red and yellow turn
The lark-becrowding field a desert grows
The brooks that sung do nothing else but mourn
For company – there long-necked cranes sojourn
Unstartled by the groups that summer gave
When reapers shepherds all with thirst did burn
And thronged its stream – aye life need little crave
For such will winter be in the unnoticed grave

AUTUMN MORNING

The autumn morning waked by many a gun
Throws o'er the fields her many-coloured light
Wood wildly touched close-tanned and stubbles dun
A motley paradise for earth's delight
Clouds ripple as the darkness breaks to light
And clover fields are hid with silver mist
One shower of cobwebs o'er the surface spread
And threads of silk in strange disorder twist
Round every leaf and blossom's bottly head
Hares in the drowning herbage scarcely steal
But on the battered pathway squats abed
And by the cart-rut nips her morning meal
Look where we may the scene is strange and new
And every object wears a changing hue

NUTTERS

The rural occupations of the year
Are each a fitting theme for pastoral song
And pleasing in our autumn paths appear
The groups of nutters as they chat along
The woodland-rides in strangest dissabille
Maids jacketed grotesque in garments ill
Hiding their elegance of shape – her ways
Her voice of music makes her woman still
Aught else the error of a careless gaze
Might fancy uncooth rustics noising bye
With laugh and chat and scraps of morning news
Till met the hazel shades and in they hie
Garbed suiting to the toil – the morning dews
Among the underwood are hardly dry

Yet down with crack and rustle branches come
And springing up like bow unloosed when free
Of their ripe clustering bunches brown – while some
Are split and broken under many a tree
Up springs the blundering pheasant with the noise
Loud brawls the maiden to her friends scared sore
And loud with mimic voice mischevous boys
Ape stranger voices to affright her more
Eccho long silent answers many a call
Straggling about the wildwood's guessing way
Till by the woodside waiting one and all
They gather homeward at the close of day
While maids with hastier step from sheperds' brawl
Speed on half-shamed of their strange dissaray

NUTTING

The sun had stooped his westward clouds to win
Like weary traveller seeking for an Inn
When from the hazelly wood we glad descried
The ivied gateway by the pasture side
Long had we sought for nutts amid the shade
Where silence fled the rustle that we made
When torn by briars and brushed by sedges rank
We left the wood and on the velvet bank
Of short-sward pasture-ground we sat us down
To shell our nutts before we reached the town
The near-hand stubble-field with mellow glower
Showed the dimmed blaze of poppys still in flower
And sweet the molehills smelt we sat upon
And now the thyme's in bloom, but where is pleasure
     gone?*

'Tis winter plain the images around
Protentious tell us of the closing year
Short grows the stupid day the moping fowl
Go roost at noon – upon the mossy barn
The thatcher hangs and lays the frequent yaum
Nudged close to stop the rain that drizzling falls
With scarce one interval of sunny sky
For weeks still leaking on that sulky gloom
Muggy and close a doubt 'twixt night and day
The sparrow rarely chirps the thresher pale
Twanks with sharp measured raps the weary flail
Thump after thump right tiresome to the ear
The hedger lonesome brustles at his toil
And shepherds trudge the fields without a song

The cat runs races with her tail – the dog
Leaps o'er the orchard hedge and knarls the grass
The swine run round and grunt and play with straw
Snatching out hasty mouthfuls from the stack
Sudden upon the elm-tree tops the crows
Unceremonious visit pays and croaks
Then swops away – from mossy barn the owl
Bobs hasty out – wheels round and scared as soon
As hastily retires – the ducks grow wild
And from the muddy pond fly up and wheel
A circle round the village and soon tired
Plunge in the pond again – the maids in haste
Snatch from the orchard hedge the mizled cloaths
And laughing hurry in to keep them dry

WOOD PICTURES IN WINTER

The woodland swamps with mosses varified
And bullrush forrests bowing by the side
Of shagroot sallows that snug shelter make
For the coy morehen in her bushy lake
Into whose tide a little runnel weaves
Such charms for silence through the choaking leaves
And whimpling melodies that but intrude
As lullabys to ancient solitude
– The wood-grass plats which last year left behind
Weaving their feathery lightness to the wind
Look now as picturesque amid the scene
As when the summer glossed their stems in green
While hasty hare* brunts through the creepy gap
Seeks their soft beds and squats in safety's lap

EMMONSAILS HEATH* IN WINTER

I love to see the old heath's withered brake
Mingle its crimpled leaves with furze and ling
While the old heron from the lonely lake
Starts slow and flaps his melancholly wing
And oddling crow in idle motion swing
On the half-rotten ash-tree's topmost twig
Beside whose trunk the gipsey makes his bed
Up flies the bouncing woodcock from the brig
Where a black quagmire quakes beneath the tread
The fieldfare chatter in the whistling thorn
And for the awe round fields and closen rove
And coy bumbarrels twenty in a drove
Flit down the hedgerows in the frozen plain
And hang on little twigs and start again

74

On Lolham Brigs* in wild and lonely mood
I've seen the winter floods their gambols play
Through each old arch that trembled while I stood
Bent o'er its wall to watch the dashing spray
As their old stations would be washed away
Crash came the ice against the jambs and then
A shudder jarred the arches – yet once more
It breasted raving waves and stood agen
To wait the shock as stubborn as before
– White foam brown-crested with the russet soil
As washed from new-ploughd lands would dart beneath
Then round and round a thousand eddies boil
On 'tother side – then pause as if for breath
One minute – and ingulphed – like life in death

Whose wrecky stains dart on the floods away
More swift then shadows in a stormy day
Straws trail and turn and steady – all in vain
The engulphing arches shoot them quickly through.
The feather dances flutters and again
Darts through the deepest dangers still afloat
Seeming as faireys whisked it from the view
And danced it o'er the waves as pleasure's boat
Light-hearted as a merry thought in May –
Trays – uptorn bushes – fence demolished rails
Loaded with weeds in sluggish motions stray
Like water-monsters lost, each winds and trails
Till near the arches – then as in affright
It plunges – reels – and shudders out of sight

Waves trough – rebound – and fury boil again
Like plunging monsters rising underneath
Who at the top curl up a shaggy main
A moment catching at a surer breath
Then plunging headlong down and down – and on
Each following boil the shadow of the last
And other monsters rise when those are gone
Crest their fringed waves – plunge onward and are past
– The chill air comes around me ocean-blea
From bank to bank the waterstrife is spread
Strange birds like snow spots o'er the huzzing sea
Hang where the wild duck hurried past and fled
On roars the flood – all restless to be free
Like trouble wandering to eternity

SNOW STORM

Winter is come in earnest and the snow
In dazzling splendour crumping underfoot
Spreads a white world all calm and where we go
By hedge or wood, trees shine from top to root
In feathered foliage flashing light and shade
Of strangest contrast – fancy's pliant eye
Delighted sees a vast romance displayed
And fairy halls descended from the sky
The smallest twig its snowy burthen bears
And woods o'erhead the dullest eyes engage
To shape strange things – where arch and pillar bears
A roof of grains fantastic arched and high
A little shed beside the spinney wears
The grotesque zemblance of an hermitage

One almost sees the hermit from the wood
Come bending with his sticks beneath his arm
And then the smoke curl up its dusky flood
From the white little roof his peace to warm
One shapes his books his quiet and his joys
And in romance's world-forgetting mood
The scene so strange so fancy's mind employs
It seems heart-aching for his solitude
Domestic spots near home and trod so oft
Seem daily – known for years – by the strange wand
Of winter's humour changed – the little croft
Left green at night when morn's loth look obtrudes
Trees bushes grass to one wild garb subdued
Are gone and left us in another land

WINTER

Old January clad in crispy rime
Comes hirpling on and often makes a stand
The hasty snowstorm ne'er disturbs his time
He mends no pace but beats his dithering hand
And Febuery like a timid maid
Smiling and sorrowing follows in his train
Huddled in cloak, of mirey roads affraid,
She hastens on to greet her home again
Then March the prophetess by storms inspired
Gazes in rapture on the troubled sky
And then in headlong fury madly fired
She bids the hail-storm boil and hurry bye
Yet 'neath the blackest cloud a sunbeam flings
Its cheering promise of returning spring

LANDSCAPES WITH FIGURES

Clare's landscape was not at all a conventionally pretty one: curious visitors who came to see the 'peasant poet' were astonished that so rich a poetry could have been inspired by so grudging a landscape, for it yielded satisfactions only to those with an unhurried and intimate knowledge.

For Clare, the landscape of his childhood was to remain throughout his life an emblem of Paradise, of Eden, and the poetry of his early and middle years – up to about 1835 – displays a clarity and acuity of observation, rooted in a preternaturally intense bond of love and an unusually vivid sense of belonging, of affinity, of sympathy and – one must add – dependency. It is as if his relationship with particular trees, streams, prospects was a very close friendship, or a love-affair.

When people figure in his landscape, they offer the possibility of an intimate social meaning: the scene need no longer offer merely picturesque spectacle but may become socially significant, encompassing a distinctive culture waiting to be interpreted. As his independence of spirit grew, such figures change from being simply appropriate human elements within a composition, and come to represent some of the strains and contradictions of English society. Clare's allegiances evolve quite clearly: he is more attuned to the company of the 'vulgar' – shepherd boys and gypsies – than to the squirearchy or the parsonage. In his mature poetry, the hierarchical conventions of taste, rooted in traditions of cultural subordination, are quietly subverted, so that 'common' is endowed with positive force, and the term 'vulgar' is applied not to the rural poor – his own social class – but to those who would use the land simply for economic gain.

His own status was paradoxical: he was both *of* the common people and also detached from them by his vocation: the term bestowed on him by the polite literary world – 'peasant poet' – expresses this contradiction. In freeing himself from this categorization he became what some few wise spirits recognized – the 'green man'; and evolved a descriptive language perfectly attuned to his own landscapes, a language that achieved a delicate marriage of 'literature' and of folk poetry – a green language, in which the term 'poetry' speaks of two sides of the same coin – both the natural world and the text committed to a loving mediation of that world. In the elegies of his middle years he discovered a world that could fail him, in which he felt adrift, alienated, even lost; what more characteristic than that of such a place he should use the adjective 'vague'?

PLEASANT PLACES

Old stone pits with veined ivy overhung
Wild crooked brooks o'er which was rudely flung
A rail and plank that bends beneath the tread
Old narrow lanes where trees meet overhead
Path stiles on which a steeple we espy
Peeping and stretching in the distant sky
And heaths o'erspread with furze blooms' sunny shine
Where wonder pauses to exclaim 'divine'
Old ponds dim-shadowed with a broken tree –
These are the picturesque of taste to me
While painting winds to make compleat the scene
In rich confusion mingles every green
Waving the sketching pencil* in their hands
Shading the living scenes to fairey lands

PLEASANT SPOTS

There is a wild and beautiful neglect
About the fields that so delights and cheers
Where nature her own feelings to effect
Is left at her own silent work for years
The simplest thing thrown in our way delights
From the wild careless feature that it wears
The very road that wanders out of sight
Crooked and free is pleasant to behold
And such the very weeds left free to flower
Corn poppys red and carlock gleaming gold
That makes the cornfields shine in summer's hour
Like painted skys – and fancy's distant eye
May well imagine armys marching bye
In all the grand array of pomp and power

How oft a summer shower hath started me
To seek for shelter in a hollow tree
Old hugh ash-dotterel wasted to a shell
Whose vigorous head still grew and flourished well
Where ten might sit upon the battered floor
And still look round discovering room for more
And he who chose a hermit life to share
Might have a door and make a cabin there
They seemed so like a house that our desires
Would call them so and make our gipsey fires
And eat field dinners of the juicey peas
Till we were wet and drabbled to the knees
But in our old tree-house rain as it might
Not one drop fell although it rained till night

THE CRAB TREE

Spring comes anew and brings each little pledge
That still as wont my childish heart decieves
I stoop again for violets in the hedge
Among the ivy and old withered leaves
And often mark amid the clumps of sedge
The pooty shells I gathered when a boy
But cares have claimed me many an evil day
And chilled the relish which I had for joy
Yet when crab-blossoms blush among the may
As wont in years gone bye I scramble now
Up mid the bramble for my old esteems
Filling my hands with many a blooming bough
Till the heart-stirring past as present seems
Save the bright sunshine of those fairy dreams

I've loved thee Swordy Well and love thee still
Long was I with thee tending sheep and cow
In boyhood ramping up each steepy hill
To play at 'roly poly' down – and now
A man I trifle o'er thee cares to kill
Haunting thy mossy steeps to botanize
And hunt the orchis tribes where nature's skill
Doth like my thoughts run into phantasys
Spider and Bee all mimicking at will
Displaying powers that fools the proudly wise
Showing the wonders of great nature's plan
In trifles insignificant and small
Puzzling the power of that great trifle man
Who finds no reason to be proud at all*

STRAY WALKS*

How pleasant are the fields to roam and think
Whole sabbaths through, unnoticed and alone
Beside the little molehill-skirted brink
Of the small brook that skips o'er many a stone
Or green woodside where many a squatting oak
Far o'er grass screeds their white-stained branches hing
Forming in pleasant close a happy seat
To nestle in while small birds chirp and sing
And the loud blackbird will its mate provoke
More louder yet its chorus to repeat
How pleasant is it thus to think and roam
The many paths, scarce knowing which to chuse
All full of pleasant scenes – then wander home
And o'er the beautys we have met to muse

'Tis Sunday and the little paths that wind
Through closen green by hedges and wood sides
And like a brook corn-crowded slope divides
Of pleasant fields – their frequent passers find
From early morn to mellow close of day
On different errands climbing many stiles
O'erhung with awthorn tempting haste to stay
And cool some moments of the road away
When hot and high the uncheckt summer smiles
Some journeying to the little hamlet hid
In dark surrounding trees to see their friends
While some sweet leisure's aimless road pursue
Wherever fancy's musing pleasure wends
To woods or lakes or church that's never out of view

EMMONSALES HEATH

In thy wild garb of other times
I find thee lingering still
Furze o'er each lazy summit climbs
At nature's easy will

Grasses that never knew a scythe
Waves all the summer long
And wild weed blossoms waken blythe
That ploughshares never wrong

Stern industry with stubborn toil
And wants unsatisfied
Still leaves untouched thy maiden soil
In its unsullied pride

The birds still find their summer shade
To build their nests again
And the poor hare its rushy glade
To hide from savage men

Nature its family protects
In thy security
And blooms that love what man neglects
Find peaceful homes in thee

The wild rose scents thy summer air
And woodbines weave in bowers
To glad the swain sojourning there
And maidens gathering flowers

Creation's steps one's wandering meets
Untouched by those of man
Things seem the same in such retreats
As when the world began

Furze ling and brake all mingling free
And grass forever green
All seem the same old things to be
As they have ever been

The brook o'er such neglected ground
One's weariness to soothe
Still wildly threads its lawless bounds
And chafes the pebble smooth

Crooked and rude as when at first
Its waters learned to stray
And from their mossy fountain burst
It washed itself a way

O who can pass such lovely spots
Without a wish to stray
And leave life's cares a while forgot
To muse an hour away

I've often met with places rude
Nor failed their sweet to share
But passed an hour with solitude
And left my blessing there

He that can meet the morning wind
And o'er such places roam
Nor leave a lingering wish behind
To make their peace his home –

His heart is dead to quiet hours
No love his mind employs
Poesy with him ne'er shares its flowers
Nor solitude its joys

O there are spots amid thy bowers
Which nature loves to find
Where spring drops round her earliest flowers
Uncheckt by winter's wind

Where cowslips wake the child's supprise
Sweet peeping ere their time
Ere April spreads her dappled skyes
Mid morning's powdered rime

I've stretched my boyish walks to thee
When Mayday's paths were dry
When leaves had nearly hid each tree
And grass greened ancle-high

And mused the sunny hours away
And thought of little things
That children mutter o'er their play
When fancy trys its wings

Joy nursed me in her happy moods
And all life's little crowd
That haunt the waters fields and woods
Would sing their joys aloud

I thought how kind that mighty power
Must in his splendour be
Who spread around my boyish hour
Such gleams of harmony

Who did with joyous rapture fill
The low as well as high
And make the pismires round the hill
Seem full as blest as I

Hope's sun is seen of every eye
The halo that it gives
In nature's wide and common sky
Cheers every thing that lives

WOOD RIDES

Who hath not felt the influence that so calms
The weary mind in summer's sultry hours
When wandering thickest woods beneath the arms
Of ancient oaks and brushing nameless flowers
That verge the little ride? Who hath not made
A minute's waste of time and sat him down
Upon a pleasant swell to gaze awhile
On crowding ferns bluebells and hazel leaves
And showers of lady smocks so called by toil
When boys sprote-gathering sit on stulps and weave
Garlands while barkmen pill the fallen tree
– Then mid the green variety to start?
Who hath not met that mood from turmoil free
And felt a placid joy refreshed at heart?

STEPPING-STONES

The stepping-stones that stride the meadow streams
Look picturesque amid spring's golden gleams
Where steps the traveller with a wary pace
And boy with laughing leisure in his face
Sits on the midmost stone in very whim
To catch the struttles that beneath him swim
While those accross the hollow lakes are bare
And winter floods no more rave dangers there
But mid the scum left where it roared and fell
The schoolboy hunts to find the pooty shell
Yet there the boisterous geese with golden broods
Hiss fierce and daring in their summer moods
The boys pull off their hats while passing bye
In vain to fright – themselves being forced to fly

WINTER FIELDS

O for a pleasant book to cheat the sway
Of winter – where rich mirth with hearty laugh
Listens and rubs his legs on corner seat
For fields are mire and sludge – and badly off
Are those who on their pudgy paths delay
There striding shepherd seeking driest way
Fearing night's wetshod feet and hacking cough
That keeps him waken till the peep of day
Goes shouldering onward and with ready hook
Progs oft to ford the sloughs that nearly meet
Accross the lands – croodling and thin to view
His loath dog follows – stops and quakes and looks
For better roads – till whistled to pursue
Then on with frequent jump he hirkles through

SNOW STORM

What a night the wind howls hisses and but stops
To howl more loud while the snow volly keeps
Insessant batter at the window pane
Making our comfort feel as sweet again
And in the morning when the tempest drops
At every cottage-door mountainious heaps
Of snow lies drifted that all entrance stops
Untill the beesom and the shovel gains
The path – and leaves a wall on either side –
The shepherd rambling valleys white and wide
With new sensations his old memorys fills
When hedges left at night, no more descried,
Are turned to one white sweep of curving hills
And trees, turned bushes, half their bodys hide

The boy that goes to fodder with supprise
Walks o'er the gate he opened yesternight
The hedges all have vanished from his eyes
E'en some tree tops the sheep could reach to bite
The novel scene emboldens new delight
And though with cautious steps his sports begin
He bolder shuffles the hugh hills of snow
Till down he drops and plunges to the chin
And struggles much and oft escape to win
Then turns and laughs but dare not further go
For deep the grass and bushes lie below
Where little birds that soon at eve went in
With heads tucked in their wings now pine for day
And little feel boys o'er their heads can stray

EVENING SCHOOLBOYS

Harken that happy shout – the school-house door
Is open thrown and out the younkers teem
Some run to leapfrog on the rushy moor
And others dabble in the shallow stream
Catching young fish and turning pebbles o'er
For mussel clams – Look in that mellow gleam
Where the retiring sun that rests the while
Streams through the broken hedge – How happy seem
Those schoolboy friendships leaning o'er the stile
Both reading in one book – anon a dream
Rich with new joys doth their young hearts beguile
And the book's pocketed most hastily
Ah happy boys well may ye turn and smile
When joys are yours that never cost a sigh

THE FODDERING BOY

The foddering boy along the crumping snows
With strawband-belted legs and folded arm
Hastens and on the blast that keenly blows
Oft turns for breath and beats his fingers warm
And shakes the lodging snows from off his cloaths
Buttoning his doublet closer from the storm
And slouching his brown beaver o'er his nose
Then faces it agen – and seeks the stack
Within its circling fence – where hungry lows
Expecting cattle making many a track
About the snows – impatient for the sound
When in hugh forkfulls trailing at his back
He litters the sweet hay about the ground
And brawls to call the staring cattle round

THE SHEPHERD BOY

Pleased in his loneliness he often lies
Telling glad stories to his dog – and e'en
His very shadow that the loss supplies
Of living company. Full oft he'll lean
By pebbled brooks and dream with happy eyes
Upon the fairey pictures spread below
Thinking the shadowed prospect real skies
And happy heavens where his kindred go
Oft we may track his haunts where he hath been
To spend the leisure which his toils bestow
By 'nine peg morris' nicked upon the green
Or flower-stuck gardens never meant to grow
Or figures cut on trees his skill to show
Where he a prisoner from a shower hath been

THE VILLAGE BOY

Free from the cottage corner see how wild
The village boy along the pastures hies
With every smell and sound and sight beguiled
That round the prospect meets his wondering eyes
Now stooping eager for the cowslip peeps
As though he'd get them all – now tired of these
Accross the flaggy brook he eager leaps
For some new flower his happy rapture sees
Now tearing mid the bushes on his knees
Or woodland banks for bluebell flowers he creeps
And now while looking up among the trees
He spies a nest and down he throws his flowers
And up he climbs with new-fed extacies
The happiest object in the summer hours

THE WOODMAN

Now evening comes and from the new-laid hedge
The woodman rustles in his leathern guise
Hiding in dyke, ylined with brustling sedge,
His bill and mattock from theft's meddling eyes
And in his wallets storing many a pledge
Of flowers and boughs from early-sprouting trees
And painted pootys from the ivied hedge
About its mossy roots, his boys to please,
Who wait with merry joy his coming home
Anticipating presents such as these
Gained far afield where they nor night nor morn
Find no school leisure long enough to go
Where flowers but rarely from their stalks are torn
And birds scarce loose a nest the season through

THE SHEPHERD'S FIRE

On the rude heath yclad in furze and ling
And oddling thorns that thick and prickly grows
Shielding the shepherd when the rude wind blows
And boys that sit right merry in a ring
Round fires upon a molehill toasting sloes
And crabs that froth and frizzle on the coals
Loud is the gabble and the laughter loud
The rabbits scarce dare peep from out their holes
Unwont to mix with such a noisey crowd
Some run to eke the fire – while many a cloud
Of smoke curls up, some on their haunches squat
With mouth for bellows puffing till it flares
Or if that fail one fans his napless hat
And when the feast is done they squabble for their
    shares

The shepherd's hut propt by the double ash
Hugh in its bulk and old in mossy age
Shadowing the dammed-up brook where plash and
    plash
The little mills did younkers' ears engage
Delightful hut rude as romances old
Where hugh old stones make each an easy chair
And brakes and ferns for luxurys manifold
And flint and steel, the all want needeth there
– The light was struck and then the happy ring
Crouched round the blaze – O these were happy times
Some telling tales and others urged to sing
Themes of old things in rude yet feeling rhymes
That raised the laugh or stirred the stifled sigh
Till pity listened in each vacant eye

Those rude old tales – man's memory augurs ill
Thus to forget the fragments of old days
Those long old songs – their sweetness haunts me still
Nor did they perish for my lack of praise
But old desciples of the pasture sward
Rude chroniclers of ancient minstrelsy
The shepherds vanished all, and disregard
Left their old music like a vagrant bee
For summer's breeze to murmur o'er and die
And in these ancient spots mind ear and eye
Turn listeners – till the very wind prolongs
The theme as wishing in its depths of joy
To reccolect the music of old songs
And meet the hut that blessed me when a boy

The shepherds and the herding swains
Keep their sabbath on the plains
They know no difference in its cares
Save that all toil has ceasd but theirs
For them the church bells vainly call
Fields are their church and house and all
Till night returns their homeward track
When soon morn's suns recall them back
Yet still they love the day's repose
And feel its peace as sweet as those
That have their freedom – and maid and clown
To walk the meadows or the town
They'll lye and catch the humming sound
That comes from steeples shining round
Enjoying in the service-time
The happy bells' delightfull chime
And oft they sit on rising ground
To view the landscap spreading round
Swimming from the following eye
In greens and stems of every dye
O'er wood and vale and fen's smooth lap
Like a richly coloured map
Square platts of clover red and white
Scented wi' summer's warm delight
And sinkfoil of a fresher stain
And different greens of varied grain
Wheat spindles bursted into ear
And browning faintly – grasses sere
In swathy seed-pods dryd by heat
Rustling when brushd by passing feet
And beans and peas of deadening green
And corn lands ribbon stripes between
And checkering villages that lye

Like light spots in a deeper sky
And woods' black greens that crowding spots
The lanscape in leaf-bearing grots
Where mingling hid lapt up to lare
The panting fox lyes cooly there
And willow grove that idly sweas
And checkering shines mid other trees
As if the morning's misty vail
Yet lingerd in their shadows pale
While from the village foliage pops
The popples tapering to their tops
That in the blue sky thinly wires
Like so many leafy spires
Thus the shepherd as he lyes
Where the heath's furze-swellings rise
Dreams o'er the scene in visions sweet
Stretching from his hawthorn seat
And passes many an hour away
Thus musing on the sabbath day
And from the fields they'll often steal
The green peas for a Sunday meal
When ne'er a farmer's on the lurch
Safe nodding o'er their books a-church
Or on their benches by the door
Telling their market profits o'er
And in snug nooks their huts beside
The gipsey blazes they provide
Braking the rotten from the trees
While some sit round to shell the peas
Or pick from hedges pilferd wood
To boil on props their stolen food
Sitting on stones or heaps of brakes
Each of the wild repast partakes
Telling to pass the hours along
Tales that to fitter days belong
While one within his scrip contains

A shatterd Bible's thumbd remains
On whose blank leaf wi' pious care
A host of names is scribbld there
Names by whom 'twas once possest
Or those in kindred bonds carresst
Childern for generations back
That doubtful memory should not lack
Their dates – 'tis there wi' care applyd
When they were born and when they dyd
From sire to son link after link
All scribbld wi' unsparing ink
This he will oft pull out and read
That takes of Sunday better heed
Then they who laugh at tale and jest
And oft he'll read it to the rest
Whose ignorance in weary mood
Pays more regard to Robin Hood
And Giant Blue Beard and such tales
That live like flowers in rural vales
Natural as last year's faded blooms
Anew wi' the fresh season comes
So these old tales from old to young
Take root and blossom where they sprung
Till age and winter bids them wane
Then fond youth takes them up again
The herdboys anxious after play
Find sports to pass the time away
Fishing for struttles in the brooks
Wi' thread for lines and pins for hooks
And stripping 'neath the willow shade
In warm and muddy ponds to bathe
And pelting wi' unerring eye
The heedless swallows starting bye
Oft breaking boughs from trees to kill
The nest of whasps beside a hill
Till one gets stung then they resort

And follow to less dangerous sport
Leaving to chance their sheep and cows
To thread the brakes and forest boughs
And scare the squirrel's lively joys
Wi' stones and sticks and shouting noise
That sat wi' in its secret place
Upon its tail to clean its face
When found they shout wi' joy to see
It hurly burly round a tree
And as they turn in sight again
It peeps and squats behind a grain
And oft they'll cut up sticks to trye
The holes where badgers darkly lye
Looking for footmark-prints about
The fresh moulds not long rooted out
And peep in burrows newly done
Where rabbits from their noses run
Where oft in terror's wild affright
They spy and startle at the sight
Rolld like a whip-thong round and round
Asleep upon the sunny ground
A snake that wakens at their play
And starts as full of fear as they
And knewt-shapd swifts that nimbly pass
And rustle in the brown heath-grass
From these in terror's fears they haste
And seek agen the scrubby waste
Where grass is pincered short by sheep
And venom creatures rarely creep
Playing at taw in sheep-beat tracks
Or leap frog o'er each other's backs
Or hump o'er hills wi' thime o'ergrown
Or mere mark's ancient mossey stone
Or run down hollows in the plain
Where steps are cut to climb again
Stone-pits that years have clothd in green
And slopd in narrow vales between

Or history's uncrowded ground
A Cromwell-trench* or Roman mound
Thus will the boys wi' makeshift joy
Their toil-taskd sabbath hours employ
And feed on fancys sweet as they
That in the town at freedom play
And pinder too is peeping round
To find a tennant for his pound
Heedless of rest or parson's prayers
He seldom to the church repairs
But thinks religion hath its due
In paying yearly for his pew
Soon as the morn puts night away
And hastening on her mantle grey
Before one sunbeam o'er the ground
Spindles its light and shadow round
He's o'er the fields as soon as morn
To see what stock are in the corn
And find what chances sheep may win
Thro' gaps the gipseys pilfer thin
Or if they've found a restless way
By rubbing at a loosend tray
Or neighing colt that trys to catch
A gate at night left off the latch
By traveller seeking home in haste
Or the clown by fancys chasd
That lasting while he made a stand
Opens each gate wi' fearful hand
Fearing a minute to remain
And put it on the latch again
And cows who often wi' their horns
Toss from the gaps the stuffing thorns
These like a fox upon the watch
He in the morning tryes to catch
And drives them to the pound for pay
Careless about the sabbath day

BIRDS AND BEASTS

Birds bees trees flowers all talked to me
incessantly louder than the busy hum of men.
Clare, 1848

Some of the most distinctive qualities of Clare's sensibility are most clearly evident in his poetry on birds and animals. It is not surprising that this should be so, for he discovered a perfectly unforced affinity between his own songs and those of the birds; and was acutely aware of the darker side of rural folk-life, in playing its cruel games with wild animals, delighting in savage killing.

As his own social identity became more and more problematic, increasingly he discovered a sense of a common condition, seeing an affinity between his own solitariness and the hermit-like lives of the shyer, quieter birds. He had a deep respect, even a reverence, for *other* forms of life, delighting in their integrity, and troubled by the spread of cultivation that ravaged their hitherto neglected territories; in exploring the territory of the more remote and private birds, he himself confessed to a sense of being an intruder, breaking into their 'secret' lives.

It is entirely inappropriate – or inadequate – to speak of Clare's poems on birds and animals as 'nature-poetry': the term fails to recognize that such poems as appear in this section are shot through not only with the delight of perception and the satisfaction of representation, but also with feelings and beliefs, perceptions and convictions that are inescapably ethical, social and political. They therefore raise in an entirely unforced manner most serious questions about the human use of the non-human natural world.

BIRDS' NESTS

How fresh the air, the birds how busy now
In every walk if I but peep I find
Nests newly made or finished all and lined
With hair and thistledown and in the bough
Of little awthorn huddled up in green
The leaves still thickening as the spring gets age
The pink's quite round and snug and closely laid
And linnet's of materials loose and rough
And still hedge-sparrow moping in the shade
Near the hedge-bottom weaves of homely stuff
Dead grass and mosses green, an hermitage
For secresy and shelter rightly made
And beautiful it is to walk beside
The lanes and hedges where their homes abide

SAND MARTIN

Thou hermit haunter of the lonely glen
And common wild and heath – the desolate face
Of rude waste landscapes far away from men
Where frequent quarrys give thee dwelling place
With strangest taste and labour undeterred
Drilling small holes along the quarry's side
More like the haunts of vermin than a bird
And seldom by the nesting boy descried
I've seen thee far away from all thy tribe
Flirting about the unfrequented sky
And felt a feeling that I can't describe
Of lone seclusion and a hermit joy
To see thee circle round nor go beyond
That lone heath and its melancholly pond

THE FERN OWL'S NEST

The weary woodman rocking home beneath
His tightly banded faggot wonders oft
While crossing over the furze-crowded heath
To hear the fern owl's cry that whews aloft
In circling whirls and often by his head
Wizzes as quick as thought and ill at rest
As through the rustling ling with heavy tread
He goes nor heeds he tramples near its nest
That underneath the furze or squatting thorn
Lies hidden on the ground and teazing round
That lonely spot she wakes her jarring noise
To the unheeding waste till mottled morn
Fills the red East with daylight's coming sounds
And the heath's echoes mocks the herding boys

THE WRYNECK'S NEST

That summer bird its oft-repeated note
Chirps from the dotterel ash and in the hole
The green woodpecker made in years remote
It makes its nest – where peeping idlers strole
In anxious plundering moods – and bye and bye
The wryneck's curious eggs as white as snow
While squinting in the hollow tree they spy
The sitting bird looks up with jetty eye
And waves her head in terror to and fro
Speckled and veined in various shades of brown
And then a hissing noise assails the clown
And quick with hasty terror in his breast
From the tree's knotty trunk he sluthers down
And thinks the strange bird guards a serpent's nest

The tame hedge-sparrow in its russet dress
Is half a robin for its gentle ways
And the bird-loving dame can do no less
Then throw it out a crumble on cold days
In early March it into gardens strays
And in the snug clipt box-tree green and round
It makes a nest of moss and hair and lays
When e'en the snow is lurking on the ground
Its eggs in number five of greenish blue
Bright beautiful and glossy shining shells
Much like the firetail's but of brighter hue
Yet in her garden-home much danger dwells
Where skulking cat with mischief in its breast
Catches their young before they leave the nest

THE WOODPIGEON'S NEST

Roaming the little path 'neath dotterel trees
Of some old hedge or spinney side I've oft
Been startled pleasantly from musing ways
By frighted dove that suddenly aloft
Sprung through the many boughs with cluttering noise
Till free from such restraints above the head
They smacked their clapping wings for very joys
And in a curious mood I've oft been led
To climb the twig-surrounded trunk and there
On some few bits of sticks two white eggs lie
As left by accident – all lorn and bare
Almost without a nest yet bye and bye
Two birds in golden down will leave the shells
And hiss and snap at wind-blown leaves that shake
Around their home where green seclusion dwells
Till fledged, and then the young adventurers take

The old ones' timid flights from oak to oak
Listening the pleasant sutherings of the shade
Nor startled by the woodman's hollow stroke
Till autumn's pleasant visions pine and fade
Then they in bolder crowds will sweep and flye
And brave the desert of a winter sky

THE RAVEN'S NEST

Upon the collar of a hugh old oak
Year after year boys mark a curious nest
Of twigs made up a faggot near in size
And boys to reach it try all sorts of schemes
But not a twig to reach with hand or foot
Sprouts from the pillared trunk and as to try
To swarm the massy bulk – 'tis all in vain
They scarce one effort make to hitch them up
But down they sluther soon as e'er they try
So long hath been their dwelling there – old men
When passing by will laugh and tell the ways
They had when boys to climb that very tree
And as it so would seem that very nest
That ne'er was missing from that selfsame spot
A single year in all their memorys
And they will say that the two birds are now
The very birds that owned the dwelling then
Some think it strange yet certainty's at loss
And cannot contradict it so they pass
As old birds living the wood's patriarchs
Old as the oldest men so famed and known
That even men will thirst into the fame
Of boys and get at schemes that now and then
May captivate a young one from the tree
With iron clamms and bands adventuring up
The mealy trunk or else by waggon ropes

Slung over the hugh grains and so drawn up
By those at bottom, one assends secure
With foot rope-stirruped – still a perrilous way
So perrilous that one and only one
In memorys of the oldest men was known
To wear his boldness to intention's end
And reach the raven's nest – and thence acchieved
A theme that wonder treasured for supprise
By every cottage-hearth the village through
Nor yet forgot though other darers come
With daring-times that scale the steeple's top
And tye their kerchiefs to the weather-cock
As trophys that the dangerous deed was done
Yet even now in these adventureous days
Not one is bold enough to dare the way
Up the old monstrous oak where every spring
Finds the two ancient birds at their old task
Repairing the hugh nest – where still they live
Through changes winds and storms and are secure
And like a landmark in the chronicles
Of village memorys treasured up yet lives
The hugh old oak that wears the raven's nest

THE SKY LARK

The rolls and harrows lie at rest beside
The battered road and spreading far and wide
Above the russet clods the corn is seen
Sprouting its spirey points of tender green
Where squats the hare to terrors wide awake
Like some brown clod the harrows failed to break
While 'neath the warm hedge boys stray far from home
To crop the early blossoms as they come
Where buttercups will make them eager run
Opening their golden caskets to the sun

To see who shall be first to pluck the prize
And from their hurry up the skylark flies
And o'er her half-formed nest with happy wings
Winnows the air – till in the clouds she sings
Then hangs a dust spot in the sunny skies
And drops and drops till in her nest she lies
Where boys unheeding passed, * ne'er dreaming then
That birds which flew so high would drop again
To nests upon the ground where any thing
May come at to destroy. Had they the wing
Like such a bird, themselves would be too proud
And build on nothing but a passing cloud
As free from danger as the heavens are free
From pain and toil – there would they build and be
And sail about the world to scenes unheard
Of and unseen – O were they but a bird –
So think they while they listen to its song
And smile and fancy and so pass along
While its low nest moist with the dews of morn
Lye safely with the leveret in the corn

THE YELLOWHAMMER'S NEST

Just by the wooden brig a bird flew up
Frit by the cowboy as he scrambled down
To reach the misty dewberry – let us stoop
And seek its nest – the brook we need not dread
'Tis scarcely deep enough a bee to drown
So it sings harmless o'er its pebbly bed
– Aye here it is, stuck close beside the bank
Beneath the bunch of grass that spindles rank
Its husk-seeds tall and high – 'tis rudely planned
Of bleached stubbles and the withered fare
That last year's harvest left upon the land
Lined thinly with the horse's sable hair

– Five eggs pen-scribbled over lilac shells
Resembling writing, scrawls which fancy reads
As nature's poesy and pastoral spells
They are the yellowhammer's and she dwells
A poet like – where brooks and flowery weeds
As sweet as Castaly to fancy seems
And that old molehill like as Parnass hill
On which her partner haply sits and dreams
O'er all his joy of song – so leave it still
A happy home of sunshine flowers and streams
Yet in the sweetest places cometh ill
A noisome weed that burthens every soil
For snakes are known with chill and deadly coil
To watch such nests and seize the helpless young
And like as though the plague became a guest
Leaving a houseless home a ruined nest
And mournful hath the little warblers sung
When such like woes hath rent its little breast

THE WREN

Why is the cuckoo's melody preferred
And nightingale's rich song so fondly praised
In poets' rhymes? Is there no other bird
Of nature's minstrelsy that oft hath raised
One's heart to extacy and mirth as well?
I judge not how another's taste is caught:
With mine, there's other birds that bear the bell
Whose song hath crowds of happy memories brought.
Such the wood-robin singing in the dell
And little wren that many a time hath sought
Shelter from showers in huts where I did dwell
In early spring the tennant of the plain
Tenting my sheep and still they come to tell
The happy stories of the past again

Accross the fallow clods at early morn
I took a random track, where scant and spare
The grass and nibbled leaves all closely shorn
Leaves a burnt flat all bleaching brown and bare
Where hungry sheep in freedom range forlorn
And 'neath the leaning willow and odd thorn
And molehill large that vagrant shade supplies
They batter round to shun the teazing flies
Trampling smooth places hard as cottage floors
Where the time-killing lonely shepherd boys
Whose summer homes are ever out of doors
Their chockholes form and chalk their marble ring
And make their clay taws at the bubbling spring
And in their rangling sport and gambling joys
They straine their clocklike shadows – when it cloys
To guess the hour that slowly runs away
And shorten sultry turmoil with their play
Here did I roam while veering overhead
The Pewet whirred in many whewing rings
And 'chewsit' screamed and clapped her flapping wings.
To hunt her nest my rambling steps was led
O'er the broad baulk beset with little hills
By moles long-formed and pismires tennanted
As likely spots – but still I searched in vain
When all at once the noisey birds were still
And on the lands a furrowed ridge between
Chance found four eggs of dingy dirty green
Deep-blotched with plashy spots of jockolate stain
Their small ends inward turned as ever found
As though some curious hand had laid them round
Yet lying on the ground with nought at all
Of soft grass withered twitch and bleached weed
To keep them from the rain storms' frequent fall
And here she broods on her unsavory bed

When bye and bye with little care and heed
Her young with each a shell upon its head
Run after their wild parents' restless cry
And from their own fears' tiney shadows run
'Neath clods and stones to cringe and snugly lie
Hid from all sight but the all-seeing sun
Till never-ceasing danger seemeth bye

THE PETTICHAP'S NEST

Well, in my many walks I rarely found
A place less likely for a bird to form
Its nest close by the rut-gulled waggon road
And on the almost bare foot-trodden ground
With scarce a clump of grass to keep it warm
And not a thistle spreads its spears abroad
Or prickly bush to shield it from harm's way
And yet so snugly made that none may spy
It out, save accident – and you and I
Had surely passed it on our walk today
Had chance not led us by it – nay e'en now
Had not the old bird heard us trampling by
And fluttered out – we had not seen it lie
Brown as the roadway side – small bits of hay
Pluckt from the old propt-haystack's pleachy brow
And withered leaves make up its outward walls
That from the snub-oak dotterel yearly falls
And in the old hedge bottom rot away
Built like an oven with a little hole
Hard to discover – that snug entrance wins
Scarcely admitting e'en two fingers in
And lined with feathers warm as silken stole
And soft as seats of down for painless ease
And full of eggs scarce bigger e'en then peas
Here's one most delicate with spots as small

As dust – and of a faint and pinky red
– We'll let them be and safety guard them well
For fear's rude paths around are thickly spread
And they are left to many dangers' ways
When green grasshopper's jump might break the shells
While lowing oxen pass them morn and night
And restless sheep around them hourly stray
And no grass springs but hungry horses bite
That trample past them twenty times a day
Yet like a miracle in safety's lap
They still abide unhurt and out of sight
– Stop, here's the bird. That woodman at the gap
Hath put it from the hedge – 'tis olive green
Well I declare it is the pettichap
Not bigger than the wren and seldom seen
I've often found their nests in chance's way
When I in pathless woods did idly roam
But never did I dream untill today
A spot like this would be her chosen home

THE NIGHTINGALE'S NEST

Up this green woodland ride let's softly rove
And list' the nightingale – she dwelleth here
Hush, let the wood-gate softly clap – for fear
The noise might drive her from her home of love
For here I've heard her many a merry year
At morn and eve nay all the live-long day
As though she lived on song – this very spot
Just where that old man's beard all wildly trails
Rude arbours o'er the road and stops the way
And where that child its blue bell flowers hath got
Laughing and creeping through the mossy rails
There have I hunted like a very boy
Creeping on hands and knees through matted
    thorns

To find her nest and see her feed her young
And vainly did I many hours employ
All seemed as hidden as a thought unborn
And where these crimping fern-leaves ramp among
The hazel's underboughs I've nestled down
And watched her while she sung and her renown
Hath made me marvel that so famed a bird
Should have no better dress then russet brown
Her wings would tremble in her extacy
And feathers stand on end as 'twere with joy
And mouth wide open to release her heart
Of its out-sobbing songs – the happiest part
Of summer's fame she shared – for so to me
Did happy fancies shapen her employ
But if I touched a bush or scarcely stirred
All in a moment stopt – I watched in vain
The timid bird had left the hazel bush
And at a distance hid to sing again
Lost in a wilderness of listening leaves
Rich extacy would pour its luscious strain
Till envy spurred the emulating thrush
To start less wild and scarce inferior songs
For cares with him for half the year remain
To damp the ardour of his speckled breast
While nightingales to summer's life belongs
And naked trees and winter's nipping wrongs
Are strangers to her music and her rest
Her joys are evergreen her world is wide
– Hark, there she is as usual let's be hush
For in this blackthorn clump if rightly guest
Her curious house is hidden – part aside
These hazel branches in a gentle way
And stoop right cautious 'neath the rustling boughs
For we will have another search today
And hunt this fern-strown thorn-clump round and
    round
And where this seeded woodgrass idly bows

We'll wade right through. It is a likely nook
In such like spots and often on the ground
They'll build where rude boys never think to look
Aye as I live her secret nest is here
Upon this whitethorn stulp – I've searched about
For hours in vain – there, put that bramble bye
Nay, trample on its branches and get near
– How subtle is the bird she started out
And raised a plaintive note of danger nigh
Ere we were past the brambles and now near
Her nest she sudden stops – as choaking fear
That might betray her home – so even now
We'll leave it as we found it – safety's guard
Of pathless solitudes shall keep it still
See there she's sitting on the old oak bough
Mute in her fears – our presence doth retard
Her joys and doubt turns every rapture chill

    Sing on sweet bird may no worse hap befall
Thy visions then the fear that now decieves
We will not plunder music of its dower
Nor turn this spot of happiness to thrall
For melody seems hid in every flower
That blossoms near thy home – these harebells all
Seems bowing with the beautiful in song
And gaping cuckoo with its spotted leaves
Seems blushing of the singing it has heard
How curious is the nest no other bird
Uses such loose materials or weaves
Their dwellings in such spots – dead oaken leaves
Are placed without and velvet moss within
And little scraps of grass – and scant and spare
Of what seems scarce materials, down and hair
For from man's haunts she seemeth nought to win
Yet nature is the builder and contrives
Homes for her childern's comfort even here
Where solitude's deciples spend their lives

Unseen save when a wanderer passes near
That loves such pleasant places – Deep adown
The nest is made an hermit's mossy cell
Snug lies her curious eggs in number five
Of deadened green or rather olive brown
And the old prickly thorn bush guards them well
And here we'll leave them still unknown to wrong
As the old woodland's legacy of song

TO THE SNIPE

Lover of swamps
The quagmire overgrown
With hassock tufts of sedge – where fear encamps
Around thy home alone

The trembling grass
Quakes from the human foot
Nor bears the weight of man to let him pass
Where thou alone and mute

Sittest at rest
In safety 'neath the clump
Of hugh flag forrest that thy haunts invest
Or some old sallow stump

Thriving on seams*
That tiney islands swell
Just hilling from the mud and rancid streams
Suiting thy nature well

For here thy bill
Suited by wisdom good
Of rude unseemly length doth delve and drill
The gelid mass for food

And here mayhap
When summer suns hath drest
The moor's rude desolate and spungy lap
May hide thy mystic nest

Mystic indeed
For isles that ocean make
Are scarcely more secure for birds to build
Then this flag-hidden lake

Boys thread the woods
To their remotest shades
But in these marshy flats these stagnant floods
Security pervades

From year to year
Places untrodden lie
Where man nor boy nor stock hath ventured near
– Nought gazed on but the sky

And fowl that dread
The very breath of man
Hiding in spots that never knew his tread
A wild and timid clan

Wigeon and teal
And wild duck – restless lot
That from man's dreaded sight will ever steal
To the most dreary spot

Here tempests howl
Around each flaggy plot
Where they who dread man's sight, the water fowl,
Hide and are frighted not

'Tis power divine
That heartens them to brave
The roughest tempest and at ease recline
On marshes or the wave

Yet instinct knows
Not safety's bounds – to shun
The firmer ground where sculking fowler goes
With searching dogs and gun

By tepid springs
Scarcely one stride accross
Though brambles from its edge a shelter flings
Thy safety is at loss

And never chuse
The little sinky foss
Streaking the moores whence spa-red waters spews
From pudges fringed with moss

Free-booters there
Intent to kill and slay
Startle with cracking guns the trepid air
And dogs thy haunts betray

From danger's reach
Here thou art safe to roam
Far as these washy flag-grown marshes stretch
A still and quiet home

In these thy haunts
I've gleaned habitual love
From the vague world where pride and folly taunts
I muse and look above

Thy solitudes
The unbounded heaven esteems
And here my heart warms into higher moods
And dignifying dreams

I see the sky
Smile on the meanest spot
Giving to all that creep or walk or flye
A calm and cordial lot

Thine teaches me
Right feelings to employ
That in the dreariest places peace will be
A dweller and a joy

WILD BEES

These childern of the sun which summer brings
As pastoral minstrels in her merry train
Pipe rustic ballads upon busy wings
And glad the cotter's quiet toils again
The white-nosed bee that bores its little hole
In mortared walls and pipes its symphonies
And never-absent couzin black as cole
That Indian-like bepaints its little thighs
With white and red bedight for holiday
Right earlily a morn do pipe and play
And with their legs stroke slumber from their eyes
And aye so fond they of their singing seem
That in their holes abed at close of day
They still keep piping in their honey dreams
And larger ones that thrum on ruder pipe
Round the sweet-smelling closen and rich woods
Where tawney white and red-flushed clover buds
Shine bonnily and beanfields blossom ripe

Shed dainty perfumes and give honey food
To these sweet poets of the summer field
Me much delighting as I stroll along
The narrow path that hay-laid meadow yields
Catching the windings of their wandering song
The black and yellow bumble first on wing
To buzz among the sallow's early flowers
Hiding its nest in holes from fickle spring
Who stints his rambles with her frequent showers
And one that may for wiser piper pass
In livery dress half sables and half red
Who laps a moss ball in the meadow grass
And hurds her stores when April showers have fled
And russet commoner who knows the face
Of every blossom that the meadow brings
Starting the traveller to a quicker pace
By threatening round his head in many rings
These sweeten summer in their happy glee
By giving for her honey melodie

INSECTS

Thou tiney loiterer on the barley's beard
And happy unit of a numerous herd
Of playfellows the laughing summer brings
Mocking the sun's face in their glittering wings
How merrily they creep and run and flye
No kin they bear to labour's drudgery
Smoothing the velvet of the pale hedge-rose
And where they flye for dinner no one knows
The dewdrops feed them not – they love the shine
Of noon whose sun may bring them golden wine
All day they're playing in their Sunday dress
Till night goes sleep and they can do no less.
Then in the heath bell's silken hood they flie

And like to princes in their slumber lie
From coming night and dropping dews and all
In silken beds and roomy painted hall
So happily they spend their summer day
Now in the corn fields now the new mown hay
One almost fancys that such happy things
In coloured moods and richly burnished wings
Are fairey folk in splendid masquerade
Disguised through fear of mortal folk affraid
Keeping their merry pranks a mystery still
Lest glaring day should do their secrets ill

FIELD-CRICKET

Sweet little minstrel of the sunny summer
Housed in the pleasant swells that front the sun
Neighbour to many a happy yearly comer
For joy's glad tidings when the winter's done
How doth thy music through the silk grass run
That cloaths the pleasant banks with herbage new
A chittering sound of healthy happiness
That bids the passer-bye be happy too
Who hearing thee feels full of pleasant moods
Picturing the cheerfulness that summer's dress
Brings to the eye with all her leaves and grass
In freshness beautified and summer's sounds
Brings to the ear in one continued flood
The luxury of joy that knows no bounds

I often pause to seek thee when I pass
Thy cottage in the sweet refreshing hue
Of sunny flowers and rich luxuriant grass
But thou wert ever hidden from the view
Brooding and piping o'er thy rural song
In all the happiness of solitude
Busy intruders do thy music wrong

And scare thy gladness dumb where they intrude
I've seen thy dwelling by the scythe laid bare
And thee in russet garb from bent to bent
Moping without a song in silence there
Till grass should bring anew thy home-content
And leave thee to thyself to sing and wear
The summer through without another care

SUMMER EVENING

The frog half-fearful jumps accross the path
And little mouse that leaves its hole at eve
Nimbles with timid dread beneath the swath
My rustling steps awhile their joys decieve
Till past – and then the cricket sings more strong
And grasshoppers in merry moods still wear
The short night weary with its fretting song
Up from behind the molehill jumps the hare
Cheat of its chosen bed – and from the bank
The yellowhammer flutters in short fears
From off its nest hid in the grasses rank
And drops again when no more noise it hears
Thus nature's human link and endless thrall:
Proud man still seems the enemy of all

HARES AT PLAY

The birds are gone to bed the cows are still
And sheep lie panting on each old molehill
And underneath the willow's grey-green bough
Like toil a-resting lies the fallow plough
The timid hares throw daylight fears away
On the lane road to dust and dance and play
Then dabble in the grain by nought deterred
To lick the dew-fall from the barley's beard

Then out they sturt again and round the hill
Like happy thoughts – dance – squat – and loiter still
Till milking maidens in the early morn
Gingle their yokes and sturt them in the corn
Through well-known beaten paths each nimbling hare
Sturts quick as fear – and seeks its hidden lair

THE MARTIN

The martin-cat long-shagged of courage good
Of weazle shape a dweller in the wood
With badger hair long-shagged and darting eyes
And lower then the common cat in size
Small head and running on the stoop
Snuffing the ground and hind-parts shouldered up
He keeps one track and hides in lonely shade
Where print of human foot is scarcely made
Save when the woods are cut. The beaten track
The woodman's dog will snuff, cock-tailed and black
Red-legged and spotted over either eye,
Snuffs barks and scrats the lice and passes bye
The great brown horned owl looks down below
And sees the shaggy martin come and go

The martin hurrys through the woodland gaps
And poachers shoot and make his skin for caps
When any woodman come and pass the place
He looks at dogs and scarcely mends his pace
And gipseys often and birdnesting boys
Look in the hole and hear a hissing noise
They climb the tree such noise they never heard
And think the great owl is a foreign bird
When the grey owl her young ones cloathed in down
Seizes the boldest boy and drives him down
They try agen and pelt to start the fray

The grey owl comes and drives them all away
And leaves the martin twisting round his den
Left free from boys and dogs and noise and men

THE HEDGEHOG

The hedgehog hides beneath the rotten hedge
And makes a great round nest of grass and sedge
Or in a bush or in a hollow tree
And many often stoops and say they see
Him roll and fill his prickles full of crabs
And creep away and where the magpie dabs
His wing at muddy dyke in aged root
He makes a nest and fills it full of fruit
On the hedge-bottom hunts for crabs and sloes
And whistles like a cricket as he goes
It rolls up like a ball or shapeless hog
When gipseys hunt it with their noisey dogs
I've seen it in their camps they call it sweet
Though black and bitter and unsavoury meat

But they who hunt the field* for rotten meat
And wash in muddy dyke and call it sweet
And eat what dogs refuse where e'er they dwell
Care little either for the taste or smell
They say they milk the cows and when they lye
Nibble their fleshy teats and make them dry
But they who've seen the small head like a hog
Rolled up to meet the savage of a dog
With mouth scarce big enough to hold a straw
Will ne'er believe what no one ever saw
But still they hunt the hedges all about
And shepherd dogs are trained to hunt them out
They hurl with savage force the stick and stone
And no one cares and still the strife goes on

The shepherd on his journey heard when nigh
His dog among the bushes barking high
The ploughman ran and gave a hearty shout
He found a weary fox and beat him out
The ploughman laughed and would have ploughed him
   in
But the old shepherd took him for the skin
He lay upon the furrow stretched and dead
The old dog lay and licked the wounds that bled
The ploughman beat him till his ribs would crack
And then the shepherd slung him at his back
And when he rested, to his dog's supprise
The old fox started from his dead disguise
And while the dog lay panting in the sedge
He up and snapt and bolted through the hedge

He scampered to the bushes far away
The shepherd called the ploughman to the fray
The ploughman wished he had a gun to shoot
The old dog barked and followed the pursuit
The shepherd threw* his hook and tottered past
The ploughman ran but none could go so fast
The woodman threw his faggot from the way
And ceased to chop and wondered at the fray
But when he saw the dog and heard the cry
He threw his hatchet but the fox was bye
The shepherd broke his hook and lost the skin
He found a badger hole and bolted in
They tryed to dig but safe from danger's way
He lived to chase the hounds another day

The badger grunting on his woodland track
With shaggy hide and sharp nose scrowed with black
Roots in the bushes and the woods and makes
A great hugh burrow in the ferns and brakes
With nose on ground he runs an awkard pace
And anything will beat him in the race
The shepherd's dog will run him to his den
Followed and hooted by the dogs and men
The woodman when the hunting comes about
Go round at night to stop the foxes out
And hurrying through the bushes ferns and brakes
Nor sees the many holes the badger makes
And often through the bushes to the chin
Breaks the old holes and tumbles headlong in

Some keep a baited badger tame as hog
And tame him till he follows like the dog
They urge him on like dogs and show fair play
He beats and scarcely wounded goes away
Lapt up as if asleep he scorns to fly
And siezes any dog that ventures nigh
Clapt like a dog he never bites the men
But worrys dogs and hurrys to his den
They let him out and turn a harrow down
And there he fights the host of all the town
He licks the patting hand and trys to play
And never trys to bite or run away
And runs away from noise in hollow trees
Burnt by the boys to get a swarm of bees

When midnight comes a host of dogs and men
Go out and track the badger to his den
And put a sack within the hole and lye
Till the old grunting badger passes bye
He comes and hears they let the strongest loose

The old fox hears the noise and drops the goose
The poacher shoots and hurrys from the cry
And the old hare half-wounded buzzes bye
They get a forked stick to bear him down
And clap the dogs and bear him to the town
And bait him all the day with many dogs
And laugh and shout and fright the scampering hogs
He runs along and bites at all he meets
They shout and hollo down the noisey streets

He turns about to face the loud uproar
And drives the rebels to their very doors
The frequent stone is hurled where e'er they go
When badgers fight and every one's a foe
The dogs are clapt and urged to join the fray
The badger turns and drives them all away
Though scarcly half as big, dimute and small,
He fights with dogs for hours and beats them all
The heavy mastiff savage in the fray
Lies down and licks his feet and turns away
The bull-dog knows his match and waxes cold
The badger grins and never leaves his hold
He drives the crowd and follows at their heels
And bites them through. The drunkard swears and reels,

The frighted women takes the boys away
The blackguard laughs and hurrys on the fray:
He tries to reach the woods, an awkard race,
But sticks and cudgels quickly stop the chace
He turns agen and drives the noisey crowd
And beats the many dogs in noises loud
He drives away and beats them every one
And then they loose them all and set them on
He falls as dead and kicked by boys and men
Then starts and grins and drives the crowd agen
Till kicked and torn and beaten out he lies
And leaves his hold and cackles groans and dies

LOVES

When, in December 1841, Clare was committed to Northampton General Lunatic Asylum by Dr Fenwick Skrimshire and Dr William Page, the certificate of insanity attributed his disorder of mind to heredity. In his poem, 'First Love', written at Northampton, Clare himself confesses that when he met Mary Joyce

> My face turned pale a deadly pale
>   My legs refused to walk away
> And when she looked what could I ail
>   My life and all seemed turned to clay
>
> And then my blood rushed to my face
>   And took my eyesight quite away
> The trees and bushes round the place
>   Seemed midnight at noon day
> I could not see a single thing
>   Words from my eyes did start
> They spoke as chords do from the string
>   And blood burnt round my heart

The benign arrow of Mary Joyce's power to excite love found a peculiarly vulnerable target in John Clare, and much of his poetry is an obsessive and pertinacious effort, sustained for forty years, to find a language that was adequate to the power of such a mixed blessing as a love that neither wearied nor degenerated into mere domestic coexistence but also tantalized and haunted him, life long, as what-might-have-been.

Nothing in Clare's poetry is more remarkable than the sheer output and intensity of his love-poems; and most of them were inspired by one woman, Mary Joyce. He married Martha 'Patty' Turner, but his true love – one might even say his only love – was Mary Joyce. The key to the intensity and persistence of this may well lie in the fact that this love was vernal and unfulfilled: the relationship ended around 1816, and she died, unmarried, in 1838, at the age of forty-one.

The consummation of Clare's love for Mary, then, was entirely vicarious: and its persisting intensity was clearly a source of deep conflict and difficulty. Married to Patty, he wrote hundreds of love poems to Mary: in order to live under the same roof as his wife, he first concealed Mary's identity by using asterisks. Over the years, she was also transformed into the divine, transcendent source of his own creative power: she became his muse.

This visionary theme is thine
From one who loves thee still
'Tis writ to thee a Valentine
But call it what you will
No more as wont thy beaming eye
To violets I compare*
Nor talk about the lily's dye
To tell thee thou art fair

The time is past when hope's sweet will
First linked thy name with mine
And the fond muse with simple skill
Chose thee its Valentine
Though some may yet their powers employ
To wreath with flowers thy brow
With me thy love's a withered joy
With hope thou'rt nothing now

The all that youth's fond spring esteems
Its blossoms pluckt in May
Are gone like flowers in summer dreams
And thoughts of yesterday
The heavenly dreams of early love
Youth's spell has broken there
And left the aching heart to prove
That earth owns nought so fair

Spring flowers were fitting hope's young songs
To grace love's earliest vow
But withered ones that autumn wrongs
Are emblems meetest now
Their perished blooms that once were green
Hope's faded tale can tell
Of shadows where a sun hath been
And suits its memory well

Then why should I on such a day
Address a song to thee
When withered hope hath died away
And love no more can be
When blinded fate that still destroys
Hath rendered all as vain
And parted from the bosom joys
'Twill never meet again

The substance of our joys hath been
Their flowers have faded long
But memory keeps the shadow green
And wakes this idle song
Then let esteem a welcome prove
That can't its place resign
And friendship take the place of love
To send a Valentine

DEDICATION TO MARY*

O Mary thou that once made all
What youthful dreams coud pleasure call
That once did love to walk with me
And own thy taste for scenery
That sat for hours by wood and brook
And stopt thy curious flowers to look
Where all that met thy artless gaze
Enjoyd thy smiles and won thy praise
O thou that did sincerely love
The cuckoo's note and cooing dove
And stood in raptures oft to hear
The blackbird's music wild and clear
That chasd sleep from thy lovely eyes
To see the morning lark arise
And made thy evening rambles long

To list' the cricket's chittering song
Thou that on sabbath noons sought bowers
To read away the sultry hours
Where roseys hung the cool to share
With thee a blossom full as fair
Oft withering from noon's scorching look
And fluttering dropping on thy book
Whispering morals as they fell
What thou ere this hath provd too well
Picturing stories sad and true
Beneath thy bright eyes beaming blue
How youth and beauty fades and dyes
The sweetest has the least to prize
How blissfull pleasures fade away
That have the shortest time to stay
As suns that blest thy eyes and mine
Are but alowd a day to shine
And fairest days without a cloud
A gloomy evening waits to shroud
So spoke the fading dropping flowers
That perishd in thy musing hours
I know not whether thou descryd
But I coud hear them by thy side
But thy warm heart tho' easy wrung
Woud not be mellancholy long:
If such was felt, the cheering day
Woud quickly chase their glooms away
For thou sought fancys sweet to look
In every hour and every nook
To thee earth swarmd with lovely things
The butterflye with spangld wings
And dragonflye and humble bee
Hummd dreams of Paradise to thee
And o thou fairest dearest still
If nature's wild mysterious skill
Beams that same rapture in thine eye

And left a love that cannot dye
If that fond taste was born to last
Nor vanishd with the summers past
If seasons as they usd to be
Still meet a favourd smile with thee
Then thou accept for memory's sake
All I can give or thou canst take
A parted record known to thee
Of what has been, no more to be
The pleasant past, the future sorrow
The blest today and sad tomorrow –
Descriptions wild of summer walks
By hedges lanes and trackless balks
And many an old familiar scene
Where thou has oft my partner been
Where thou, enrapt in wild delight,
Hast lingerd morning noon and night
And where to fancy's rapturd thrill
Thy lovely memory lingers still
Thy flowers still bloom and look the while
As tho' they witnessd Mary's smile
The birds still sing thy favourd lays
As tho' they sung for Mary's praise
And bees hum glad and fearless by
As tho' their tender friend was nigh
O if with thee those raptures live
Accept the trifle which I give
Tho' lost to pleasures witnessd then
Tho' parted ne'er to meet agen
My aching heart is surely free
To dedicate its thoughts to thee
Then thou accept and if a smile
Lights on the page thou reads the while
If aught bespeaks those banishd hours
Of beauty in thy favourd flowers
Or scenes recall of happy days

That claims as wont thy ready praise
Tho' I so long have lost the claim
To joys which wear thy gentle name
Tho' thy sweet face so long unseen
Seems types of charms that ne'er hath been
Thy voice so long in silence bound
To me that I forget the sound
And tho' thy presence warms my theme
Like beauty floating in a dream
Yet I will think that such may be
Tho' buried secrets all to me
And if it be as hopes portray
Then will thy smiles like dews of heaven
Cheer my lone walks my toils repay
And all I ask be given

FIRST LOVE'S RECOLLECTIONS

First love will with the heart remain
When all its hopes are bye
As frail rose blossoms still retain
Their fragrance till they die
And joy's first dreams will haunt the mind
With shades from whence they sprung
As summer leaves the stems behind
On which spring's blossoms hung

Mary I dare not call thee dear
I've lost that right so long
Yet once again I vex thine ear
With memory's idle song
Had time and change not blotted out
The love of former days
Thou wert the last that I should doubt
Of pleasing with my praise

When honied tokens from each tongue
Told with what truth we loved
How rapturous to thy lips I clung
Whilst nought but smiles reproved
But now methinks if one kind word
Were whispered in thine ear
Thou'dst startle like an untamed bird
And blush with wilder fear

How loath to part how fond to meet
Had we two used to be
At sunset with what eager feet
I hastened on to thee
Scarce nine days passed us ere we met*
In spring nay wintry weather
Now nine years' suns* have risen and set
Nor found us once together

Thy face was so familiar grown
Thyself so often bye
A moment's memory when alone
Would bring thee to mine eye
But now my very dreams forget
That witching look to trace.
Though there thy beauty lingers yet
It wears a stranger face

I felt a pride to name thy name
But now that pride hath flown
My words e'en seem to blush for shame
That own I love thee on
I felt I then thy heart did share
Nor urged a binding vow
But much I doubt if thou couldst spare
One word of kindness now

And what is now my name to thee
Though once nought seemed so dear
Perhaps a jest in hours of glee
To please some idle ear
And yet like counterfeits with me
Impressions linger on
Though all the gilded finery
That passed for truth is gone

Ere the world smiled upon my lays
A sweeter meed was mine
Thy blushing look of ready praise
Was raised at every line
But now methinks thy fervent love
Is changed to scorn severe
And songs that other hearts approve
Seem discord to thine ear

When last thy gentle cheek I prest
And heard thee feign adieu
I little thought that seeming jest
Would prove a word so true
A fate like this hath oft befell
E'en loftier hopes than ours
Spring bids full many buds to swell
That ne'er can grow to flowers

BALLAD*

Where is the heart thou once hast won
Can cease to care about thee?
Where is the eye thou'st smiled upon
Can look for joy without thee?

Lorn is the lot one heart hath met
That's lost to thy caressing
Cold is the hope that loves thee yet
Now thou art past possessing
    Fare thee well

We met, we loved, we've met the last
The farewell word is spoken
O Mary canst thou feel the past
And keep thy heart unbroken
To think how warm we loved and how
Those hopes should blossom never
To think how we are parted now
And parted oh for ever
    Fare thee well

Thou wert the first my heart to win
Thou art the last to wear it
And though another claims akin
Thou must be one to share it
Oh had we known when hopes were sweet
That hopes would once be thwarted
That we should part no more to meet
How sadly we had parted
    Fare thee well

THE MILKING HOUR

The sun had grown on lessening day
A table large and round
And in the distant vapours grey
Seemed leaning on the ground
When Mary like a lingering flower
Did tenderly agree
To stay beyond her milking hour
And talk awhile with me

We wandered till the distant town
Had silenced nearly dumb
And lessened on the quiet ear
Small as a beetle's hum
She turned her buckets upside-down
And made us each a seat
And there we talked the evening brown
Beneath the rustling wheat

And while she milked her breathing cows
I sat beside the streams
In musing o'er our evening joys
Like one in pleasant dreams
The bats and owls to meet the night
From hollow trees had gone
And e'en the flowers had shut for sleep
And still she lingered on

We mused in rapture side by side
Our wishes seemed as one
We talked of time's retreating tide
And sighed to find it gone
And we had sighed more deeply still
O'er all our pleasures past
If we had known what now we know
That we had met the last

———————

I've ran the furlongs to thy door
And thought the way as miles
With doubts that I should see thee not
And scarcely staid for stiles
Lest thou should think me past the time
And change thy mind to go
Some other where to pass the time
The quickest speed was slow

But when thy cottage came in sight
And showed thee at the gate
The very scene was one delight
And though we parted late
Joy scarcely seemed a minute long
When hours their flight had ta'en
And parting welcomed from thy tongue
'Be sure and come again'

For thou wert young and beautiful
A flower but seldom found
That many hands were fain to pull
Who wouldn't care to wound
But there was no delight to meet
Where crowds and folly be
The fields found thee companion meet
And kept love's heart for me

To folly's ear 'twas little known
A secret in a crowd
And only in the fields alone
I spoke thy name aloud
And if to cheer my walk along
A pleasant book was mine
Then beauty's name in every song
Seemed nobody's but thine

Far far from all the world I found
Thy pleasant home and thee
Heaths woods a stretching circle round
Hid thee from all but me
And o so green those ways when I
On Sundays used to seek
Thy company they gave me joy
That cheered me all the week

And when we parted with the pledge
Right quickly to return
How lone the wind sighed through the hedge
Birds singing seemed to mourn
My old home was a stranger place
If told the story plain
My home was in thy happy face
That saw me soon again

THE ENTHUSIAST: A DAYDREAM
IN SUMMER*

'Daydreams of summers gone'   *White**

Wearied with his lonely walk
Hermit-like with none to talk
And cloyed with often seen delight
His spirits sickened at the sight
Of life's realitys, and things
That spread around his wanderings
Of wood and heath in brambles clad
That seemed like him in silence sad
The lone enthusiast weary worn
Sought shelter from the heats of morn
And in a cool nook by the stream
Beside the bridge-wall dreamed a dream
And instant from his half-closed eye
Reality seemed fading bye
Dull fields and woods that round him lay
Like curtains to his dreaming play
All slided by and on his sight
New scenes appeared in fairy light
The skys lit up a fairer sun
The birds a cheery song begun
And flowers bloomed fair and wildly round

As ever grew on dreaming ground
And mid the sweet enchanting view
Created every minute new
He swooned at once from care and strife
Into the poesy of life
A stranger to the thoughts of men
He felt his boyish limbs again
Revelling in all the glee
Of life's first fairy infancy
Chasing by the rippling spring
Dragonflyes of purple wing
Or setting mushroom-tops afloat
Mimmicing the sailing boat
Or vainly trying by supprise
To catch the settling butterflyes
And oft with rapture driving on
Where many partner-boys had gone
Wading through the rustling wheat
Red and purple flowers to meet
To weave and trim a wild cockade
And play the soldier's gay parade
Then searched the ivy-haunted dell
To seek the pooty's painted shell
And scaled the trees with burning breast
Mid scolding crows to rob their nest
Heart bursting with unshackled joys
The only heritage of boys
That from the haunts of manhood flye
Like songbirds from a winter sky
And now tore through the clinging thorns
Seeking kecks for bugle horns
Thus with the schoolboy's heart again
He chased and halooed o'er the plain
Till the old church clock counted one
And told us freedom's hour was gone.
In its dull humming drowsy way

It called us from our sports and play
How different did the sound appear
To that which brought the evening near
That lovely humming happy strain
That brought them liberty again
– The desk the books were all the same
Marked with each well-known little name
And many a cover blotched and blurred
With shapeless forms of beast and bird
And the old master white with years
Sat there to waken boyish fears
While the tough scepter of his sway
That awed to silence all the day
The peeled wand acting to his will
Hung o'er the smoak-stained chimney still
– The church yard still its trees possest
And jackdaws sought their ancient nest
In whose old trunks they did acquire
Homes safe as in the mossy spire
The school they shadowed as before
With its white dial o'er the door
And bees hummed round in summer's pride
In its time-crevised walls to hide
The gravestones childhood eager reads
Peeped o'er the rudely clambering weeds
Where cherubs gilt that represent
The slumbers of the innoscent
Smiled glittering to the slanting sun
As if death's peace with heaven was won
All, all was blest, and peace and plays
Brought back the enthusiast's fairy days
And leaving childhood unpercieved
Scenes sweeter still his dream relieved
Life's calmest spot that lingers green
Manhood and infancy between
When youth's warm feelings have their birth

Creating angels upon earth
And fancying woman born for joy
With nought to wither and destroy
That picture of past youth's delight
Was swimming now before his sight
And love's soft thrills of pleasant pain
Was whispering its deciets again
And Mary, pride of pleasures gone,
Was at his side to lead him on
And on they went through field and lane
Haunts of their loves to trace again
Clung to his arm she skipt along
With the same music on her tongue
The self-same voice as soft and dear
As that which met his youthful ear
The sunny look the witching grace
Still blushed upon her angel face
As though one moment's harmless stay
Had never stole a charm away
That self-same bloom and in her eye
That blue of thirteen summers bye*
She took his hand to climb the stiles
And looked as wont her winning smiles
And as he met her looks divine
More tender did their blushes shine
Her small hand peeped within his own
Thrilled pleasures life hath never known
His heart beat as it once had done
And felt as love had just begun
As they'd ne'er told their minds before
Or parted long to meet no more
The pleasant spots where they had met
All shone as nought had faded yet
The sun was setting o'er the hill
The thorn bush it was blooming still
As it was blooming on the day

When last he reached her boughs of may
And pleased he clumb the thorny grain
To crop its firstling buds again
And claimed in eager extacys
Love's favours as he reached the prize
Marking her heart's uneasy rest
The while he placed them on her breast
And felt warm love's o'erbounding thrill
That it could beat so tender still
And all her artless winning ways
Were with her as of other days
Her fears such fondness to reveal
Her wishes struggling to consceal
Her cheeks love's same warm blushes burned
And smiled when he its warmth returned
O he did feel as he had done
When Mary's bosom first was won
And gazed upon her eyes of blue
And blest her tenderly and true
As she sat by his side to rest
Feeling as then that he was blest
The talk, the whisper, met his ears
The same sweet tales of other years
That as they sat or mused along
Melted like music from her tongue
Objects of summer all the same
Were nigh her gentle praise to claim
The lark was rising from his nest
To sing the setting sun to rest
And her fair hand was o'er her eyes
To see her favourite in the skies
And oft his look was turned to see
If love still felt that melody
And blooming flowers were at her feet
Her bending lovely looks to meet
The blooms of spring and summer days

Lingering as to wait her praise
And though she showed him weeds the while
He praised and loved them for a smile
The cuckoo sung in soft delight
Its ditty to departing light
And murmuring childern far away
Mockt the music in their play
And in the ivied tree the dove
Breathed its soothing song to love
And as her praise she did renew
He smiled and hoped her heart as true
She blushed away in maiden pride
Then nestled closer to his side
He loved to watch her wistful look
Following white moths down the brook
And thrilled to mark her beaming eyes
Brightening in pleasure and surprise
To meet the wild mysterious things
That evening's soothing presence brings
And stepping on with gentle feet
She strove to shun the lark's retreat
And as he near the bushes prest
And scared the linnet from its nest
Fond chidings from her bosom fell
Then blessed the bird and wished it well
His heart was into rapture stirred
His very soul was with the bird
He felt that blessing by her side
As only to himself applied
'Tis woman's love makes earth divine
And life its rudest cares resign
And in his rapture's gushing whim
He told her it was meant for him
She ne'er denied but looked the will
To own as though she blest him still
Yet he had fearful thoughts in view

Joy seemed too happy to be true
He doubted if 'twas Mary by
Yet could not feel the reason why
He loitered by her as in pain
And longed to hear her voice again
And called her by her witching name
She answered – 'twas the very same
And looked as if she knew his fears
Smiling to cheer him through her tears
And whispering in a tender sigh
''Tis youth and Mary standing by'
His heart revived yet in its mirth
Felt fears that they were not of earth
That all were shadows of the mind
Picturing the joys it wished to find
Yet he did feel as like a child
And sighed in fondness till she smiled
Vowing they ne'er would part no more
And act so foolish as before
She nestled closer by his side
And vowed 'We never will' and sighed
He grasped her hand, it seemed to thrill,
And whispered 'No, we never will'
And thought in rapture's mad extream
To hold her though it proved a dream
And instant as that thought begun
Her presence seemed his love to shun
And deaf to all he had to say
Quick turned her tender face away
When her small waist he strove to clasp
She shrunk like water from his grasp.
He woke – all lonely as before
He sat beside the rilling streams
And felt that aching joy once more
Akin to thought and pleasant dreams

BALLAD

Fair maiden when my love began
Ere thou thy beauty knew
I fearless owned my passion then
Nor met reproof from you

But now perfection wakes thy charms
And strangers turn to praise
Thy pride my faint-grown heart alarms
And I scarce dare to gaze

Those lips to which mine own did grow
In love's glad infancy
With ruby ripeness now doth glow
As gems too rich for me

The full-blown rose thy cheeks doth wear
Those lilys on thy brow
Forget whose kiss their buds did wear
And bloom above me now

Those eyes whose first sweet timid light
Did my young hopes inspire
Like midday suns in splendour bright
Now burn me with their fire

Nor can I weep what I bemoan
As great as are my fears
Too burning is my passion grown
To e'er be quenched by tears

BALLAD

O sigh no more, love, sigh no more
Nor pine for earthly treasure
Who fears a shipwreck on the shore
Or meets despair with pleasure

Let not our wants our troubles prove
Although 'tis winter weather
Nor singly strive with what our love
Can better brave together

Thy love is proved thy worth is such
It cannot fail to bless me
If I loose thee I can't be rich
Nor poor if I possess thee

BALLAD*

The spring returns, the pewet screams
Loud welcomes to the dawning
Though harsh and ill as now it seems
'Twas music last May morning
The grass so green – the daisy gay
Wakes no joy in my bosom
Although the garland last Mayday
Wore not a finer blossom

For by this bridge my Mary sat
And praised the screaming plover
As first to hail the day – when I
Confessed myself her lover
And at that moment stooping down
I pluckt a daisy blossom
Which smilingly she called her own
May-garland for her bosom

And in her heart she hid it there
As true love's happy omen
Gold had not claimed a safer care
I thought love's name was woman
I claimed a kiss, she laughed away
I sweetly sold the blossom
I thought myself a king that day
My throne was beauty's bosom

And little thought an evil hour
Was bringing clouds around me
And least of all that little flower
Would turn a thorn to wound me –
She showed me after many days
Though withered – how she prized it
And then she leaned to wealthy praise
And my poor love – despised it

Aloud the whirring pewet screams
The daisy blooms as gaily
But where is Mary? Absence seems
To ask that question daily
Nowhere on earth where joy can be
To glad me with her pleasure
Another name she owns – to me
She is as stolen treasure

When lovers part – the longest mile
Leaves hope of some returning
Though mine's close bye – no hope the while
Within my heart is burning
One hour would bring me to her door
Yet sad and lonely-hearted
If seas between us both should roar
We were not further parted

Though I could reach her with my hand
Ere sun* the earth goes under,
Her heart from mine – the sea and land
Are not more far asunder
The wind and clouds, now here, now there,
Hold not such strange dominion
As woman's cold perverted will
And soon-estranged opinion

CHANGES AND CONTRADICTIONS

If the satisfactions of Clare's earlier poetry derives from a richly sensuous registration of his perceptions of a stable world, his maturity, from as early as 1821, and increasingly through the 1820s and early 1830s, incorporated or absorbed this achievement within a more complex reflectiveness: the syntax slowly veers from simple to elaborate as it comes to interweave many complex and contradictory discoveries: discoveries derived not so much from sheer observation as from sustained painful reflection, centred on his experience of changes and contradictions.

He came to explore the social, political and aesthetic meanings of economic changes and agricultural innovations – matters that changed fundamentally the relationships between the members of his own society and their environment. So he evolved a sense of a heritage, of being heir to natural blessings that were not merely a matter of sensory gratification or of physical well-being but, rather, of moral and spiritual import: fundamentally a matter of a wise love between the individual and his environment. Against such 'natural' virtue, Clare sets the cant and greed, the mania for improvement and the insensitivity of those for whose interests such a document as the following was framed:

And be it further Enacted, That no Horses, Beasts, Asses, Sheep, Lambs, or other Cattle, shall at any Time within the first Ten Years after the said Allotments shall be directed to be entered upon by the respective Proprietors thereof, be kept in any of the public Carriage Roads or Ways to be set out and fenced off on both Sides, or Laned out in pursuance of this Act. *From: An Act for Inclosing Lands in the Parishes of Maxey . . . and Helpstone, in the County of Northampton,* 49 Geo. III. Sess. 1809.

In the process, he shaped a poetry that integrates a number of urgent and passionate questions, all centred on the question of what makes a life worth living. Simultaneously, he developed a sense of personal history *as* social and economic history: thus many of his strongest poems from the 1820s and 1830s tend to take the form of elegiac lament or social complaint, asserting his own pre-enclosure years as inherently pre-lapsarian, Edenic or paradisal. Enmeshed in such mythic framing is the equally urgent theme of first love unfulfilled and of disenchantment. The result is a poetry that is inescapably rooted in a particular epoch, a crisis in English history, but which also expresses the predicaments of one who found his world increasingly undependable, not to be trusted, in an extreme degree.

The delicate balance of his vulnerable mind was irrevocably disturbed by the scheme of well-meaning friends and patrons, who persuaded him to escape in 1832 from his 'blue devils' by leaving his birthplace, to move to a superior cottage in a nearby village. Henceforth, he felt himself to be in exile, in limbo.

Sauntering at ease I often love to lean
O'er old bridge-walls and mark the flood below
Whose ripples through the weeds of oily green
Like happy travellers mutter as they go
And mark the sunshine dancing on the arch
Time keeping to the merry waves beneath
And on the banks see drooping blossoms parch
Thirsting for water in the day's hot breath
Right glad of mud-drops plashed upon their leaves
By cattle plunging from the steepy brink
While water-flowers more than their share recieve
And revel to their very cups in drink.
Just like the world some strive and fare but ill
While others riot and have plenty still

MIDSUMMER

Midsummer's breath gives ripeness to the year
Of beautiful and picturesque and grand
Tinting the mountain with the hues of fear
Bare climbing dizziness – where bushes stand
Their breakneck emminence with danger near
Like lives in peril – though they wear a smile
'Tis sickly green as in a homeless dream
Of terror at their fate – while underhand
Smiles with home hues as rich as health to toil
In mellow greens and darker lights that cheer
The ploughman turning up the healthy soil
And health and pleasure glistens every where
– So high ambitions dwell as danger's guests
And quiet minds as small birds in their nests

THE SHEPHERD'S TREE

Hugh elm thy rifted trunk all notched and scarred
Like to a warrior's destiny – I love
To stretch me often on such shadowed sward
And hear the laugh of summer leaves above
Or on thy buttressed roots to sit and lean
In careless attitude and there reflect
On times and deeds and darings that have been
Old castaways now swallowed in neglect
While thou art towering in thy strength of heart
Stirring the soul to vain imaginings
In which life's sordid being hath no part
The wind of that eternal ditty sings
Humming of future things that burns the mind
To leave some fragment of itself behind

THE MEADOW GRASS

Delicious is a leisure hour
Among the sweet green fields to be
So sweet indeed I have no power
To tell the joys I feel and see
See here the meadows how they lie
So sunny, level, and so green
The grass is waving ancle-high
A sweeter rest was never seen

I look around and drop me down
And feel delight to be alone
Cares hardly dare to show a frown
While May's sweet leisure is my own.
Joy, half a stranger, comes to me
And gives me thoughts to profit bye
I think how happy worlds must be
That dwell above that peaceful sky

That happy sky with here and there
A little cloud that would express
By the slow motions that they wear
They live with peace and quietness
I think so as I see them glide
Thoughts earthly tumults can't destroy
So calm, so soft, so smooth, they ride
I'm sure their errands must be joy

The sky is all serene and mild
The sun is gleaming far away
So sweet, so rich – the very child
Would feel its maker brought the may
For heaven's ways are pleasant ways
Of silent quietness and peace
And he who musing hither strays
Finds all in such a scene as this

Where no strife comes but in the songs
Of birds half frantic in their glee
Hid from the rude world's many wrongs
How can they else but happy be
In places where the summer seems
Entirely out of trouble's way
Where joy o'er outdoor leisure dreams
As if 'twas Sunday every day

For nature here in self-delight
Bestows her richest gifts – the green
Luxuriance all around – the light
Seems more then any common scene –
And yet appears no looker-on
Left to herself and solitude
I seem myself the only one
Intruding on her happy mood

Intruding as of wont to meet
That joyousness she throws around
To feel the grass beneath my feet
Heart-cheered to hear its brushing sound
Pit-patting at one's legs, to feel
Their seeded heads then bounce away
There's something more then joy to steal
A walk o'er meadows in the may

A noise now comes on joy's repose
That May's right welcome visit brings
Up from the bush the blackbird goes
The fanned leaves dance beneath his wings
And up with yet a louder noise
Woodpigeons flusker – roadway cows
Brouze there – and soon the herdboy shows
His head amid the shaking boughs

There's something more to fill the mind
Then words can paint to ears and eyes
A calmness quiet loves to find
In these green summer reveries
A freshness giving youth to age
A health to pain and troubles drear
The world has nought but wars to wage
Peace comes and makes her dwelling here

I feel so calm I seem to find
A world I never felt before
And heaven fills my clouded mind
As though it would be dull no more
An endless sunshine glows around
A meadow like a waveless sea
Glows green in many a level ground
A very Paradise to me

'Tis sweeter than the sweetest book
That ever met the poet's eye
To read in this delightful nook
The scenes that round about me lie
And yet they are but common things
Green hedges bowering o'er the grass
And one old tree that stoops and flings
Its boughs o'er water smooth as glass

And on a ledge of gravel crags
Those golden blooms so nobly towers
Though but the yellow water-flags
They're fine enough for garden-flowers
And overhead the breadth of sky
Goes spreading gladness everywhere
Yet on this meadow-grass to lie
Nowhere so happy seems as here

THE ROBIN'S NEST*

Come luscious spring come with thy mossy roots
Thy weed-strown banks – young grass – and tender
    shoots
Of woods new-plashed sweet smells of opening blooms
Sweet sunny mornings and right glorious dooms
Of happiness – to seek and harbour in
Far from the ruder world's inglorious din
Who see no glory but in sordid pelf
And nought of greatness but its little self
Scorning the splendid gift that nature gives
Where nature's glory ever breathes and lives
Seated in crimping ferns uncurling now
In russet fringes ere in leaves they bow
And moss as green as silk – there let me be
By the grey-powdered trunk of old oak-tree

Buried in green delights to which the heart
Clings with delight and beats as loath to part
The birds unbid come round about to give
Their music to my pleasures – wild flowers live
About as if for me – they smile and bloom
Like uninvited guests that love to come
Their wild fragrant offerings all to bring
Paying me kindness like a throned king
Lost in such extacys in this old spot
I feel that rapture which the world hath not
That joy like health that flushes in my face
Amid the brambles of this ancient place
Shut out from all but that superior power
That guards and glads and cheers me every hour
That wraps me like a mantle from the storm
Of care and bids the coldest hope be warm
That speaks in spots where all things silent be
In words not heard but felt – each ancient tree
With lickens deckt – time's hoary pedigree
Becomes a monitor to teach and bless
And rid me of the evils cares possess
And bids me look above the trivial things
To which pride's mercenary spirit clings
The pomps, the wealth, and artificial toys
That men call wealth beleagued with strife and noise
To seek the silence of their ancient reign
And be myself in memory once again
To trace the path of briar-entangled holt
Or bushy closen where the wanton colt
Crops the young juicey leaves from off the hedge
In this old wood where birds their passions pledge
And court and build and sing their under-song
In joy's own cue that to their hearts belong
Having no wish or want unreconsiled
But spell-bound to their homes within the wild
Where old neglect lives patron and befriends

Their homes with safety's wildness – where nought
    lends
A hand to injure, root up or disturb
The things of this old place – there is no curb
Of interest, industry, or slavish gain
To war with nature, so the weeds remain
And wear an ancient passion that arrays
One's feelings with the shadows of old days
The rest of peace the sacredness of mind
In such deep solitudes we seek and find
Where moss grows old and keeps an evergreen
And footmarks seem like miracles when seen
So little meddling toil doth trouble here
The very weeds as patriarchs appear
And if a plant one's curious eyes delight
In this old ancient solitude we might
Come ten years hence of trouble dreaming ill
And find them like old tennants peaceful still
Here the wood robin rustling on the leaves
With fluttering step each visitor recieves
Yet from his ancient home he seldom stirs
In heart content on these dead teazle-burs
He sits and trembles o'er his under-notes
So rich – joy almost chokes his little throat
With extacy and from his own heart flows
That joy himself and partner only knows
He seems to have small fear but hops and comes
Close to one's feet as if he looked for crumbs
And when the woodman strinkles some around
He leaves the twig and hops upon the ground
And feeds untill his little daintys cloy
Then claps his little wings and sings for joy
And when in woodland solitudes I wend
I always hail him as my hermit friend
And naturally enough, whene'er they come
Before me, search my pockets for a crumb

At which he turns his eye and seems to stand
As if expecting somthing from my hand
And thus these feathered heirs of solitude
Remain the tennants of this quiet wood
And live in melody and make their home
And never seem to have a wish to roam.
Beside this ash-stulp where in years gone bye
The thrush had built and taught her young to flye
Where still the nest half-filled with leaves remains
With moss still green amid the twisting grains
Here on the ground and sheltered at its foot
The nest is hid close at its mossy root
Composed of moss and grass and lined with hair
And five brun-coloured eggs snug sheltered there
And bye and bye a happy brood will be
The tennants of this woodland privacy

THE MOORHEN'S NEST

O poesy's power, thou overpowering sweet
That renders hearts that love thee all unmeet
For this rude world, its trouble, and its care
Loading the heart with joys it cannot bear
That warms and chills and burns and bursts at last
O'er broken hopes and troubles never past,
I pay thee worship at a rustic shrine
And dream o'er joys I still imagine mine
I pick up flowers and pebbles and by thee
As gems and jewels they appear to me
I pick out pictures round the fields that lie
In my mind's heart like things that cannot die
Like picking hopes and making friends with all
Yet glass will often bear a harder fall
As bursting bottles loose the precious wine
Hope's casket breaks and I the gems resign

Pain shadows on till feeling's self decays
And all such pleasures leave me is their praise
And thus each fairy vision melts away
Like evening landscapes from the face of day
Till hope returns with April's dewy reign
And then I start and seek for joys again
And pick her fragments up to hurd anew
Like fancy-riches pleasure loves to view
And these associations of the past
Like summer pictures in a winter blast
Renews my heart to feelings as the rain
Falls on the earth and bids it thrive again
Then e'en the fallow fields appear so fair
The very weeds make sweetest gardens there
And summer there puts garments on so gay
I hate the plough that comes to dissaray
Her holiday delights – and labour's toil
Seems vulgar curses on the sunny soil
And man the only object that distrains
Earth's garden into deserts for his gains
Leave him his schemes of gain – 'tis wealth to me
Wild heaths to trace – and note their broken tree*
Which lightening shivered – and which nature tries
To keep alive for poesy to prize
Upon whose mossy roots my leisure sits
To hear the birds pipe o'er their amorous fits
Though less beloved for singing then the taste
They have to choose such homes upon the waste –
Rich architects – and then the spots to see
How picturesque their dwellings make them be
The wild romances of the poet's mind
No sweeter pictures for their tales can find
And so I glad my heart and rove along
Now finding nests – then listening to a song
Then drinking fragrance whose perfuming cheats
Tinges life's sours and bitters into sweets

That heart-stirred fragrance when the summer's rain
Lays the road-dust and sprouts the grass again
Filling the cracks up on the beaten paths
And breathing insence from the mower's swaths
Insence the bards and prophets of old days
Met in the wilderness to glad their praise
And in these summer walks I seem to feel
These Bible pictures in their essence steal
Around me – and the ancientness of joy
Breathe from the woods till pleasures even cloy
Yet holy breathing manna seemly falls
With angel answers if a trouble calls
And then I walk and swing my stick for joy
And catch at little pictures passing bye
A gate whose posts are two old dotterel trees
A close with molehills sprinkled o'er its leas
A little footbrig with its crossing rail
A wood-gap stopt with ivy-wreathing pale
A crooked stile each path-crossed spinny owns
A brooklet forded by its stepping-stones
A wood-bank mined with rabbit-holes – and then
An old oak leaning o'er a badger's den
Whose cave-mouth enters 'neath the twisted charms
Of its old roots and keeps it safe from harms
Pickaxes, spades, and all its strength confounds
When hunted foxes hide from chasing hounds
– Then comes the meadows where I love to see
A floodwashed bank support an aged tree
Whose roots are bare – yet some with foothold good
Crankle and spread and strike beneath the flood
Yet still it leans as safer hold to win
On 'tother side and seems as tumbling in
While every summer finds it green and gay
And winter leaves it safe as did the may
Nor does the morehen find its safety vain
For on its roots their last year's homes remain

And once again a couple from the brood
Seek their old birth-place and in safety's mood
Lodge there their flags and lay – though danger comes
It dares and tries and cannot reach their homes
And so they hatch their eggs and sweetly dream
On their shelfed nests that bridge the gulphy stream
And soon the sutty brood from fear elopes
Where bulrush-forrests give them sweeter hopes
Their hanging nest that aids their wishes well
Each leaves for water as it leaves the shell
And dive and dare and every gambol trie
Till they themselves to other scenes can fly

THE ETERNITY OF NATURE

Leaves from eternity are simple things
To the world's gaze – whereto a spirit clings
Sublime and lasting – trampled underfoot
The daisy lives and strikes its little root
Into the lap of time – centurys may come
And pass away into the silent tomb
And still the child hid in the womb of time
Shall smile and pluck them when this simple rhyme
Shall be forgotten like a churchyard-stone
Or lingering lie unnoticed and alone
When eighteen hundred years our common date
Grows many thousands in their marching state
Aye still the child with pleasure in his eye
Shall cry 'The daisy!' – a familiar cry –
And run to pluck it – in the self-same state
As when time found it in his infant date
And like a child himself when all was new
Wonder might smile and make him notice too
– Its little golden bosom frilled with snow
Might win e'en Eve to stoop adown and show

Her partner Adam in the silky grass
This little gem that smiled where pleasure was
And loving Eve from Eden followed ill
And bloomed with sorrow and lives smiling still
As once in Eden under Heaven's breath
So now on blighted earth and on the lap of death
It smiles for ever – cowslaps' golden blooms
That in the closen and the meadow comes
Shall come when kings and empires fade and die
And in the meadows as time's partners lie
As fresh two thousand years to come as now
With those five crimson spots upon its brow
And little brooks that hum a simple lay
In green unnoticed spots from praise away
Shall sing when poets in time's darkness hid
Shall lie like memory in a pyramid
Forgetting yet not all forgot – tho' lost
Like a thread's end in ravelled windings crost
And the small bumble bee shall hum as long
As nightingales, for time protects the song
And nature is their soul to whom all clings
Of fair or beautiful in lasting things
The little robin in the quiet glen
Hidden from fame and all the strife of men
Sings unto time a pastoral and gives
A music that lives on and ever lives
Both spring and autumn, years rich bloom and fade
Longer then songs that poets ever made
And think ye these time's playthings – pass, proud skill,
Time loves them like a child and ever will
And so I worship them in bushy spots
And sing with them when all else notice not
And feel the music of their mirth agree
With that sooth quiet that bestirreth me
And if I touch aright that quiet tone
That soothing truth that shadows forth their own

Then many a year shall grow in after days
And still find hearts to love my quiet lays
Yet cheering mirth with thoughts sung not for fame
But for the joy that with their utterance came
That inward breath of rapture urged not loud
– Birds singing lone flie silent past the crowd
So in these pastoral spots which childish time
Makes dear to me I wander out and ryhme
What time the dewy morning's infancy
Hangs on each blade of grass and every tree
And sprents the red thighs of the bumble bee
Who 'gins by times unwearied minstrelsy
Who breakfasts, dines, and most divinely sups
With every flower save golden buttercups
On their proud bosoms he will never go
And passes by with scarcely 'How do ye do'
So in their showy gaudy shining cells
Maybe the summer's honey never dwells
– Her ways are mysterys all, yet endless youth
Lives in them all unchangable as truth
With the odd number five. Strange nature's laws
Plays many freaks nor once mistakes the cause
And in the cowslap-peeps this very day
Five spots appear which time ne'er wears away
Nor once mistakes the counting – look within
Each peep and five nor more nor less is seen
And trailing bindweed with its pinky cup
Five lines of paler hue goes streaking up
And birds a many keep the rule alive
And lay five eggs nor more nor less than five
And flowers how many own that mystic power
With five leaves ever making up the flower
The five-leaved grass trailing its golden cup
Of flowers – five leaves make all for which I stoop
And briony in the hedge that now adorns
The tree to which it clings and now the thorns

Own five star-pointed leaves of dingy white
Count which I will all make the number right
And spreading goosegrass trailing all abroad
In leaves of silver green about the road
Five leaves make every blossom all along
I stoop for many, none are counted wrong
'Tis nature's wonder and her maker's will
Who bade earth be and order owns him still
As that superior power who keeps the key
Of wisdom, power, and might through all eternity

SONG'S ETERNITY

What is song's eternity?
Come and see
Can it noise and bustle be?
Come and see
Praises sung or praises said,
Can it be?
Wait awhile and these are dead
Sigh sigh
Be they high or lowly bred
They die

What is song's eternity?
Come and see
Melodys of earth and sky
Here they be
Songs once sung to Adam's ears
Can it be?
– Ballads of six thousand years
Thrive thrive
Songs awakened with the spheres
Alive

Mighty songs that miss decay
What are they?
Crowds and citys pass away
Like a day
Books are writ and books are read
What are they?
Years will lay them with the dead
Sigh sigh
Trifles unto nothing wed
They die

Dreamers list' the honey bee
Mark the tree
Where the blue cap, tootle tee,
Sings a glee
Sung to Adam and to Eve
Here they be
When floods covered every bough
Noah's ark
Heard that ballad singing now
Hark hark

Tootle tootle tootle tee
Can it be
Pride and fame must shadows be?
Come and see
Every season own her own
Bird and bee
Sing creation's music on
Nature's glee
Is in every mood and tone
Eternity

The eternity of song
Liveth here
Nature's universal tongue

Singeth here
Songs I've heard and felt and seen
Everywhere
Songs like the grass are evergreen
The giver
Said live and be, and they have been
For ever

PASTORAL POESY

True poesy is not in words
But images that thoughts express
By which the simplest hearts are stirred
To elevated happiness

Mere books would be but useless things
Where none had taste or mind to read
Like unknown lands where beauty springs
And none are there to heed

But poesy is a language meet
And fields are everyone's employ
The wild flower neath the shepherd's feet
Looks up and gives him joy

A language that is ever green
That feelings unto all impart
As awthorn blossoms soon as seen
Give May to every heart

The pictures that our summer minds
In summer's dwellings meet
The fancys that the shepherd finds
To make his leisure sweet

The dustmills that the cowboy delves
In banks for dust to run
Creates a summer in ourselves
He does as we have done

An image to the mind is brought
Where happiness enjoys
An easy thoughtlessness of thought
And meets excess of joys

The world is in that little spot
With him – and all beside
Is nothing. All a life forgot
In feelings satisfied

And such is poesy. Its power
May varied lights employ
Yet to all minds* it gives the dower
Of self-creating joy

And whether it be hill or moor
I feel where e'er I go
A silence that discourses more
Then any tongue can do

Unruffled quietness hath made
A peace in every place
And woods are resting in their shade
Of social loneliness

The storm from which the shepherd turns
To pull his beaver down
While he upon the heath sojourns
Which autumn bleaches brown

Is music aye and more indeed
To those of musing mind
Who through the yellow woods proceed
And listen to the wind

The poet in his fitful glee
And fancy's many moods
Meets it as some strange melody
And poem of the woods

It sings and whistles in his mind
And then it talks aloud
While by some leaning tree reclined
He shuns a coming cloud

That sails its bulk against the sun
A mountain in the light
He heeds not for the storm begun
But dallys with delight

And now a harp that flings around
The music of the wind
The poet often hears the sound
When beauty fills the mind

The morn with saffron stripes* and grey
Or blushing to the view
Like summer fields when run away
In weeds of crimson hue

Will simple shepherds' hearts imbue
With nature's poesy
Who inly fancy while they view
How grand must heaven be

With every musing mind she steals
Attendance on their way
The simplest thing her heart reveals
Is seldom thrown away

The old man full of leisure hours
Sits cutting at his door
Rude fancy sticks to tye his flowers
– They're sticks and nothing more

With many passing by his door,
But pleasure has its bent
With him 'tis happiness and more
Heart-satisfied content

Those box-edged borders that imprint
Their fragrance near his door
Hath been the comfort of his heart
For sixty years and more

That mossy thatch above his head
In winter's drifting showers
To him and his old partner made
A music many hours

It patted to their hearts a joy
That humble comfort made
A little fire to keep them dry
And shelter over head

And such no matter what they call
Each, all are nothing less
Then poesy's power that gives to all
A cheerful blessedness

So would I my own mind employ
And my own heart impress
That poesy's self's a dwelling joy
Of humble quietness

So would I for the biding joy
That to such thoughts belong
That I life's errand may employ
As harmless as a song

THE FALLEN ELM

Old elm that murmured in our chimney top
The sweetest anthem autumn ever made
And into mellow whispering calms would drop
When showers fell on thy many-coloured shade
And when dark tempests mimic thunder made
While darkness came as it would strangle light
With the black tempest of a winter night
That rocked thee like a cradle to thy root
How did I love to hear the winds upbraid
Thy strength without – while all within was mute
It seasoned comfort to our hearts' desire
We felt thy kind protection like a friend
And edged our chairs up closer to the fire
Enjoying comforts that was never penned
Old favourite tree thou'st seen time's changes lower
Though change till now did never injure thee
For time beheld thee as her sacred dower
And nature claimed thee her domestic tree
Storms came and shook thee many a weary hour
Yet stedfast to thy home thy roots hath been
Summers of thirst parched round thy homely bower
Till earth grew iron – still thy leaves was green
The childern sought thee in thy summer shade

And made their play-house rings of sticks and stone
The mavis sang and felt himself alone
While in thy leaves his early nest was made
And I did feel his happiness mine own
Nought heeding that our friendship was betrayed
Friend not inanimate – though stocks and stones
There are and many formed of flesh and bones –
Thou owned a language by which hearts are stirred
Deeper than by a feeling cloathed in words
And speakest now what's known of every tongue
Language of pity and the force of wrong
What cant assumes, what hypocrites will dare
Speaks home to truth and shows it what they are
I see a picture which thy fate displays
And learn a lesson from thy destiny
Self-interest saw thee stand in freedom's ways
So thy old shadow must a tyrant be
Thou'st heard the knave abusing those in power
Bawl freedom loud and then opress the free
Thou'st sheltered hypocrites in many a shower
That when in power would never shelter thee
Thou'st heard the knave supply his canting powers
With wrong's illusions when he wanted friends
That bawled for shelter when he lived in showers
And when clouds vanished made thy shade amends
With axe at root he felled thee to the ground
And barked of freedom – O I hate the sound
Time hears its visions speak and age sublime
Had made thee a deciple unto time
– It grows the cant term of enslaving tools
To wrong another by the name of right
It grows the liscence of o'erbearing fools
To cheat plain honesty by force of might
Thus came enclosure – ruin was its guide
But freedom's clapping hands enjoyed the sight
Though comfort's cottage soon was thrust aside

And workhouse prisons raised upon the site
E'en nature's dwellings far away from men,
The common heath, became the spoilers' prey
The rabbit had not where to make his den
And labour's only cow was drove away
No matter – wrong was right and right was wrong
And freedom's bawl was sanction to the song
– Such was thy ruin, music-making elm
The rights of freedom was to injure thine
As thou wert served, so would they overwhelm
In freedom's name the little that is mine
And there are knaves that brawl for better laws
And cant of tyranny in stronger powers
Who glut their vile unsatiated maws
And freedom's birthright from the weak devours

THE MORES

Far spread the moorey ground a level scene
Bespread with rush and one eternal green
That never felt the rage of blundering plough
Though centurys wreathed spring's blossoms on its
    brow
Still meeting plains that stretched them far away
In uncheckt shadows of green, brown, and grey
Unbounded freedom ruled the wandering scene
Nor fence of ownership crept in between
To hide the prospect of the following eye
Its only bondage was the circling sky
One mighty flat undwarfed by bush and tree
Spread its faint shadow of immensity
And lost itself, which seemed to eke its bounds
In the blue mist the horizon's edge surrounds

Now this sweet vision of my boyish hours
Free as spring clouds and wild as summer flowers
Is faded all – a hope that blossomed free,
And hath been once, no more shall ever be
Inclosure came and trampled on the grave
Of labour's rights and left the poor a slave
And memory's pride ere want to wealth did bow
Is both the shadow and the substance now
The sheep and cows were free to range as then
Where change might prompt nor felt the bonds of men
Cows went and came, with evening morn and night,
To the wild pasture as their common right
And sheep, unfolded with the rising sun,
Heard the swains shout and felt their freedom won
Tracked the red fallow field and heath and plain
Then met the brook and drank and roamed again
The brook that dribbled on as clear as glass
Beneath the roots they hid among the grass
While the glad shepherd traced their tracks along
Free as the lark and happy as her song
But now all's fled and flats of many a dye
That seemed to lengthen with the following eye
Moors, loosing from the sight, far, smooth, and blea,
Where swopt the plover in its pleasure free
Are vanished now with commons wild and gay
As poet's visions of life's early day
Mulberry-bushes where the boy would run
To fill his hands with fruit are grubbed and done
And hedgrow-briars – flower-lovers overjoyed
Came and got flower-pots – these are all destroyed
And sky-bound mores in mangled garbs are left
Like mighty giants of their limbs bereft
Fence now meets fence in owners' little bounds
Of field and meadow large as garden grounds
In little parcels little minds to please
With men and flocks imprisoned ill at ease

Each little path that led its pleasant way
As sweet as morning leading night astray
Where little flowers bloomed round a varied host
That travel felt delighted to be lost
Nor grudged the steps that he had ta'en as vain
When right roads traced his journeys and again –
Nay, on a broken tree he'd sit awhile
To see the mores and fields and meadows smile
Sometimes with cowslaps smothered – then all white
With daiseys – then the summer's splendid sight
Of cornfields crimson o'er the headache bloomd
Like splendid armys for the battle plumed
He gazed upon them with wild fancy's eye
As fallen landscapes from an evening sky
These paths are stopt – the rude philistine's thrall
Is laid upon them and destroyed them all
Each little tyrant with his little sign
Shows where man claims earth glows no more divine
But paths to freedom and to childhood dear
A board sticks up to notice 'no road here'
And on the tree with ivy overhung
The hated sign by vulgar taste is hung*
As tho' the very birds should learn to know
When they go there they must no further go
Thus, with the poor, scared freedom bade goodbye
And much they feel it in the smothered sigh
And birds and trees and flowers without a name
All sighed when lawless law's enclosure came
And dreams of plunder in such rebel schemes
Have found too truly that they were but dreams

Petitioners are full of prayers
To fall in pity's way
But if her hand the gift forbears
They'll sooner swear than pray
They're not the worst to want who lurch
On plenty with complaints
No more then those who go to church
Are e'er the better saints

I hold no hat to beg a mite
Nor pick it up when thrown
Nor limping leg I hold in sight
But pray to keep my own
Where profit gets his clutches in
There's little he will leave
Gain stooping for a single pin
Will stick it on his sleeve

For passers-by I never pin
No troubles to my breast
Nor carry round some names to win*
More money from the rest
I'm Swordy Well a piece of land
That's fell upon the town
Who worked me till I couldn't stand
And crush me now I'm down

In parish bonds I well may wail
Reduced to every shift
Pity may grieve at trouble's tale
But cunning shares the gift
Harvests with plenty on his brow
Leaves losses' taunts with me
Yet gain comes yearly with the plough
And will not let me be

Alas dependance thou'rt a brute
Want only understands
His feelings wither branch and root
That falls in parish hands.
The muck that clouts the ploughman's shoe
The moss that hides the stone,
Now I'm become the parish due,
Is more then I can own

Though I'm no man yet any wrong
Some sort of right may seek
And I am glad if e'en a song
Gives me the room to speak
I've got among such grubbling geer
And such a hungry pack
If I brought harvests twice a year
They'd bring me nothing back

When war their tyrant-prices got
I trembled with alarms
They fell and saved my little spot
Or towns had turned to farms
Let profit keep an humble place
That gentry may be known
Let pedigrees their honours trace
And toil enjoy its own

The silver springs grown naked dykes
Scarce own a bunch of rushes
When grain got high the tasteless tykes
Grubbed up trees, banks, and bushes
And me, they turned me inside out
For sand and grit and stones
And turned my old green hills about
And pickt my very bones

These things that claim my own as theirs
Were born by yesterday
But ere I fell to town affairs
I were as proud as they
I kept my horses, cows, and sheep
And built the town below
Ere they had cat or dog to keep
And then to use me so

Parish allowance gaunt and dread
Had it the earth to keep
Would even pine the bees to dead
To save an extra keep
Pride's workhouse is a place that yields
From poverty its gains
And mines a workhouse for the fields
A-starving the remains

The bees flye round in feeble rings
And find no blossom bye
Then thrum their almost weary wings
Upon the moss and die
Rabbits that find my hills turned o'er
Forsake my poor abode
They dread a workhouse like the poor
And nibble on the road

If with a clover bottle now
Spring dares to lift her head
The next day brings the hasty plough
And makes me misery's bed
The butterflyes may wir and come
I cannot keep 'em now
Nor can they bear my parish home
That withers on my brow

No, now not e'en a stone can lie
I'm just what e'er they like
My hedges like the winter flye
And leave me but the dyke
My gates are thrown from off the hooks
The parish thoroughfare
Lord he that's in the parish books
Has little wealth to spare

I couldn't keep a dust of grit
Nor scarce a grain of sand
But bags and carts claimed every bit
And now they've got the land
I used to bring the summer's life
To many a butterflye
But in oppression's iron strife
Dead tussocks bow and sigh

I've scarce a nook to call my own
For things that creep or flye
The beetle hiding 'neath a stone
Does well to hurry bye
Stock eats my struggles every day
As bare as any road
He's sure to be in something's way
If e'er he stirs abroad

I am no man to whine and beg
But fond of freedom still
I hang no lies on pity's peg
To bring a grist to mill
On pity's back I needn't jump
My looks speak loud alone
My only tree they've left a stump
And nought remains my own

My mossy hills gain's greedy hand
And more then greedy mind
Levels into a russet land
Nor leaves a bent behind
In summers gone I bloomed in pride
Folks came for miles to prize
My flowers that bloomed nowhere beside
And scarce believed their eyes

Yet worried with a greedy pack
They rend and delve and tear
The very grass from off my back
I've scarce a rag to wear
Gain takes my freedom all away
Since its dull suit I wore
And yet scorn vows I never pay
And hurts me more and more

And should the price of grain get high –
Lord help and keep it low –
I shan't possess a single flye
Or get a weed to grow
I shan't possess a yard of ground
To bid a mouse to thrive
For gain has put me in a pound
I scarce can keep alive

I own I'm poor like many more
But then the poor mun live
And many came for miles before
For what I had to give
But since I fell upon the town
They pass me with a sigh
I've scarce the room to say 'Sit down'
And so they wander bye

Though now I seem so full of clack
Yet when ye're riding bye
The very birds upon my back
Are not more fain to flye
I feel so lorn in this disgrace
God send the grain to fall
I am the oldest in the place
And the worst-served of all

Lord bless ye I was kind to all
And poverty in me
Could always find a humble stall
A rest and lodging free
Poor bodys with an hungry ass
I welcomed many a day
And gave him tether-room and grass
And never said him nay

There was a time my bit of ground
Made freemen of the slave
The ass no pindar'd dare to pound
When I his supper gave
The gipsey's camp was not affraid
I made his dwelling free
Till vile enclosure came and made
A parish slave of me

The gipseys further on sojourn
No parish bounds they like
No sticks I own and would earth burn
I shouldn't own a dyke
I am no friend to lawless work
Nor would a rebel be
And why I call a Christian turk
Is they are turks to me

And if I could but find a friend
With no deciet to sham
Who'd send me some few sheep to tend
And leave me as I am
To keep my hills from cart and plough
And strife of mongerel men
And as spring found me find me now
I should look up agen

And save his Lordship's woods, that past
The day of danger dwell,
Of all the fields I am the last
That my own face can tell
Yet what with stone pits' delving holes
And strife to buy and sell
My name will quickly be the whole
That's left of Swordy Well

DECAY

Amidst the happiest joy a shade of grief
Will come – to mark in summer's prime a leaf
Tinged with the autumn's visible decay
As pining to forgetfulness away
Aye blank forgetfulness that coldest lot
To be – and to have been – and then be not
E'en beauty's self, love's essence, heaven's prime –
Mate for eternity in joys sublime,
Earth's most divinest, is a mortal thing
And nurses time's sick autumn from its spring
And fades and fades till wonder knows it not
And admiration hath all praise forgot
Coldly forsaking an unheeding past
To fade and fall and die like common things at last

Old tree, oblivion doth thy life condemn
Blank and recordless as that summer wind
That fanned the first few leaves on thy young stem
When thou wert one year's shoot – and who can find
Their homes of rest or paths of wandering now?
So seems thy history to a thinking mind
As now I gaze upon thy sheltering bough
Thou grew unnoticed up to flourish now
And leave thy past as nothing all behind
Where many years and doubtless centurys lie
That ewe beneath thy shadow – nay that flie
Just settled on a leaf – can know with time
Almost as much of thy blank past as I
Thus blank oblivion reigns as earth's sublime

NOTHINGNESS OF LIFE

I never pass a venerable tree
Pining away to nothingness and dust
Ruin's vain shades of power I never see
Once dedicated to time's cheating trust
But warm reflection makes the saddest thought
And views life's vanity in cheerless light
And sees earth's bubbles youth so eager sought
Burst into emptiness of lost delight
And all the pictures of life's early day
Like evening's striding shadows haste away
Yet there's a glimmering of pleasure springs
From such reflections of earth's vanity
That pines and sickens o'er life's mortal things
And leaves a relish for eternity

The past it is a majic word
Too beautiful to last
It looks back like a lovely face
Who can forget the past?
There's music in its childhood
That's known in every tongue
Like the music of the wildwood
All chorus to the song

The happy dream the joyous play
The life without a sigh
The beauty thoughts can ne'er pourtray
In those four letters lye
The painters' beauty-breathing arts
The poets' speaking pens
Can ne'er call back a thousand part
Of what that word contains

And fancy at its sweetest hour
What e'er may come to pass
Shall find that majic thrill no more
Time broke it like his glass
The sweetest joy the fairest face
The treasure most preferred
Have left the honours of their place
Locked in that silent word

When we look back on what we were
And feel what we are now
A fading leaf is not so drear
Upon a broken bough
A winter seat without a fire
A cold world without friends
Doth not such chilly glooms impart
As that one word portends

Like withered wreaths in banquet halls
When all the rout is past
Like sunshine that on ruins falls
Our pleasures are at last
The joy is fled the love is cold
And beauty's splendour too
Our first believings all are old
And faith itself untrue

When beauty met love's budding spring
In artless witcherys
It were not then an earthly thing
But an angel in disguise
Where are they now of youth's esteems?
All shadows passed away
Flowers blooming but in summer dreams
And thoughts of yesterday

Our childhood soon a trifle gets
Yet like a broken toy
Grown out of date it reccolects
Our memorys into joy
The simple catalogue of things
That reason would despise
Starts in the heart a thousand springs
Of half-forgotten joys

When we review that place of prime
That childhood's joys endow
That seemed more green in winter time
Than summer grass does now
Where oft the task of skill was put
For other boys to match
To run along the churchyard wall
Or balls to cuck and catch

How oft we clomb the porch to cut
Our names upon the leads
Though fame nor anything akin
Was never in our heads
Where hands and feet were rudely drawn
And names we could not spell
And thought no artist in the world
Could ever do as well

We twirled our tops that spun so well
They scarce could tumble down
And thought they twirled as well again
When riddled on the crown
And bee-spell marbles bound to win
As by a potent charm
Was often wetted in the mouth
To show the dotted swarm

We pelted at the weathercock
And he who pelted o'er
Was reckoned as a mighty man
And even somthing more
We leapt accross 'cat gallows sticks'
And mighty proud was he
Who overshot the famous nicks
That reached above his knee

And then each other's tasks we did
And great ambition grew
We ran so swift, so strong we leaped
We almost thought we flew
We ran across the broken brig
Whose wooden rail was lost
And loud the victor's feat was hailed
Who dared the danger most

And hopskotch too a spur to joy
We thought the task divine
To hop and kick the stone right out
And never touch a line
And then we walked on mighty stilts
Scarce seven inches high
Yet on we stalked and thought ourselves
Already at the sky

Our pride to reason would not shrink
In these exalted hours
A jiant's was a pigmy link
To statures such as ours
We even fancied we could flye
And fancy then was true
So with the clouds upon the sky
In dreams at night we flew

We shot our arrows from our bows
Like any archers proud
And thought when lost they went so high
To lodge upon a cloud
And these seemed feats that none before
Ourselves could e'er attain
And Wellington with all his feats
Felt never half so vain

And oft we urged the barking dog
For mischief was our glee
To chace the cat up weed-green walls
And mossy apple-tree
When her tail stood like a bottle-brush
With fear – we laughed again
Like tyrants we could purchase mirth
And ne'er alow for pain

And then our playpots sought and won
For uses and for show
That Wedgewood's self with all his skill
Might guess in vain to know
And pallaces of stone and stick
In which we could not creep
Which Nash himself ne'er made so quick
And never half so cheap

Our fancys made us great and rich
No bounds our wealth could fix
A stool drawn round the room was soon
A splendid coach and six
The majic of our minds was great
And even pebbles they
Soon as we chose to call them gold
Grew guineas in our play

And carriages of oyster-shells
Though filled with nought but stones
Grew instant ministers of state
While clay kings filled their thrones
Like Cinderella's fairey queen
Joy would our wants bewitch
If wealth was sought the dust and stones
Turned wealth and made us rich

The mallow-seed became a cheese
The henbanes loaves of bread
A burdock leaf our table cloth
On a table stone was spread
The bindweed flower that climbs the hedge
Made us a drinking-glass
And there we spread our merry feast
Upon the summer grass

A henbane root could scarcely grow
A mallow shake its seeds
The insects that might feed thereon
Found famine in the weeds
But like the pomp of princely taste
That humbler life anoys
We thought not of our neighbours' wants
While we were wasting joys

We often tried to force the snail
To leave his harvest horn
By singing that the beggarman
Was coming for his corn
We thought we forced the lady-cow
To tell the time of day
'Twas one o'clock and two o'clock
And then she flew away

We bawled to beetles as they ran
That their childern were all gone
Their houses down and door-key hid
Beneath the golden stone
They seemed to haste as fast again
While we shouted as they passed
With mirth half-mad to think our tale
Had urged their speed so fast

The stonecrop that on ruins comes
And hangs like golden balls
How oft to reach its shining blooms
We scaled the mossy walls
And weeds – we gathered weeds as well
Of all that bore a flower
And tied our little poseys up
Beneath the eldern bower

Our little gardens there we made
Of blossoms all arow
And though they had no roots at all
We hoped to see them grow
And in the cart rutt after showers
Of sudden summer rain
We filled our tiney waterpots
And cherished them in vain

We pulled the moss from apple trees
And gathered bits of straws
When weary twirling of our tops
And shooting of our taws
We made birds' nests and thought that birds
Would like them ready-made
And went full twenty times a day
To see if eggs were laid

The long and swaily willow-row
Where we for whips would climb
How sweet their shadows used to grow
In merry harvest time
We pulled boughs down and made a swee
Snug hid from toil and sun
And up we tossed right merrily
Till weary with the fun

On summer eves with wild delight
We bawled the bat to spy
Who in the 'I spy' dusky light
Shrieked loud and flickered bye
And up we tossed our shuttlecocks
And tried to hit the moon
And wondered bats should flye so long
And they come down so soon

We sought for nutts in secret nook
We thought none else could find
And listened to the laughing brook
And mocked the singing wind
We gathered acorns ripe and brown
That hung too high to pull
Which friendly winds would shake adown
Till all had pockets full

Then loading home at day's decline
Each sought his corner stool
Then went to bed till morning came
And crept again to school
Yet there by pleasure unforsook
In nature's happy moods
The cuts in Fenning's Spelling Book
Made up for fields and woods

Each noise that breathed around us then
Was majic all and song
Where ever pastime found us then
Joy never led us wrong
The wild bees in the blossom hung
The coy bird's startled call
To find its home in danger – there
Was music in them all

And o'er the first bumbarrel's nest
We wondered at the spell
That birds who served no prenticeship
Could build their nests so well
And finding linnets' moss was green
And finches chusing grey
And every finches' nest alike
Our wits was all away

Then blackbirds lining theirs with grass
And thrushes theirs with dung –
So for our lives we could not tell
From whence the wisdom sprung
We marvelled much how little birds
Should ever be so wise
And so we guessed some angel came
To teach them from the skys

In winter too we traced the fields
And still felt summer joys
We sought our hips and felt no cold
Cold never came to boys
The sloes appeared as choice as plumbs
When bitten by the frost
And crabs grew honey in the mouth
When apple time was past

We rolled in sunshine lumps of snow
And called them mighty men
And tired of pelting Bouneparte
We ran to slide again
And ponds for glibbest ice we sought
With shouting and delight
And tasks of spelling all were left
To get by heart at night

And when it came – and round the fire
We sat – what joy was there
The kitten dancing round the cork
That dangled from a chair
While we our scraps of paper burnt
To watch the flitting sparks
And Collect books were often torn
For parsons and for clerks

Nought seemed too hard for us to do
But the sums upon our slates
Nought seemed too hard for us to win
But the master's chair of state
The 'Town of Troy' we tried and made
When our sums we could not try
While we envied e'en the sparrows wings
From our prison house to flye

When twelve o'clock was counted out
The joy and strife began
The shut of books the hearty shout
As out of doors we ran
Sunshine and showers who could withstand
Our food and rapture they
We took our dinners in our hands
To loose no time in play

The morn when first we went to school
Who can forget the morn
When the birchwhip lay upon the stool
And our hornbook it was torn
We tore the little pictures out
Less fond of books than play
And only took one letter home
And that the letter 'A'

I love in childhood's little book
To read its lessons through
And o'er each pictured page to look
Because they read so true
And there my heart creates anew
Love for each trifling thing
— Who can disdain the meanest weed
That shows its face at spring

The daisey looks up in my face
As long ago it smiled
It knows no change but keeps its place
And takes me for a child
The chaffinch in the hedgerow thorn
Cries 'pink pink pink' to hear
My footsteps in the early morn
As though a boy was near

I seek no more the finches' nest
Nor stoop for daisey-flowers
I grow a stranger to myself
In these delightful hours
Yet when I hear the voice of spring
I can but call to mind
The pleasures which they used to bring
The joys I used to find

The firetail on the orchard wall
Keeps at its startled cry
Of 'tweet tut tut' nor sees the morn
Of boyhood's mischief bye
It knows no change of changing time
By sickness never stung
It feeds on hope's eternal prime
Around its brooded young

Ponds where we played at 'Duck and Drake'
Where the ash with ivy grew
Where we robbed the owl of all her eggs
And mocked her as she flew
The broad tree in the spinney-hedge
'Neath which the gipseys lay
Where we our fine oak apples got
On the twenty-ninth of May*

These all remain as then they were
And are not changed a day
And the Ivy's crown's as near to green
As mine is to the grey
It shades the pond, o'erhangs the stile
And the oak is in the glen
But the paths of joy are so worn out
I can't find one agen

The merry wind still sings the song
As if no change had been
The birds build nests the summer long
The trees look full as green
As e'er they did in childhood's joy
Though that hath long been bye
When I a happy roving boy
In the fields had used to lye

To tend the restless roving sheep
Or lead the quiet cow
Toils that seemed more than slavery then
How more then freedom now
Could we but feel as then we did
When joy too fond to flye
Would flutter round as soon as bid
And drive all troubles bye

But rainbows on an April cloud
And blossoms pluckt in May
And painted eves that summer brings
Fade not so fast away
Tho' grass is green though flowers are gay
And everywhere they be
What are the leaves on branches hung
Unto the withered tree?

Life's happiest gifts, and what are they?
Pearls by the morning strung
Which ere the noon are swept away –
Short as a cuckoo's song
A nightingale's the summer is
Can pleasure make us proud
To think when swallows fly away
They leave her in her shroud?

Youth revels at his rising hour
With more than summer joys
And rapture holds the fairey flower
Which reason soon destroys
O sweet the bliss which fancy feigns
To hide the eyes of truth
And beautious still the charm remains
Of faces loved in youth

And spring returns the blooming year
Just as it used to be
And joys in youthful smiles appear
To mock the change in me
Each sight leaves memory ill at ease
And stirs an aching bosom
To think that seasons sweet as these
With me are out of blossom

The fairest summer sinks in shade
The sweetest blossom dies
And age finds every beauty fade
That youth esteemed a prize
The play breaks up, the blossom fades,
And childhood dissapears
For higher dooms ambitions aims
And care grows into years

But time we often blame him wrong
That rude destroying time
And follow him with sorrow's song
When he hath done no crime
Our joys in youth are often sold
In folly's thoughtless fray
And many feel their hearts grow old
Before their heads are grey

The past – there lyes in that one word
Joys more than wealth can crown
Nor could a million call them back
Though muses wrote them down
The sweetest joys imagined yet
The beautys that surpast
All life or fancy ever met
Are there among the past

THE OLD MAN'S SONG*

Youth has no fear of ill by no cloudy days anoyed
But the old man's all hath fled and his hopes have met
    their doom
The bud hath burst to bloom and the flower been long
    destroyed
The root too is withered and no more can look for
    bloom
So I have said my say and I have had my day
And sorrow like a young storm creeps dark upon my
    brow
Hopes like to summer winds they have all blown away
And the world's sunny side is turned over with me now
And left me like a lame bird upon a withered bough

I look upon the past, 'tis as black as winter days
But the worst it is not over there is blacker days to come
O would I had but known of the wide world's many
  ways
But futurity is blind so I e'en must share my doom
Joy once reflected brightly of prospects overcast
But now like a looking-glass that's turned to the wall
Life is nothing but a blank and the sunny shining past
Is overspread with glooms that doth every hope enthrall
While troubles daily thicken in the wind ere they fall

Life smiled upon me once as the sun upon the rose
My heart so free and open guessed every face a friend
Though the sweetest flower must fade and the sweetest
  season close
Yet I never gave it thought that my happiness would
  end
Till the warmest-seeming friends grew the coldest at the
  close
As the sun from lonely night hides its haughty shining
  face
Yet I could not think them gone for they turned not
  open foes
While memory fondly mused, former favours to
  retrace,
And I turned but only found that my shadow kept its
  place

And this is nought but common life, what everybody
  finds
As well as I, or more's the luck of those that better speed
I'll mete my lot to bear with the lot of kindred minds
And grudge not those who say they for sorrow have no
  need
Why should I when I know that it will not aid a nay?
For summer is the season, even then the little flye

Finds friends enew indeed, both for leisure and for play
But on the winter window, why they crawl alone to die
Such is life and such am I, a wounded and a winter-
    stricken flie

REMEMBRANCES*

Summer's pleasures they are gone like to visions every one
And the cloudy days of autumn and of winter cometh on
I tried to call them back but unbidden they are gone
Far away from heart and eye and for ever far away
Dear heart and can it be that such raptures meet decay
I thought them all eternal when by Langley Bush I lay
I thought them joys eternal when I used to shout and
    play
On its banks at clink and bandy chock and taw and
    ducking stone
Where silence sitteth now on the wild heath as her own
Like a ruin of the past all alone

When I used to lye and sing by old Eastwell's boiling
    spring
When I used to tie the willow boughs together for a
    swing
And fish with crooked pins and thread and never catch a
    thing
With heart just like a feather – now as heavy as a stone –
When beneath old Lea Close Oak I the bottom branches
    broke
To make our harvest cart like so many working folk
And then to cut a straw at the brook to have a soak
O I never dreamed of parting or that trouble had a sting
Or that pleasures like a flock of birds would ever take to
    wing
Leaving nothing but a little naked spring

When jumping time away on old Crossberry Way
And eating awes like sugar plumbs ere they had lost the
   may
And skipping like a leveret before the peep of day
On the rolly-poly up and down of pleasant Swordy Well
When in Round Oak's narrow lane as the South got
   black again
We sought the hollow ash that was shelter from the rain
With our pockets full of pease we had stolen from the grain
How delicious was the dinner-time on such a showery day
O words are poor reciepts for what time hath stole away
The ancient pulpit-trees and the play

When for school o'er little field with its brook and
   wooden brig
Where I swaggered like a man though I was not half so big
While I held my little plough though 'twas but a willow
   twig
And drove my team along made of nothing but a name
'Gee hep' and 'hoit' and 'woi' – O I never call to mind
Those pleasant names of places but I leave a sigh behind
While I see the little mouldiwarps* hang sweeing to the
   wind
On the only aged willow that in all the field remains
And nature hides her face while they're sweeing in their
   chains
And in a silent murmuring complains

Here was commons for their hills where they seek for
   freedom still
Though every common's gone and though traps are set
   to kill
The little homeless miners – O it turns my bosom chill
When I think of old Sneap Green, Puddock's Nook, and
   Hilly Snow
Where bramble bushes grew and the daisey gemmed in
   dew

And the hills of silken grass like to cushions on the view
Where we threw the pismire crumbs when we'd
    nothing else to do
All leveled like a desert by the never-weary plough
All banished like the sun where that cloud is passing
    now
And settled here for ever on its brow

O I never thought that joys would run away from boys
Or that boys should change their minds and forsake
    mid-summer joys
But alack I never dreamed that the world had other toys
To petrify first feelings, like the fable, into stone
Till I found the pleasure past and a winter come at last
Then the fields were sudden bare and the sky got
    overcast
And boyhood's pleasing haunts like a blossom in the
    blast
Was shrivelled to a withered weed and trampled down
    and done
Till vanished was the morning spring and set the
    summer sun
And winter fought her battle-strife and won

By Langley Bush I roam but the bush hath left its hill
On Cowper Green I stray, 'tis a desert strange and chill
And spreading Lea Close Oak ere decay had penned its
    will
To the axe of the spoiler and self-interest fell a prey
And Crossberry Way and old Round Oak's narrow lane
With its hollow trees like pulpits I shall never see again
Inclosure like a Buonaparte let not a thing remain
It levelled every bush and tree and levelled every hill
And hung the moles for traitors – though the brook is
    running still
It runs a naked stream cold and chill

O had I known as then joy had left the paths of men
I had watched her night and day, besure, and never slept
   agen
And when she turned to go O I'd caught her mantle
   then
And wooed her like a lover by my lonely side to stay
Aye, knelt and worshiped on, as love in beauty's bower
And clung upon her smiles as a bee upon a flower
And gave her heart my poesys all cropt in a sunny hour
As keepsakes and pledges all to never fade away
But love never heeded to treasure up the may
So it went the common road to decay

THE FLITTING*

I've left mine own old home of homes
Green fields and every pleasant place
The summer like a stranger comes
I pause and hardly know her face
I miss the hazel's happy green
The bluebell's quiet hanging blooms
Where envy's sneer was never seen
Where staring malice never comes

I miss the heath its yellow furze
Molehills and rabbit-tracks* that lead
Through beesom ling and teazle burrs
That spread a wilderness indeed
The woodland oaks and all below
That their white-powdered branches shield
The mossy paths – the very crow
Croaks music in my native field

I sit me in my corner chair
That seems to feel itself from home
And hear bird-music here and there
From awthorn hedge and orchard come
I hear, but all is strange and new
– I sat on my old bench in June
The sailing puddock's shrill 'peelew'
O'er Royce Wood seemed a sweeter tune

I walk adown the narrow lane
The nightingale is singing now
But like to me she seems at loss
For Royce Wood and its shielding bough
I lean upon the window sill
The trees and summer happy seem
Green, sunny green, they shine – but still
My heart goes far away, to dream

Of happiness, and thoughts arise
With home-bred pictures many a one
Green lanes that shut out burning skies
And old crooked stiles to rest upon
Above them hangs the maple tree
Below grass swells a velvet hill
And little footpaths sweet to see
Goes seeking sweeter places still

With bye and bye a brook to cross
O'er which a little arch is thrown
No brook is here I feel the loss
From home and friends and all alone
– The stone pit with its shelvy sides
Seemed hanging rocks in my esteem
I miss the prospect far and wide
From Langley Bush, and so I seem

Alone and in a stranger scene
Far far from spots my heart esteems
The closen with their ancient green
Heaths woods and pastures' sunny streams
The awthorns here were hung with may
But still they seem in deader green
The sun e'en seems to loose its way
Nor knows the quarter it is in

I dwell on trifles like a child
I feel as ill becomes a man
And still my thoughts like weedlings wild
Grow up to blossom where they can
They turn to places known so long
And feel that joy was dwelling there
So home-fed pleasures fill the song
That has no present joys to heir

I read in books for happiness
But books are like the sea to joy
They change – as well give age the glass
To hunt its visage when a boy
For books they follow fashions new
And throw all old esteems away
In crowded streets flowers never grew
But many there hath died away

Some sing the pomps of chivalry
As legends of the ancient time
Where gold and pearls and mystery
Are shadows painted for sublime
But passions of sublimity
Belong to plain and simpler things
And David underneath a tree
Sought, when a shepherd, Salem's springs

Where moss did into cushions spring
Forming a seat of velvet hue
A small unnoticed trifling thing
To all but heaven's hailing dew
And David's crown hath passed away
Yet poesy breathes his shepherd skill
His palace lost – and to this day
The little moss is blooming still

Strange scenes mere shadows are to me
Vague unpersonifying things
I love with my old home to be
By quiet woods and gravel springs
Where little pebbles wear as smooth
As hermit's beads by gentle floods
Whose noises doth my spirits soothe
And warms them into singing moods

Here every tree is strange to me
All foreign things where e'er I go
There's none where boyhood made a swee
Or clambered up to rob a crow
No hollow tree or woodland bower
Well-known when joy was beating high
Where beauty ran to shun a shower
And love took pains to keep her dry

And laid the shoaf upon the ground
To keep her from the dripping grass
And ran for stowks and set them round
Till scarce a drop of rain could pass
Through – where the maidens they reclined
And sung sweet ballads now forgot
Which brought sweet memorys to the mind
But here no memory knows them not

There have I sat by many a tree
And leaned o'er many a rural stile
And conned my thoughts as joys to me
Nought heeding who might frown or smile
'Twas nature's beauty that inspired
My heart with raptures not its own
And she's a fame that never tires
How could I feel myself alone?

No – pasture molehills used to lie
And talk to me of sunny days
And then the glad sheep resting bye
All still in ruminating praise
Of summer, and the pleasant place
And every weed and blossom too
Was looking upward in my face
With friendship's welcome 'How do ye do'

All tennants of an ancient place
And heirs of noble heritage
Coeval they with Adam's race
And blest with more substantial age
For when the world first saw the sun
There little flowers beheld him too
And when his love for earth begun
They were the first his smiles to woo

There little lambtoe bunches springs
In red-tinged and begolden dye
For ever, and like China kings
They come but never seem to die
There may-blooms with its little threads
Still comes upon the thorny bowers
And ne'er forgets those pinky threads
Like fairy pins amid the flowers

And still they bloom as on the day
They first crowned wilderness and rock
When Abel haply crowned with may
The firstlings of his little flock
And Eve might from the matted thorn
To deck her lone and lovely brow
Reach that same rose that heedless scorn
Misnames as the dog-rosey now

Give me no highflown fangled things
No haughty pomp in marching chime
Where muses play on golden strings
And splendour passes for sublime
Where citys stretch as far as fame
And fancy's straining eye can go
And piled untill the sky for shame
Is stooping far away below

I love the verse that mild and bland
Breathes of green fields and open sky
I love the muse that in her hand
Bears wreaths of native poesy
Who walks nor skips the pasture brook
In scorn – but by the drinking horse
Leans o'er its little brig to look
How far the sallows lean accross

And feels a rapture in her breast
Upon their root-fringed grains to mark
A hermit morehen's sedgy nest
Just like a naiad's summer bark
She counts the eggs she cannot reach
Admires the spot and loves it well
And yearns, so nature's lessons teach,
Amid such neighbourhoods to dwell

I love the muse who sits her down
Upon the molehill's little lap
Who feels no fear to stain her gown
And pauses by the hedgrow gap
Not with that affectation, praise
Of song to sing, and never see
A field flower grow in all her days
Or e'en a forest's aged tree

E'en here my simple feelings nurse
A love for every simple weed
And e'en this little 'shepherd's purse'
Grieves me to cut it up – Indeed
I feel at times a love and joy
For every weed and every thing
A feeling kindred from a boy
A feeling brought with every spring

And why – this 'shepherd's purse' that grows
In this strange spot – In days gone bye
Grew in the little garden rows
Of my old home now left – And I
Feel what I never felt before
This weed an ancient neighbour here
And though I own the spot no more
Its every trifle makes it dear

The Ivy at the parlour end
The woodbine at the garden gate
Are all and each affection's friend
That rendered parting desolate
But times will change and friends must part
And nature still can make amends
Their memory lingers round the heart
Like life whose essence is its friends

Time looks on pomp with careless moods
Or killing apathy's disdain
– So where old marble citys stood
Poor persecuted weeds remain
She feels a love for little things
That very few can feel beside
And still the grass eternal springs
Where castles stood and grandeur died

DECAY

O poesy is on the wane
For fancy's visions all unfitting
I hardly know her face again
Nature herself seems on the flitting
The fields grow old and common things
The grass, the sky, the winds a-blowing
And spots where still a beauty clings
Are sighing 'Going, all a-going'
O poesy is on the wane
I hardly know her face again

The bank with brambles overspread
And little molehills round about it
Was more to me than laurel shades
With paths and gravel finely clouted
And streaking here and streaking there
Through shaven grass and many a border
With rutty lanes had no compare
And heaths were in a richer order
But poesy is in its wane
I hardly know her face again

I sat with love by pasture stream
Aye beauty's self was sitting by
Till fields did more than Edens seem
Nor could I tell the reason why
I often drank when not a-dry
To pledge her health in draughts divine
Smiles made it nectar from the sky
Love turned e'en water into wine
O poesy is on the wane
I cannot find her face again

The sun those mornings used to find
When clouds were other-country-mountains
And heaven looked upon the mind
With groves and rocks and mottled fountains
These heavens are gone – the mountains grey
Turned mist – the sun a homeless ranger
Pursues a naked weary way
Unnoticed like a very stranger
O poesy is on its wane
Nor love nor joy is mine again

Love's sun went down without a frown
For every joy it used to grieve us
I often think that West is gone
Ah cruel time to undeceive us
The stream it is a naked stream
Where we on Sundays used to ramble
The sky hangs o'er a broken dream
The bramble's dwindled to a bramble
O poesy is on its wane
I cannot find her haunts again

Mere withered stalks and fading trees
And pastures spread with hills and rushes
Are all my fading vision sees
Gone gone is rapture's flooding gushes
When mushrooms they were fairy bowers
Their marble pillars overswelling
And danger paused to pluck the flowers
That in their swathy rings were dwelling
But poesy's spells are on the wane
Nor joy nor fear is mine again

Aye poesy hath passed away
And fancy's visions undecieve us
The night hath ta'en the place of day
And why should passing shadows grieve us?
I thought the flowers upon the hills
Were flowers from Adam's open gardens
And I have had my summer thrills
And I have had my heart's rewardings
So poesy is on the wane
I hardly know her face again

And friendship it hath burned away
Just like a very ember cooling
A make-believe on April-day*
That sent the simple heart a-fooling
Mere jesting in an earnest way
Decieving on and still decieving
And hope is but a fancy play
And joy the art of true believing
For poesy is on the wane
O could I feel her faith again

'MADHOUSES, PRISONS,
WHORESHOPS . . .'

I myself left many Byron Poems behind me but I did
not stay to know or hear what became of them, and I
have written some since I returned, with an account of
my escape from Essex.

November 1841, Letters, p. 652

My poetry has been the world's Hornbook for many
years

Clare to Mary Joyce, 1841

If one wishes to write a poem, one must first invent the
poet. For over twenty years, despite some early short-
lived acclaim, Clare had been inventing himself to little
or no avail: his *Shepherd's Calendar* of 1827 and *Rural Muse*
of 1835 had caused him almost intolerable distress:
editors and patrons had ridden over him rough-shod, and
both books had failed to find a sufficient readership. In
the spring of 1841, Cyrus Redding, founder editor of *The
English Journal*, visited Clare in Allen's Asylum. When
the conversation turned to Byron, Clare asked Redding
to send him a volume of Byron's poetry. Redding re-
sponded to Clare's request generously, and as a result
Clare re-invented himself not only as Byron but also as
Jack Randall, the celebrated prizefighter who, in Clare's
memory,* was intimately connected with the poet. The
collocation may appear odd, but Clare's experiences in
London in 1824 had sowed the seeds for his adoption of
these two personas, albeit strange bedfellows.

By 'becoming' Byron, Clare reclaimed his poetic
vocation; by 'becoming' Randall, he asserted his right to
challenge those who would render him powerless.

When, therefore, in early summer, 1841, he began to write as Byron, he was engaged not in imitation or forgery, but in a self-transformation, constructing an effective and productive self by 'becoming' that epitome of sexual adventurer, political and social libertine and satirist, literary lion, and aristocratic hero in the cause of freedom: a piquant case of the top and bottom united against the middle.

While appropriating Byron's titles for his most ambitious asylum poems, he also kept his own titles up his sleeve, and I have chosen to restore these, adding the Byronic titles after them.

'Old Wigs and Sundries' ('Don Juan') is a perfectly uncharacteristic text, exploiting a dashingly licentious bravura and flamboyance in order to express repressed fears, impulses, desires, anxieties and rages. It is also an account of a sensitive inmate's confinement in an enclosed institution, elbowed by outrageous fellow-patients. It ranges from suggestive jokes at the expense of Queen Victoria to compelling accounts of sexual perversities, not to mention anal and oral sex. Throughout, the Juanesque/Byronic voice is dominant, in some extravagantly managed rhyme-schemes, a tone of reckless insouciance and some outrageous punning.

'Prison Amusements' ('Child Harold') is Byronic only in its borrowed title (minus the 'e') and its stanza-form: in all other respects it is quintessential Clare. Auden once remarked on the maladroitness of Byron's choice of the nine-line Spenserian stanza for a fast-moving poem, but Clare uses it to good effect: he seems to have found the nine-line stanza almost infinitely flexible as a medium for offering a measured sequence of unhurried speculative meditations, and Byron's poem showed him how he could punctuate these with the changes of pace and voice afforded by lyrical songs. Nature is still powerfully present in the poems of this time, both as a presence, chthonic and transcendent, and also as vividly rendered minutiae of colour, sound, motion, light and shade; but it is now an elusive, momentary, nervously charged phenomenon, dynamic but unstable.

By the time Clare escaped from Allen's institution, in July 1841, 'Old Wigs and Sundries' was almost complete; but he continued to write 'Prison Amusements' at Northborough, incorporating into it songs written immediately after his return home and meditations on that place and time, before he was removed, in December, to Northampton. At that time, the poem was left unfinished, but in 1844 he took both poems up again, even though by that time Burns had displaced Byron as his dominant persona. 'Old Wigs and Sundries' he brought up to date, and 'Prison Amusements' he extended further.

Maid of Walkherd, meet again,*
By the wilding in the glen,
By the oak against the door,
Where we often met before.
By thy bosom's heaving snow,
By thy fondness none shall know,
Maid of Walkherd, meet again,
By the wilding in the glen.

By thy hand of slender make,
By thy love I'll ne'er forsake,
By thy heart I'll ne'er betray,
Let me kiss thy fears away!
I will live and love thee ever,
Leave thee and forsake thee never!
Though far in other lands to be,
Yet never far from love and thee.

THE FRIGHTENED PLOUGHMAN

I went in the fields with the leisure I got,
The stranger might smile but I heeded him not;
The hovel was ready to screen from a shower
And the book in my pocket was read in an hour.

The bird came for shelter but soon flew away;
The horse came to look and seemed happy to stay,
He stood up in quiet and hung down his head
And seemed to be hearing the poem I read.

The ploughman would turn from his plough in the day,
And wonder what *being* had come in his way,
To lie on a molehill, and read the day long,
And laugh out aloud when he finished his song.

The peewit turned over and stooped o'er my head,
Where the raven croaked loud, like the ploughman
    ill-bred,
But the lark high above charmed me all the day long
So I sat down and joined in the chorus of song.

The foolhardy ploughman I well could endure,
His praise was worth nothing, his censure was poor;
Fame bade me go on and I toiled the day long,
Till the fields where he lived should be known in my
    song.

THE GIPSY CAMP*

The snow falls deep; the Forest lies alone:
The boy goes hasty for his load of brakes,
Then thinks upon the fire and hurries back;
The Gipsy knocks his hands and tucks them up,
And seeks his squalid camp, half hid in snow,
Beneath the oak, which breaks away the wind,
And bushes close, with snow like hovel warm:
There stinking mutton roasts upon the coals,
And the half-roasted dog squats close and rubs,
Then feels the heat too strong and goes aloof;
He watches well, but none a bit can spare,
And vainly waits the morsel thrown away:
'Tis thus they live – a picture to the place;
A quiet, pilfering, unprotected race.

———————

Nigh Leopard's Hill* stand All-n's hells
The public know the same
Where lady sods and buggers dwell
To play the dirty game

A man there is a prisoner there
Locked up from week to week
He's very fond they do declare
To play at hide and seek

With sweethearts so they seem to say
And such like sort of stuff
Well – one did come the other day
With half a pound of snuff

The snuff went here the snuff went there
And is not that a bad house
To cheat a prisoner of his fare
In a well-ordered madhouse

They'll cheat you of your money, friend,
By takeing too much care o't
And if your wives their cun-ys send
They're sure to have a share o't

Now where this snuff could chance to stop
Perhaps gifts hurded are up
Till Mat and steward open shop
And have a jolly flare-up

Madhouses they must shut up shop
And tramp to fairs and races
Master and men as madmen stop
Life lives by changing places

BALLAD — FRAGMENT*

O Lord God Almighty How Usefull Art Thou
To Darn The Knave's Cloak And To Paint The
 Thieve's Brow

As Good As A Laundress Thy Kindness Has Been
To Help Starving Sinners And Wash The Unclean
Thou'rt As Good As A Nurse To the Sickly And Lame
That Live In Bad Houses And Die In Ill Fame
For The Worst In The World Have A Passport For
 Heaven
While The Best Go To Hell Like A Deed Unforgiven

And I'll Hazard Hell Upon Life's Roughest Waves
Before I'll Be Cheated By Ruffians and Knaves
Plain Honesty Still Is The Truth Of My Song
And I'll Still Stick For Right To Be Out Of The Wrong
The Honest And True My Example Shall Be
For While A Man's Honest His Conscience Is Free

Part of
THE SALE OF OLD WIGS AND SUNDRIES,
or
DON JUAN*

'Poets are born' – and so are whores – the trade is
Grown universal – in these canting days
Women of fashion must of course be ladies
And whoreing is the business that still pays
Playhouses Ballrooms – there the masquerade is
– To do what was of old – and nowadays
Their maids – nay wives so innocent and blooming
Cuckold their spouses to seem honest women

Milton sung Eden and the fall of man
Not woman for the name implies a wh—e
And they would make a ruin of his plan
Falling so often they can fall no lower
Tell me a worse delusion if you can
For innoscence – and I will sing no more
Wherever mischief is, 'tis woman's brewing
Created from manself – to be man's ruin

The flower in bud hides from the fading sun
And keeps the hue of beauty on its cheek
But when full-blown they into riot run
The hue turns pale and lost each ruddy streak
So 'tis with woman who pretends to shun
Immodest actions which they inly seek
Night hides the wh—e – and cupboards tart and pasty
Flora was p-x-d – and woman's quite as nasty

Marriage is nothing but a driveling hoax
To please old codgers when they're turned of forty
I wed and left my wife like other folks
But not untill I found her false and faulty
O woman fair – the man must pay thy jokes
Such makes a husband very often naughty
Who falls in love will seek his own undoing
The road to marriage is – 'the road to ruin'

Love worse then debt or drink or any fate
It is the damnest smart of matrimony
A hell incarnate is a woman-mate
The knot is tied – and then we loose the honey
A wife is just the prototype to hate
Commons for stock and warrens for the coney
Are not more tresspassed over in right's plan
Then this incumberance on the rights of man

There's much said about love and more of women
I wish they were as modest as they seem
Some borrow husbands till their cheeks are blooming
Not like the red rose blush – but yellow cream
Lord what a while those good days are in coming
Routs Masques and Balls – I wish they were a dream
– I wish for poor men luck – an honest praxis
Cheap food and cloathing – no corn laws or taxes

I wish – but there is little got bye wishing
I wish that bread and great coats ne'er had risen
I wish that there was some such word as 'pishun'
For rhymes' sake for my verses must be dizen
With dresses fine – as hooks with baits for fishing
I wish all honest men were out of prison
I wish M.P's. would spin less yarn – nor doubt
But burn false bills and cross bad taxes out

I wish young married dames were not so frisky
Nor hide the ring to make believe they're single
I wish small beer was half as good as whiskey
And married dames with buggers would not mingle
There's some too cunning far and some too frisky
And here I want a rhyme – so write down 'jingle'
And there's such putting in – in whores' crim. con.
Some mouths would eat forever and eat on

Childern are fond of sucking sugar-candy
And maids of sausages – larger the better
Shopmen are fond of good sigars and brandy
And I of blunt* – and if you change the letter
To C or K it would be quite as handy
And throw the next away – but I'm your debtor
For modesty – yet wishing nought between us
I'd hawl close to a she as Vulcan did to Venus

I really can't tell what this poem will be
About – nor yet what trade I am to follow
I thought to buy old wigs – but that will kill me
With cold starvation – as they're beaten hollow*
Long speeches in a famine will not fill me
And madhouse-traps still take me by the collar
So old wig bargains now must be forgotten
The oil that dressed them fine has made them rotten

I wish old wigs were done with ere they're mouldy
I wish – but here's the papers large and lusty
With speeches that full fifty times they've told ye
– Noble Lord John* to sweet Miss Fanny Fusty
Is wed – a lie good reader I ne'er sold ye
– Prince Albert goes to Germany and must he
Leave the Queen's snuff-box where all fools are
     strumming
From addled eggs no chickens can be coming

Whigs strum state fiddle-strings untill they snap
With cuckoo cuckold cuckoo year by year
The razor plays it on the barber's strap
– The sissars grinder thinks it rather quere
That labour won't afford him 'one wee drap'
Of ale or gin or half and half or beer
– I wish Prince Albert and the noble dastards
Who wed the wives – would get the noble bastards

I wish Prince Albert on his German journey
I wish the Whigs were out of office and
Pickled in law books of some good atorney
For ways and speeches few can understand
They'll bless ye when in power – in prison scorn ye
And make a man rent his own house and land –
I wish Prince Albert's Queen was undefiled
– And every man could get his *wife* with child

I wish the devil luck with all my heart
As I would any other honest body
His bad name passes bye me like a f—t
Stinking of brimstone – then, like a whisky toddy,
We swallow sin which seems to warm the heart
– There's no imputing any sin to God – he
Fills hell with work – and isn't it a hard case
To leave old whigs and give to hell the carcass

Me-b—ne may throw his wig to little Vicky
And so resign* his humbug and his power
And she with the young princess* mount the dickey
On ass-milk diet for her German tour
Asses like ministers are rather tricky
I and the country proves it every hour
W-ll—gt-n and M-lb—ne in their station
Coblers to queens – are phisic to the nation

These batch of toadstools on this rotten tree
Shall be the cabinet of any queen
Though not such coblers as her servants be
They're of Gods making – that is plainly seen
Nor red nor green nor orange – they are free
To thrive and flourish as the Whigs have been
But come tomorrow – like the Whigs forgotten
You'll find them withered, stinking, dead and rotten

Death is an awfull thing, it is, by God
I've said so often and I think so now
'Tis rather droll to see an old wig nod
Then doze and die the devil don't know how
Odd things are wearisome and this is odd –
'Tis better work then kicking up a row
I'm weary of old Whigs and old whigs' heirs
And long been sick of teazing God with prayers

I've never seen the cow turn to a bull
I've never seen a horse become an ass
I've never* seen an old brawn cloathed in wool
But I have seen full many a bonny lass
And wish I had one now beneath the cool
Of these high elms – Muse tell me where I was
O – talking of turning I've seen Whig and Tory
Turn imps of hell and all for England's glory

I love good fellowship and wit and punning
I love 'true love' and, God my taste defend,
I hate most damnably all sorts of cunning –
I love the Moor and Marsh and Ponders End* –
I do not like the song of 'Cease your funning'*
I love a modest wife and trusty friend
– Bricklayers want lime as I want rhyme for fillups
– So here's a health to sweet Eliza Phillips*

Song

Eliza now the summer tells
Of sports where love and beauty dwells
Come and spend a day with me
Underneath the forest tree
Where the restless water flushes
Over mosses, mounds and rushes
And where love and freedom dwells
With orchis flowers and foxglove bells
Come dear Eliza set me free
And o'er the forest roam with me

Here I see the morning sun
Among the beachtree's shadows run
That into gold the short sward turns
Where each bright yellow blossom burns

With hues that would his beams outshine
Yet nought can match those smiles of thine
I try to find them all the day
But none are nigh when thou'rt away
Though flowers bloom now on every hill
Eliza is the fairest still

The sun wakes up the pleasant morn
And finds me lonely and forlorn
Then wears away to sunny noon
The flowers in bloom the birds in tune
While dull and dowie all the year
No smiles to see no voice to hear
I in this forest prison lie
With none to heed my silent sigh
And underneath this beachen tree
With none to sigh for Love but thee . . .

There's Doctor Bottle,* imp who deals in urine,
A keeper of state-prisons for the queen
As great a man as is the Doge of Turin
And save in London is but seldom seen
Yclep'd old A–ll–n – mad-brained ladies curing
Some p–x–d like Flora and but seldom clean
The new road o'er the forest is the right one
To see red hell and, further on, the white one*

Earth hells or b–gg–r sh–ps or what you please
Where men close prisoners are and women ravished
I've often seen such dirty sights as these
I've often seen good money spent and lavished
To keep bad houses up for doctors' fees
And I have known a b–gg–r's tally travers'd
Till all his good intents began to falter
– When death brought in his bill and left the halter . . .

Now this day is the eleventh of July
And being Sunday I will seek no flaw
In man or woman – but prepare to die.
In two days more I may that ticket draw
And so may thousands more as well as I
Today is here – the next who ever saw?
And In a madhouse I can find no mirth pay
– Next Tuesday* used to be Lord Byron's birthday

'Lord Byron? Poh, – the man wot rites the werses?'*
And is just what he is and nothing more?'
Who with his pen lies like the mist disperses
And makes all nothing as it was before
Who wed two wives* and oft the truth rehearses
And might have had some twenty thousand more
Who has been dead, so fools their lies are giving,
And still in Allen's madhouse caged and living . . .

I have two wives and I should like to see them
Both by my side before another hour
If both are honest I should like to be them
For both are fair and bonny as a flower
And one o Lord – now do bring in the tea, mem.
Were bards' pens steamers, each of ten horse-power,
I could not bring her beautys fair to weather
So I've towed both in harbour blest together

Now i'n't this canto worth a single pound
From anybody's pocket? Who will buy?
As thieves are worth a halter I'll be bound
Now honest reader take the book and try
And if as I have said it is not found
I'll write a better canto bye and bye
So reader now the money-till, unlock it,
And buy the book* and help to fill my pocket

PRISON AMUSEMENTS,
or
CHILD HAROLD*

Many are poets* – though they use no pen
To show their labours to the shuffling age
Real poets must be truly honest men
Tied to no mongrel laws or flattery's page
No zeal* have they for wrong or party rage
– The life of labour is a rural song
That hurts no cause – nor warfare tries to wage
Toil like the brook in music wears along –
Great little minds* claim right to act the wrong

Ballad

Summer morning is risen
And to even it wends
And still I'm in prison
Without any friends

I had joy's assurance
Though in bondage I lie
– I am still left in durance
Unwilling to sigh

Still the forest is round me
Where the trees bloom in green
As if chains ne'er had bound me
Or cares had ne'er been

Nature's love is eternal
In forest and plain
Her course is diurnal
To blossom again

For homes and friends vanished
I have kindness not wrath
For in days care has banished
My heart possessed both

My hopes are all hopeless
My skys have no sun
Winter fell in youth's Mayday
And still freezes on

But Love like the seed is
In the heart of a flower
It will blossom with truth
In a prosperous hour

True love is eternal
For God is the giver
And love like the soul will
Endure – and forever

And he who studies nature's volume through
And reads it with a pure unselfish mind
Will find God's power all round in every view
As one bright vision of the almighty mind
His eyes are open though the world is blind
No ill from him creation's works deform
The high and lofty one is great and kind
Evil may cause the blight and crushing storm
His is the sunny glory and the calm

Song

The sun has gone down with a veil on her brow
While I in the forest sit museing alone
The maiden has been o'er the hills for her cow
While my heart's affections are freezing to stone
Sweet Mary I wish that the day was my own
To live in a cottage with beauty and thee
The past I will not as a mourner bemoan
For abscence leaves Mary still dearer to me

How sweet are the glooms of the midsummer even
Dark night in the bushes seems going to rest
And the bosom of Mary with fancys is heaving
Where my sorrows and feelings for seasons were blest
Nor will I repine though in love we're divided
She in the Lowlands* and I in the glen
Of these forest beeches – by nature we're guided
And I shall find rest on her bosom again

How soft the dew falls on the leaves of the beeches
How fresh the wild flower seems to slumber below
How sweet are the lessons that nature still teaches
For truth is her tidings wherever I go
From schooldays of boyhood her image was cherished
In manhood sweet Mary was fairer then flowers
Nor yet has her name or her memory perished
Though absence like winter o'er happiness lowers

Though cares still will gather like clouds in my sky
Though hopes may grow hopeless and fetters recoil
While the sun of existance sheds light in my eye
I'll be free in a prison and cling to the soil
I'll cling to the spot where my first love was cherished
Where my heart nay my soul unto Mary I gave
And when my last hope and existance is perished
Her memory will shine like a sun on my grave

Mary thou ace of hearts thou muse of song
The pole-star of my being and decay
Earth's coward-foes my shattered bark may wrong
Still thou'rt the sunrise of my natal day
Born to misfortunes – where no sheltering bay
Keeps off the tempest* – wrecked where e'er I flee
I struggle with my fate – in trouble strong –
Mary thy name loved long still keeps me free
Till my lost life becomes a part of thee

Song

I've wandered* many a weary mile
Love in my heart was burning
To seek a home in Mary's smile
But cold is love's returning
The cold ground was a feather-bed
Truth never acts contrary
I had no home above my head
My home was love and Mary

I had no home in early youth
When my first love was thwarted
But if her heart still beats with truth
We'll never more be parted
And changing as her love may be
My own shall never vary
Nor night nor day I'm never free
But sigh for abscent Mary

Nor night nor day nor sun nor shade
Week month nor rolling year
Repairs the breach wronged love hath made
There madness – misery here
Life's lease was lengthened by her smiles
– Are truth and love contrary?
No ray of hope my life beguiles
I've lost love home and Mary

Love is the main spring of existance–It
Becomes a soul wherebye I live to love
On all I see that dearest name is writ
Falsehood is here* – but truth has life above
Where every star that shines exists in love
Skys vary in their clouds – the seasons vary
From heat to cold – change cannot constant prove
The South is bright – but smiles can act contrary
My guide-star gilds the North – and shines with Mary

Song

Here's where Mary loved to be
And here are flowers she planted
Here are books she loved to see
And here the kiss she granted

Here on the wall with smileing brow
Her picture used to cheer me
Both walls and rooms are naked now
No Mary's nigh to hear me

The church-spire* still attracts my eye
And leaves me broken-hearted
Though grief hath worn their channels dry
I sigh o'er days departed

The churchyard where she used to play
My feet could wander hourly
My school-walks there was every day
Where she made winter flowery

But where is angel Mary now?
Love's secrets, none disclose 'em
Her rosey cheeks and broken vow
Live in my aching bosom

My life hath been one love – no blot it out
My life hath been one chain of contradictions
Madhouses Prisons wh–re shops – never doubt
But that my life hath had some strong convictions
That such was wrong – religion makes restrictions
I would have followed – but life turned a bubble
And clumb the giant stile of maledictions
They took me from my wife and to save trouble
I wed again and made the error double

Yet abscence claims them both and keeps them too
And locks me in a shop in spite of law
Among a low-lived set and dirty crew
Here let the Muse* oblivion's curtain draw
And let man think – for God hath often saw
Things here too dirty for the light of day
For in a madhouse there exists no law –
Now stagnant grows my too refined clay
I envy birds their wings to flye away

How servile is the task to please alone
Though beauty woo and love inspire the song
Mere painted beauty* with her heart of stone
Thinks the world worships while she flaunts along
The flower of sunshine, butterflye of song
Give me the truth of heart in woman's life
The love to cherish one – and do no wrong
To none – o peace of every care and strife
Is true love in an estimable wife

How beautifull this hill of fern swells on
So beautifull the chappel peeps between
The hornbeams – with its simple bell – alone

I wander here hid in a palace green
Mary is abscent – but the forest queen
Nature is with me – morning noon and gloaming
I write my poems in these paths unseen
And when among these brakes and beeches roaming
I sigh for truth and home and love and woman

I sigh for one and two – and still I sigh
For many are the whispers I have heard
From beauty's lips – love's soul in many an eye
Hath pierced my heart with such intense regard
I looked for joy and pain was the reward
I think of them I love, each girl and boy,
Babes of two mothers – on this velvet sward
And nature thinks – in her so sweet employ
While dews fall on each blossom weeping joy

Here is the chappel-yard enclosed with pales
And oak trees nearly top its little bell
Here is the little bridge with guiding rail
That leads me on to many a pleasant dell
The fernowl chitters like a startled knell
To nature – yet 'tis sweet at evening still –
A pleasant road curves round the gentle swell
Where nature seems to have her own sweet will
Planting her beech and thorn about the sweet fern-hill

I have had many loves – and seek no more –
These solitudes my last delights shall be
The leaf-hid forest – and the lonely shore
Seem to my mind like beings that are free
Yet would I had some eye to smile on me
Some heart where I could make a happy home in
Sweet Susan that was wont my love to be
And Bessey* of the glen – for I've been roaming
With both at morn and noon and dusky gloaming

Cares gather round I snap their chains in two
And smile in agony and laugh in tears
Like playing with a deadly serpent – who
Stings to the death – there is no room for fears
Where death would bring me happiness – his sheers
Kills cares that hiss to poison many a vein
The thought to be extinct my fate endears
Pale death the grand phisician cures all pain
The dead rest well – who lived for joys in vain

Written in a Thunderstorm* July 15th 1841

The heavens are wrath – the thunder's rattling peal
Rolls like a vast volcano in the sky
Yet nothing starts the apathy I feel
Nor chills with fear eternal destiny

My soul is apathy – a ruin vast
Time cannot clear the ruined mass away
My life is hell – the hopeless die is cast
And manhood's prime is premature decay

Roll on, ye wrath of thunders – peal on peal
Till worlds are ruins and myself alone
Melt heart and soul cased in obdurate steel
Till I can feel that nature is my throne

I live in love, sun of undying light,
And fathom my own heart for ways of good
In its pure atmosphere day without night
Smiles on the plains the forest and the flood

Smile on ye elements of earth and sky
Or frown in thunders as ye frown on me
Bid earth and its delusions pass away
But leave the mind as its creator free

This twilight seems a veil of gause and mist
Trees seem dark hills between the earth and sky
Winds sob awake and then a gusty hist
Fanns through the wheat like serpents gliding bye
I love to stretch my length 'tween earth and sky
And see the inky foliage o'er me wave
Though shades are still my prison where I lie
Long use grows nature which I easy brave
And think how sweet cares rest within the grave

Remind me not of other years or tell
My broken hopes of joys they are to meet
While thy own falshood rings the loudest knell
To one fond heart that aches too cold to beat
Mary how oft* with fondness I repeat
That name alone to give my troubles rest
The very sound though bitter seemeth sweet –
In my love's home and thy own faithless breast
Truth's bonds are broke and every nerve distrest

Life is to me a dream that never wakes
Night finds me on this lengthening road alone
Love is to me a thought that ever aches
A frost-bound thought that freezes life to stone
Mary in truth and nature still my own
That warms the winter of my aching breast
Thy name is joy nor will I life bemoan –
Midnight when sleep takes charge of nature's rest
Finds me awake and friendless – not distrest

Tie all my cares up in thy arms, O sleep,
And give my weary spirits peace and rest
I'm not an outlaw in this midnight deep
If prayers are offered from sweet woman's breast
One and one only made my being blest
And fancy shapes her form in every dell
On that sweet bosom I've had hours of rest

Though now, through years of abscence doomed to dwell,
Day seems my night and night seems blackest hell

England my country though my setting sun
Sinks in the ocean-gloom and dregs of life
My muse can sing my Mary's heart was won
And joy was heaven when I called her wife
The only harbour in my days of strife
Was Mary when the sea roiled mountains high
When joy was lost and every sorrow rife
To her sweet bosom I was wont to flye
To undecieve by truth life's treacherous agony

Friend of the friendless from a host of snares
From lying varlets and from friendly foes
I sought thy quiet truth to ease my cares
And on the blight of reason found repose
But when the strife of nature ceased her throes
And other hearts would beat for my return
I trusted fate to ease my world of woes
Seeking love's harbour – where I now sojourn
– But hell is heaven, could I cease to mourn

For her, for one whose very name is yet
My hell or heaven – and will ever be.
Falsehood is doubt – but I can ne'er forget
Oaths virtuous falsehood volunteered to me
To make my soul new bonds which God made free
God's gift is love and do I wrong the giver
To place affections wrong from God's decree?*
– No, when farewell upon my lips did quiver
And all seemed lost – I loved her more than ever

I loved her in all climes beneath the sun
Her name was like a jewel in my heart
'Twas heaven's own choice – and so God's will be
  done

Love-ties that keep unbroken cannot part
Nor can cold abscence sever or desert
That simple beauty blessed with matchless charms
Oceans have rolled between us – not to part
E'en Iceland's snows true love's delirium warms
For there I've dreamed – and Mary filled my arms

Song

O Mary sing thy songs to me
Of love and beauty's melody
My sorrows sink beneath distress
My deepest griefs are sorrowless
So used to glooms and cares am I
My fearless troubles seem as joy
O Mary sing thy songs to me
Of love and beauty's melody

'To be beloved* is all I need
And them I love are loved indeed'
The soul of woman is my shrine
And Mary made my songs divine
O for that time that happy time
To hear thy sweet piano's chime
In music so divine and clear
That woke my soul in heaven to hear

But heaven itself without thy face
To me would be no resting-place
And though the world was one delight
No joy would live but in thy sight
The soul of woman is my shrine
Then Mary make those songs divine
For music, love, and melody
Breathe all of thee and only thee

Song

Lovely Mary when we parted
I ne'er felt so lonely-hearted
As I do now in field and glen
When hope says 'we shall meet agen'
And by yon spire that points to heaven
Where my earliest vows was given
By each meadow field and fen
I'll love thee till we meet agen

True as the needle to the pole
My life I love thee heart and soul
Wa'n't thy love in my heart enrolled
Though love was fire 'twould soon be cold
By thy eyes of heaven's own blue
My heart for thine was ever true
By sun and moon, by sea and shore,
My life I love thee more and more

And by that hope that lingers last
For heaven when life's hell is past
By time the present – past and gone
I've loved thee – and I love thee on
Thy beauty made youth's life divine
Till my soul grew a part of thine
Mary I mourn no pleasures gone –
The past has made us both as one

———————

Now melancholly autumn* comes anew
With showery clouds and fields of wheat tanned brown
Along the meadow banks I peace pursue
And see the wild flowers gleaming up and down

Like sun and light – the ragwort's golden crown
Mirrors like sunshine when sunbeams retire
And silver yarrow – there's the little town
And o'er the meadows gleams that slender spire
Reminding me of one – and waking fond desire

I love thee nature in my inmost heart
Go where I will thy truth seems from above
Go where I will thy landscape forms a part
Of heaven – e'en these fens where wood nor grove
Are seen – their very nakedness I love
For one dwells nigh that secret hopes prefer
Above the race of women – like the dove
I mourn her abscence – fate, that would deter
My hate for all things, strengthens love for her

Thus saith the great and high and lofty one
Whose name is holy – home, eternity:
'In the high and holy place I dwell alone
And with them also that I wish to see
Of contrite humble spirits – from sin free –
Who trembles at my word – and good receive.'
– Thou high and lofty one – O give to me
Truth's low estate and I will glad believe
If such I am not – such I'm feign to live

That form from boyhood loved and still loved on
That voice – that look – that face of one delight
Love's register for years, months, weeks – time past and
    gone
Her looks was ne'er forgot or out of sight
– Mary the muse of every song I write
Thy cherished memory never leaves my own
Though care's chill winter doth my manhood blight
And freeze like Niobe* my thoughts to stone –
Our lives are two – our end and aim is one

Ballad

Sweet days while God your blessings send
I call your joys my own
— And if I have an only friend
I am not left alone

She sees the fields the trees the spires
Which I can daily see
And if true love her heart inspires
Life still has joys for me

She sees the wild flower in the dells
That in my rambles shine
The sky that o'er her homestead dwells
Looks sunny over mine

The cloud that passes where she dwells
In less then half an hour
Darkens around these orchard dells
Or melts a sudden shower

The wind that leaves the sunny South
And fans the orchard tree
Might steal the kisses from her mouth
And waft her voice to me

O when will autumn bring the news
Now harvest browns the fen
That Mary as my vagrant muse
And I shall meet again

'Tis pleasant now day's hours begin to pass
To dewy eve – To walk down narrow close
And feel one's feet among refreshing grass
And hear the insects in their homes discourse
And startled blackbird flye from covert close
Of whitethorn hedge with wild fear's fluttering wings
And see the spire and hear the clock toll hoarse
And whisper names – and think o'er many things
That love hurds up in truth's imaginings

Fame blazed upon me like a comet's glare
Fame waned and left me like a fallen star
Because I told the evil what they are
And truth and falsehood never wished to mar
My Life hath been a wreck – and I've gone far
For peace and truth – and hope – for home and rest
– Like Eden's gates – fate throws a constant bar –
Thoughts may o'ertake the sunset in the West
– Man meets no home within a woman's breast

Though they are blazoned in the poet's song
As all the comforts which our lives* contain
I read and sought such joys my whole life long
And found the best of poets sung in vain
But still I read and sighed and sued again
And lost no purpose where I had the will
I almost worshiped when my toils grew vain
Finding no antidote my pains to kill
I sigh a poet and a lover still

Song

Dying gales of sweet even
How can you sigh so
Though the sweet day is leaving

And the sun sinketh low
How can you sigh so
For the wild flower is gay
And her dew-gems all glow
For the abscence of day

Dying gales of sweet even
Breathe music from toil
Dusky eve is love's heaven
And meets beauty's smile
Love leans on the stile
Where the rustic brooks flow
Dying gales all the while
How can you sigh so

Dying gales round a prison
To fancy may sigh
But day here hath risen
Over prospects of joy
Here Mary would toy
When the sun it got low
Even gales whisper joy
And never sigh so

Labour lets man his brother
Retire to his rest
The babe meets its mother
And sleeps on her breast –
The sun in the West
Has gone down in the ocean
Dying gales gently sweep
O'er the heart's ruffled motion
And sing it to sleep

Song

The spring may forget that he reigns in the sky
And winter again hide her flowers in the snow
The summer may thirst when her fountains are dry
But I'll think of Mary wherever I go
The bird may forget that her nest is begun
When the snow settles white on the new-budding tree
And nature in tempests forget the bright sun
But I'll ne'er forget her – that was plighted to me

How could I – how should I – that loved her so early
Forget – when I've sung of her beauty in song
How could I forget – what I've worshiped so dearly
From boyhood to manhood – and all my life long –
As leaves to the branches in summer comes duly
And blossoms will bloom on the stalk and the tree
To her beauty I'll cling – and I'll love her as truly
And think of sweet Mary wherever I be

Song

No single hour can stand for nought
No moment-hand* can move
But calenders an aching thought
Of my first lonely love

Where silence doth the loudest call
My secrets to betray
As moonlight holds the night in thrall
As suns reveal the day

I hide it in the silent shades
Till silence finds a tongue
I make its grave where time invades
Till time becomes a song

I bid my foolish heart be still
But hopes will not be chid
My heart will beat – and burn – and chill
First love will not be hid

When summer ceases to be green
And winter bare and blea –
Death may forget what I have been
But I must cease to be

When words refuse before the crowd
My Mary's name to give
The muse in silence sings aloud
And there my love will live

————————

Now harvest smiles embrowning all the plain
The sun of heaven o'er its ripeness shines
'Peace-plenty'* has been sung nor sung in vain
As all bring forth the maker's grand designs
– Like gold that brightens in some hidden mines
His nature is the wealth that brings increase
To all the world – his sun forever shines
– He hides his face and troubles they increase
He smiles – the sun looks out in wealth and peace

This life* is made of lying and grimace
This world is filled with whoring and decieving
Hypocrisy ne'er masks an honest face
Stories are told – but seeing is believing
And I've seen much from which there's no retrieving
I've seen deception take the place of truth
I've seen knaves flourish – and the country grieving
Lies was the current gospel in my youth
And now a man – I'm further off from truth

They ne'er read the heart
Who would read it in mine
That love can desert
The first truth on his shrine
Though in Lethe I steep it
And sorrows prefer
In my heart's core I keep it
And keep it for her

For her and her only
Through months and through years
I've wandered thus lonely
In sorrow and fears
My sorrows I smother
Though troubles anoy
In this world and no other
I cannot meet joy

No peace nor yet pleasure
Without her will stay
Life looses its treasure
When Mary's away
Though the nightingale often
In sorrow may sing
– Can the blast of the winter
Meet blooms of the spring

Thou first, best, and dearest
Though dwelling apart
To my heart still the nearest
Forever thou art
And thou wilt be the dearest
Though our joys may be o'er
And to me thou art nearest
Though I meet thee no more

Song

Did I know where to meet thee
Thou dearest in life
How soon would I greet thee
My true love and wife
How soon would I meet thee
At close of the day
Though cares would still cheat me
If Mary would meet me
I'd kiss her sweet beauty and love them away

And when evening discovers
The sun in the West
I long like true lovers
To lean on thy breast
To meet thee my dearest
 – Thy eyes beaming blue
Abscent pains the severest
Feel Mary's the dearest
And if Mary's abscent – how can I be true?

How dull the glooms cover
This meadow and fen
Where I as a lover
Seek Mary agen
But silence is teazing
Wherever I stray
There's nothing seems pleasing
Or aching thoughts easing
Though Mary lives near me – she seems far away

O would these gales murmur
My love in her ear
Or a bird's note inform her
While I linger here
But nature, contrary,
Turns night into day
No bird – gale – or fairy
Can whisper to Mary
To tell her who seeks her – while Mary's away

———————

Dull must that being live who sees unmoved
The scenes and objects that his childhood knew
The school-yard and the maid he early loved
The sunny wall where long the old Elms grew
The grass that e'en till noon retains the dew
Beneath the wallnut shade I see them still
Though not such fancys do I now pursue
Yet still the picture turns my bosom chill
And leaves a void – nor love nor hope may fill

After long abscence how the mind recalls
Pleasing associations of the past
Haunts of his youth – thorn-hedges and old walls
And hollow trees that sheltered from the blast
And all that map of boyhood overcast
With glooms and wrongs and sorrows not his own
That o'er his brow like the scathed lightening passed
That turned his spring to winter and alone
Wrecked name and fame and all – to solitude unknown

So on he lives in glooms and living death
A shade like night forgetting and forgot
Insects that kindle in the spring's young breath
Take hold of life and share a brighter lot
Then he the tennant* of the hall and Cot

The princely palace too hath been his home
And Gipsey's camp when friends would know him not
In midst of wealth a beggar still to roam
Parted from one whose heart was once his home

And yet not parted – still love's hope illumes
And like the rainbow brightest in the storm
It looks for joy beyond the wreck of tombs
And in life's winter keeps love's embers warm
The ocean's roughest tempest meets a calm
Care's thickest cloud shall break in sunny joy
O'er the parched waste, showers yet shall fall like balm
And she the soul of life for whom I sigh
Like flowers shall cheer me when the storm is bye

Song

O Mary dear, three springs* have been
Three summers too have blossomed here
Three blasting winters crept between
Though abscence is the most severe
Another summer blooms in green
But Mary never once was seen

I've sought her in the fields and flowers
I've sought her in the forest groves
In avanues and shaded bowers
And every scene that Mary loves
E'en round her home I seek her there*
But Mary's abscent everywhere

'Tis autumn and the rustling corn
Goes loaded on the creaking wain
I seek her in the early morn
But cannot meet her face again
Sweet Mary she is abscent still
And much I fear she ever will

The autumn morn looks mellow as the fruit
And ripe as harvest – every field and farm
Is full of health and toil – yet never mute
With rustic mirth and peace the day is warm
The village maid with gleans upon her arm
Brown as the hazel-nut from field to field
Goes cheerily – the valley's native charm –
I seek for charms that autumn best can yield
In mellowing wood and time ybleaching field

Song

'Tis autumn now and nature's scenes
The pleachy fields and yellowing trees
Looses their blooming hues and greens
But nature finds no change in me
The fading woods the russet grange
The hues of nature may desert
But nought in me shall find a change
To wrong the angel of my heart
For Mary is my angel still
Through every month and every ill

The leaves they loosen from the branch
And fall upon the gusty wind
But my heart's silent love is staunch
And nought can tear her from my mind
The flowers are gone from dell and bower
Though crowds from summer's lap was given

244

But love is an eternal flower
Like purple amaranths in heaven
To Mary first my heart did bow
And if she's true she keeps it now

Just as the summer keeps the flower
Which spring conscealed in hoods of gold
Or unripe harvest met the shower
And made earth's blessings manifold
Just so my Mary lives for me
A silent thought for months and years
The world may live in revellry
Her name my lonely quiet cheers
And cheer it will what e'er may be
While Mary lives to think of me

———————

Sweet comes the misty mornings in September
Among the dewy paths how sweet to stray
Greensward or stubbles, as I well remember
I once have done – the mist curls thick and grey
As cottage smoke – like net-work on the spray
Or seeded grass the cobweb draperies run
Beaded with pearls of dew at early day
And o'er the pleachy stubbles peeps the sun
The lamp of day when that of night is done

What mellowness these harvest days unfold
In the strong glances of the midday sun
The homestead's very grass seems changed to gold
The light in golden shadows seems to run
And tinges every spray it rests upon
With that rich harvest hue of sunny joy
Nature life's sweet companion cheers alone –
The hare starts up before the shepherd-boy
And partridge coveys wir on russet wings of joy

The meadow flags now rustle bleached and dank
And misted o'er with down as fine as dew
The sloe and dewberry shine along the bank
Where weeds in bloom's luxuriance lately grew
Red rose the sun and up the morehen flew
From bank to bank* the meadow-arches stride
Where foamy floods in winter tumbles through
And spread a restless ocean foaming wide
Where now the cowboys sleep nor fear the coming tide

About the meadows now I love to sit
On banks, bridge-walls, and rails, as when a boy
To see old trees bend o'er the flaggy pit
With hugh roots bare that time does not destroy
Where sits the angler at his day's employ
And there the ivy* leaves the bank to climb
The tree – and now how sweet to weary joy
– Aye nothing seems so happy and sublime
As sabbath-bells and their delightfull chime

Sweet solitude thou partner of my life
Thou balm of hope and every pressing care
Thou soothing silence o'er the noise of strife
These meadow-flats and trees – the autumn air
Mellows my heart to harmony – I bear
Life's burthen happily – these fenny dells
Seem Eden in this sabbath rest from care
My heart with love's first early memory swells
To hear the music of those village bells

For in that hamlet lives my rising sun
Whose beams hath cheered me all my lorn life long
My heart to nature there was early won
For she was nature's self – and still my song
Is her through sun and shade through right and wrong
On her my memory forever dwells
The flower of Eden – evergreen of song
Truth in my heart the same love-story tells
– I love the music of those village bells

Song

Here's a health* unto thee bonny lassie O
Leave the thorns o' care wi' me
And whatever I may be
Here's happiness to thee
Bonny lassie O

Here's joy unto thee bonny lassie O
Though we never meet again
I well can bear the pain
If happiness is thine
Bonny lassie O

Here is true love unto thee bonny lassie O
Though abscence cold is ours
The spring will come wi' flowers
And love will wait for thee
Bonny lassie O

So here's love unto thee bonny lassie O
Aye wherever I may be
Here's a double health to thee
Till life shall cease to love
Bonny lassie O

The blackbird startles from the homestead-hedge
Raindrops and leaves fall yellow as he springs
Such images are nature's sweetest pledge
To me there's music in his rustling wings
'Prink prink' he cries and loud the robin sings
The small hawk like a shot drops from the sky
Close to my feet for mice and creeping things
Then swift as thought again he suthers bye
And hides among the clouds from the pursueing eye

Song

Her cheeks are like roses
Her eyes they are blue
And her beauty is mine
If her heart it is true

Her cheeks are like roses –
And though she's away
I shall see her sweet beauty
On some other day

Ere the flowers of the spring
Deck the meadow and plain
If there's truth in her bosom
I shall see her again.

I will love her as long
As the brooks they shall flow
For Mary is mine
Wheresoever I go

Honesty and good intentions are
So mowed and hampered in with evil lies
She hath not room to stir a single foot
Or even strength to break a spider's web
– So lies keep climbing round love's sacred stem
Blighting fair truth whose leaf is evergreen
Whose roots are the heart's fibres and whose sun
The soul that cheers and smiles it into bloom
Till heaven proclaims that truth can never die

The lightening's vivid flashes rend the cloud
That rides like castled crags along the sky
And splinters them to fragments – while aloud
The thunders, heaven's artillery, vollies bye
Trees crash, earth trembles – beasts prepare to flye
Almighty, what a crash – yet man is free
And walks unhurt while danger seems so nigh –
Heaven's archway now the rainbow seems to be
That spans the eternal round of earth and sky and sea

A shock, a moment, in the wrath of God
Is long as hell's eternity to all
His thunderbolts leave life but as the clod
Cold and inanimate – their temples fall
Beneath his frown to ashes – the eternal pall
Of wrath sleeps o'er the ruins where they fell
And nought of memory may their creeds recall
The sin of Sodom was a moment's yell
Fire's death-bed theirs, their first grave the last hell

The towering willow with its pliant boughs
Sweeps its grey foliage to the autumn wind
The level grounds where oft a group of cows
Huddled together close – or propped behind

An hedge or hovel ruminate and find
The peace – as walks and health and I pursue
For nature's every place is still resigned
To happiness – new life's in every view
And here I comfort seek and early joys renew

The lake that held a mirror to the sun
Now curves with wrinkles in the stillest place
The autumn wind sounds hollow as a gun
And water stands in every swampy place
Yet in these fens peace, harmony, and grace,
The attributes of nature, are allied
The barge with naked mast in sheltered place
Beside the brig, close to the bank, is tied
While small waves plashes by its bulky side

Song

The floods come o'er the meadow leas
The dykes are full and brimming
Field–furrows reach the horses' knees
Where wild ducks oft are swimming
The skyes are black the fields are bare
The trees their coats are loosing
The leaves are dancing in the air
The sun its warmth refusing

Brown are the flags and fadeing sedge
And tanned the meadow plains
Bright yellow is the osier hedge
Beside the brimming drains
The crows sit on the willow tree
The lake is full below
But still the dullest thing I see
Is self that wanders slow

The dullest scenes are not so dull
As thoughts I cannot tell
The brimming dykes are not so full
As my heart's silent swell
I leave my troubles to the winds
With none to share a part
The only joy my feeling finds
Hides in an aching heart

Absence in love is worse then any fate
Summer is winter's desert and the spring
Is like a ruined city desolate
Joy dies and hope retires on feeble wing
Nature sinks heedless, birds unheeded sing
'Tis solitude in citys,* crowds all move
Like living death though all to life still cling
The strongest bitterest thing that life can prove
Is woman's undisguise of hate and love

Song

I think of thee at early day
And wonder where my love can be
And when the evening shadow's grey
O how I think of thee

Along the meadow banks I rove
And down the flaggy fen
And hope, my first and early love,
To meet thee once again

I think of thee at dewy morn
And at the sunny noon
And walks with thee – now left forlorn
Beneath the silent moon

I think of thee I think of all
How blest we both have been –
The sun looks pale upon the wall
And autumn shuts the scene

I can't expect to meet thee now
The winter floods begin
The wind sighs through the naked bough
Sad as my heart within

I think of thee the seasons through
In spring when flowers I see
In winter's lorn and naked view
I think of only thee

While life breathes on this earthly ball
What e'er my lot may be
Whether in freedom or in thrall
Mary I think of thee

———————

'Tis winter and the fields are bare and waste
The air one mass of 'vapour clouds and storms'
The sun's broad beams are buried and o'ercast
And chilly glooms the midday light deforms
Yet comfort now the social bosom warms
Friendship of nature which I hourly prove
Even in this winter scene of frost and storms
Bare fields, the frozen lake, and leafless grove
Are nature's grand religion and true love

Thou'rt dearest to my bosom
As thou wilt ever be
While the meadows wear a blossom
Or a leaf is on the tree
I can forget thee never
While the meadow grass is green
While the flood rolls down the river
Thou art still my bonny queen

While the winter swells the fountain
While the spring awakes the bee
While the chamois loves the mountain
Thou'lt be ever dear to me
Dear as summer to the sun
As spring is to the bee
Thy love was soon as won
And so 'twill ever be

Thou'rt love's eternal summer
The dearest maid I prove
With bosom white as ivory
And warm as virgin love
No falsehood gets between us
There's nought the tie can sever
As Cupid dwells with Venus
Thou'rt my own love forever

Song

In this cold world without a home
Disconsolate I go
The summer looks as cold to me
As winter's frost and snow
Though winter's scenes are dull and drear
A colder lot I prove
No home had I through all the year
But Mary's honest love

But Love inconstant as the wind
Soon shifts another way
No other home my heart can find
Life wasting day by day
I sigh and sit and sit and sigh
For better days to come
For Mary was my hope and joy
Her truth and heart my home

Her truth and heart was once my home
And May was all the year
But now through seasons as I roam
'Tis winter everywhere
Hopeless I go through care and toil
No friend I e'er possest
To reccompence for Mary's smile
And the love within her breast

My love was ne'er so blest as when
It mingled with her own
Told often to be told agen
And every feeling known
But now love's hopes are all bereft
A lonely man I roam
And abscent Mary long hath left
My heart without a home

The Paigles Bloom* In Showers In Grassy Close
How Sweet To Be Among Their Blossoms Led
And Hear Sweet Nature To Herself Discourse
While Pale The Moon Is Bering Over Head
And Hear The Grazeing Cattle Softly Tread
Cropping The Hedgerow's Newly Leafing Thorn
Sounds Soft As Visions Murmured O'er In Bed
At Dusky Eve or Sober Silent Morn
For Such Delights 'Twere Happy Man Was Born

Green bushes and green trees where fancy feeds
On the retireing solitudes of May
Where the sweet foliage like a volume reads
And weeds are gifts too choice to throw away
How sweet the evening now succeeds the day
The velvet hillock forms a happy seat
The whitethorn bushes bend with snowey may
Dwarf furze in golden blooms and violets sweet
Make this wild scene a pleasure-ground's retreat

Where are my friends and childern where are they
The childern of two mothers born in joy
One roof has held them – all have been at play
Beneath the pleasures of a mother's eye
– And are my late hopes blighted – need I sigh?
Hath care commenced his long perpetual reign?
The spring and summer hath with me gone bye
Hope views the bud a flower and not in vain
Long is the night that brings no morn again

Now Come The Balm And Breezes Of The Spring
Not With The Pleasures Of My Early Days
When Nature Seemed One Endless Song To Sing
A Joyous Melody And Happy Praise
Ah Would They Come Agen – But Life Betrays
Quicksands and Gulphs And Storms That Howl And
    Sting

All Quiet Into Madness And Delays
Care Hides The Sunshine With Its Raven Wing
And Hell Glooms Sadness O'er The Songs Of Spring

Like Satan's Warcry First In Paradise
When Love Lay Sleeping On The Flowery Slope
Like Virtue Wakeing In The Arms Of Vice
Or Death's Sea Bursting In The Midst Of Hope
Sorrows Will Stay – And Pleasures Will Elope
In The Uncertain Certainty Of Care
Joy's Bounds Are Narrow But A Wider Scope
Is Left For Trouble Which Our Life Must Bear
Of Which All Human Life Is More Or Less The Heir

My Mind Is Dark And Fathomless And Wears
The Hues Of Hopeless Agony And Hell
No Plummet Ever Sounds The Soul's Affairs
There Death Eternal Never Sounds The Knell
There Love Imprisoned Sighs The Long Farewell
And Still May Sigh In Thoughts No Heart Hath Penned
Alone In Loneliness Where Sorrows Dwell
And Hopeless Hope Hopes On And Meets No End
Wastes Without Springs And Homes Without A Friend

Song

Say What Is Love – To Live In Vain
To Live And Die And Live Again

Say What Is Love – Is It To Be
In Prison Still And Still Be Free

Or Seem As Free – Alone And Prove
The Hopeless Hopes Of Real Love

Does Real Love On Earth Exist
'Tis Like A Sunbeam On The Mist

That Fades And No Where Will Remain
And Nowhere Is O'ertook Again

Say What Is Love – A Blooming Name
A Rose Leaf On The Page Of Fame

That Blooms Then Fades – To Cheat No More
And Is What Nothing Was Before

Say What Is Love – What E'er It be
It Centers Mary Still With Thee

What is the Orphan Child Without A Friend
That Knows No Father's Care Or Mother's Love
No Leading Hand His Infant Steps Defend
And None To Notice But His God Above
No Joys Are Seen His Little Heart To Move
Care Turns All Joys to Dross And Nought To Gold
And He In Fancy's Time May Still Disprove
Growing To Cares And Sorrows Menifold
Bird Of The Waste A Lamb Without A Fold

No Mother's Love or Father's Care Have They
Left To The Storms Of Fate Like Creatures Wild
They Live Like Blossoms In The Winter's Day
E'en Nature Frowns Upon The Orphan Child
On Whose Young Face A Mother Never Smiled
Foolhardy Care Increasing With His Years
From Friends And Joys Of Every Kind Exiled
Even Old In Care The Infant Babe Appears
And Many A Mother Meets Its Face In Tears

The Dog Can Find A Friend And Seeks His Side
The Ass Can Know Its Owner And Is Fed
But None Are Known To Be The Orphan's Guide
Toil Breaks His Sleep And Sorrow Makes His Bed
No Mother's Hand Holds Out The Sugared Bread
To Fill His Little Hand – He Hears No Song
To Please His Pouting Humours – Love Is Dead
With Him And Will Be All His Whole Life Long
Lone Child Of Sorrow And Perpetual Wrong

But Providence That Grand Eternal Calm
Is With Him Like The Sunshine In The Sky
Nature Our Kindest Mother Void Of Harm
Watches The Orphan's Lonely Infancy
Strengthening The Man When Childhood's Cares Are
    Bye
She Nurses Still Young Unreproached Distress
And Hears The Lonely Infant's Every Sigh
Who Finds At Length To Make Its Sorrows Less
Mid Earth's Cold Curses There Is One To Bless

Sweet Rural Maids Made Beautifull By Health
Brought Up Where Nature's Calm Encircles All
Where Simple Love Remains As Sterling Wealth
Where Simple Habits Early Joys Recall
Of Youthfull Feelings Which No Wiles Enthrall
The Happy Milk Maid* In Her Mean Array
Fresh As The New-Blown Rose Outblooms Them All
E'en Queens Might Sigh To Be As Blest As They
While Milkmaids Laugh And Sing Their Cares Away

How Doth Those Scenes Which Rural Mirth Endears
Revise Old Feelings That My Youth Hath Known
And Paint The Faded Bloom Of Earlier Years
And Soften Feelings Petrefied To Stone
Joy Fled And Care Proclaimed Itself My Own

Farewells I Took Of Joys In Earliest Years
And Found The Greatest Bliss To Be Alone
My Manhood Was Eclipsed But Not In Fears
– Hell Came In Curses And She Laugh'd At Tears

But Memory Left Sweet Traces Of Her Smiles
Which I Remember Still And Still Endure
The Shadows Of First Loves My Heart Beguiles
Time Brought Both Pain and Pleasure But No Cure
Sweet Bessey Maid Of Health And Fancys Pure
How Did I Woo Thee Once – Still Unforgot
But Promises In Love Are Never Sure
And Where We Met How Dear Is Every Spot
And Though We Parted Still I Murmur Not

For Loves However Dear Must Meet With Clouds
And Ties Made Tight Get Loose And May Be Parted
Spring's First Young Flowers The Winter Often
   Shrouds
And Love's First Hopes Are Very Often Thwarted
E'en Mine Beat High And Then Fell Broken-Hearted
And Sorrow Mourned In Verse to Reconscile
My Feelings To My Fate Though Lone And Parted
Love's Enemies Are Like The Scorpion Vile
That O'er Its Ruined Hopes Will Hiss And Smile

Ballad

The Blackbird Has Built In The Pasture Agen
And The Thorn O'er The Pond Shows A Delicate
   Green
Where I Strolled With Patty Adown In The Glen
And Spent Summer Evenings And Sundays Unseen
How Sweet The Hill Brow
And The Low Of The Cow

And The Sunshine That Gilded The Bushes So Green
When Evening Brought Dews Nature's Thirst To Allay
And Clouds Seemed To Nestle Round Hamlets And
   Farms
While In The Green Bushes We Spent The Sweet Day
And Patty Sweet Patty Was Still in My Arms

The Love Bloom That Redded Upon Her Sweet Lips
The Love Light That Glistened Within Her Sweet Eye
The Singing Bees There That The Wild Honey Sips
From Wild Blossoms Seemed Not So Happy As I
How Sweet Her Smile Seemed
While The Summer Sun Gleamed
And The Laugh Of The Spring Shadowed Joys From
   On High
While The Birds Sung About Us And Cattle Grazed
   Round
And Beauty Was Blooming On Hamlets and Farms
How Sweet Steamed The Inscence Of Dew From The
   Ground
While Patty Sweet Patty Sat Locked In My Arms

Yet Love Lives On In Every Kind Of Weather
In Heat And Cold In Sunshine And In Gloom
Winter May Blight And Stormy Clouds May Gather
Nature Invigorates And Love Will Bloom
It Fears No Sorrow In A Life To Come
But Lives Within Itself From Year To Year
As Doth The Wild Flower In Its Own Perfume
As In The Lapland Snows Spring's Blooms Appear
So True Love Blooms And Blossoms Every Where

Ballad

The Rose Of The World Was Dear Mary To Me
In The Days Of My Boyhood And Youth
I Told Her In Songs Where My Heart Wished To Be
And My Songs Were The Language Of Truth

I Told Her In Looks When I Gazed In Her Eyes
That Mary Was Dearest To Me
I Told Her In Words And The Language Of Sighs
Where My Whole Heart's Affections Would Be

I Told her in love that all nature was true
I convinced her that nature was kind
But love in his trials had labour to do
          Mary would be in the mind*

Mary met me in spring where the speedwell-knots grew
And the kingcups were shining like flame
I chose her all colours red yellow and blue
But my love was one hue and the same

Spring summer and winter and all the year through
In the sunshine the shower and the blast
I told the same tale and she knows it all true
And Mary's my blossom at last

Love is of heaven still the first akin
'Twas born in Paradise and left its home
For desert lands stray hearts to nurse and win
Though pains like plagues pursue them where they
   roam

Its joys are evergreen and blooms at home
The sailor rocking on the giddy mast
The soldier when the cannons cease to boom
And every heart its doubts or dangers past
Beats on its way for love and home at last

Nature thou truth of heaven if heaven be true
Falsehood may tell her ever changeing lie
But nature's truth looks green in every view
And love in every Landscape glads the eye
How beautiful these slopeing thickets lie
Woods on the hills and plains all smooth and even
Through which we see the ribboned evening sky
Though Winter here in floods and snows was driven
Spring came like God and turned it all to heaven

There Is A Tale For Every Day To Hear
For Every Heart To Feel And Tongue To Tell
The Daughter's Anxious Dread The Lover's Fear
Pains That In Cots And Palaces May Dwell
Not Short And Passing Like The Friend's Farewell
Where Tears May Fall And Leave A Smile Beneath
Eternal Grief Rings In The Passing-Bell
'Tis Not The Sobs of Momentary Breath
Ties Part Forever In The Tale Of Death

The Dew falls on the weed and on the flower
The rose and thistle bathe their heads in dew
The lowliest heart may have its prospering hour
The saddest bosom meet its wishes true
E'en I may joy, love, happiness renew
Though not the sweets of my first early days
When one sweet face was all the loves I knew
And my soul trembled on her eyes to gaze
Whose very censure seemed intended praise

A soul within the heart that loves the more
Giving to pains and fears eternal life
Burning the flesh till it consumes the core
So Love is still the eternal calm of strife
Thou soul within a soul thou life of life
Thou Essence of my hopes and fears and joys
M—y my dear first love and early wife
And still the flower my inmost soul enjoys
Thy love's the bloom no canker-worm destroys

Flow on my verse though barren thou mayest be
Of thought – Yet sing and let thy fancys roll
In Early days thou swept a mighty sea
All calm in troublous deeps and spurned controul
Thou fire and iceberg to an aching soul
And still an angel in my gloomy way
Far better opiate than the draining bowl
Still sing my muse to drive care's fiends away
Nor heed what loitering listener hears the lay

My themes be artless cots and happy plains
Though far from man my wayward fancies flee
Of fields and woods rehearse in willing strains
And I mayhap may feed on joys with thee
These cowslip-fields, this sward, my pillow be
So I may sleep the sun into the West
My cot this awthorn hedge, this spreading tree
– Mary and Martha* once my daily guests
And still as mine both wedded, loved, and blest

I rest my wearied life in these sweet fields
Reflecting every smile in nature's face
And much of joy this grass, these hedges yields
Not found in citys where crowds daily trace.

Heart-pleasures there hath no abideing place
The star-gemmed early morn, the silent even
Hath pleasures that our broken hopes deface
To love too well leaves nought to be forgiven
The Gates of Eden is the bounds of heaven

The apathy that fickle love wears through
The doubts and certaintys are still akin
Its every joy has sorrow in the view
Its holy truth like Eve's beguileing sin
Seems to be losses even while we win
Tormenting joys and cheating into wrong
And still we love – and fall into the gin
My sun of love was short – and clouded long
And now its shadow fills a feeble song

Song

I saw her in my spring's young choice
Ere love's hopes looked upon the crowd
Ere love's first secrets found a voice
Or dared to speak the name aloud

I saw her in my boyish hours
A Girl as fair as heaven above
When all the world seemed strewn with flowers
And every pulse and look was love

I saw her when her heart was young
I saw her when my heart was true
When truth was all the themes I sung
And Love the only muse I knew

Ere infancy had left her brow
I seemed to love her from her birth
And thought her then as I do now
The dearest angel upon earth

O she was more then fair – divinely fair
Can language paint the soul in those blue eyes?
Can fancy read the feelings painted there
– Those hills of snow that on her bosom lies,
Or beauty speak for all those sweet replies
That through love's visions like the sun is breaking,
Wakeing new hopes and fears and stifled sighs?
From first love's dreams my love is scarcely waking
The wounds might heal but still the heart is aching

Her looks was like the spring, her very voice
Was spring's own music more then song to me
Choice of my boyhood, nay, my soul's first choice
From her sweet thralldom I am never free
Yet here my prison is a spring to me
Past memories bloom like flowers where e'er I rove
My very bondage, though in snares, is free
I love to stretch me in this shadey grove
And muse upon the memories of love

Hail, Solitude, still Peace, and Lonely good
Thou spirit of all joys to be alone
My best of friends these glades and this green wood
Where nature is herself and loves her own
The heart's hid anguish here I make it known
And tell my troubles to the gentle wind
Friends' cold neglects have froze my heart to stone
And wrecked the voyage of a quiet mind
With wives and friends and every hope disjoined

Wrecked of all hopes save one to be alone
Where Solitude becomes my wedded mate
Sweet Forest with rich beauties overgrown
Where solitude is queen and riegns in state
Hid in green trees I hear the clapping gate*
And voices calling to the rambling cows
I Laugh at Love and all its idle fate
The present hour is all my lot alows
An age of sorrow springs from lovers' vows

Sweet is the song of Birds for that restores
The soul to harmony the mind to love
Tis nature's song of freedom out of doors
Forests beneath, free winds and clouds above
The Thrush and Nightingale and timid dove
Breathe music round me where the gipseys dwell –
Pierced hearts left burning in the doubts of love
Are desolate where crowds and citys dwell –
The splendid palace seems the gates of hell

Lord hear my prayer when trouble glooms
Let sorrow find a way
And when the day of trouble comes
Turn not thy face away
My bones like hearth-stones burn away
My life like vapoury smoke decays

My heart is smitten like the grass
That withered lies and dead
And I so lost to what I was
Forget to eat my bread
My voice is groaning all the day
My bones prick through this skin of clay

The wilderness's pelican
The desert's lonely owl
I am their like, a desert man*
In ways as lone and foul
As sparrows on the cottage top
I wait till I with faintness drop

I bear my enemies' reproach
All silently I mourn
They on my private peace encroach
Against me they are sworn
Ashes as bread my trouble shares
And mix my food with weeping cares

Yet not for them is sorrow's toil
I fear no mortal's frown
But thou hast held me up awhile
And thou hast cast me down
My days like shadows waste from view
I mourn like withered grass in dew

But thou Lord shalt endure forever
All generations through
Thou shalt to Zion be the giver
Of joy and mercey too
Her very stones are in their trust
Thy servants reverence her dust

Heathens shall hear and fear thy name
All kings of earth thy glory know
When thou shalt build up Zion's fame
And live in glory there below
He'll not despise their prayers though mute
But still regard the destitute

'Tis Martinmass* from rig to rig
Ploughed fields and meadow lands are blea
In hedge and field each restless twig
Is dancing on the naked tree
Flags in the dykes are bleached and brown
Docks by its sides are dry and dead
All but the ivy-boughs are brown
Upon each leaning dotterel's head

Crimsoned with awes the awthorns bend
O'er meadow-dykes and rising floods
The wild geese seek the reedy fen
And dark the storm comes o'er the woods
The crowds of lapwings load the air
With buzes of a thousand wings
There flocks of starnels too repair
When morning o'er the valley springs

'THE ENGLISH BASTILLE'*

I have nothing to write about for I see Nothing and
hear nothing

Letter to his son, Charles, 8 July 1850

I have written a good lot and as I should think nearly
sufficient.

Letter to W. F. Knight, 11 April 1851

8 March 1860

Dear Sir

I am in a Madhouse and quite forget your Name or
who you are. You must excuse me for I have nothing
to communicate or tell of and why I am shut up I don't
know. I have nothing to say so I conclude

Yours respectfully
John Clare

For five months – July to December 1841 – Clare lived
with his wife and children in Northborough, by now
convinced that he was married to two women – his 'first'
wife, Mary, and his second wife, Martha. The biblical
resonances of their names were not lost on him, as he
continued to work on his 'Prison Amusements' ('Child
Harold'), and continued to deny that Mary was in fact
dead.

The tensions soon proved too much for his family and
friends, and on 28 December, Dr Page and Dr Skrimshire
certified that Clare was 'in a state of Lunacy': to the
question, 'Was it preceded by any severe or long con-
tinued mental emotion or exertion?' the answer given
was: 'after years addicted to Poetical prossing' (*sic*).

Clare was taken to Northampton General Lunatic
Asylum the following day, and remained there for
twenty-three years, until his death. His shifts of identity

– his changes of persona – proliferated: some days he was
Nelson (a friend of Clare's former patron, Admiral Lord
Radstock): on others, Randall or Ben Caunt (pugilists);
Shakespeare; or, above all, Robert Burns: in the manu-
script in which he wrote his continuation of 'Prison
Amusements,' he noted:

> Anecdotes of Burns Poems the 'On the daisey'
> and 'The Mouse'
> On turning up a mouse with the plough
> This poem was written on the west wide of Royce
> Wood while driving Plough for my brother Jem
> occasioned by turning one up with a Plough
>
> Robt Burns
> On the daisey on burying one under the furrow was
> written in the same field at Royce wood end which
> had been part of the green or Cowpasture
>
> Robt Burns
> Tam O'Shanter was written in a part of the same field
> called Tenters Nook* while at work in a garden of his
> master a Publican of the Bluebell Public house
>
> Robt Burns
> (MS 19, p. 119)

Internal evidence suggests that Clare was writing this
sequence from the spring of 1844 to the early summer of
1845, clearly envisaging it as a continuation of the 1841
sequence; the Byronic persona was still available, but was
mingled with that of Burns: as a result, the songs that
occur in the continuation of 'Prison Amusements' were
mostly written in the Scots English of Burns, often with
unfelicitous results. For this reason, I have included only
a selection of them in this edition.

Clare's conduct in this sequence is exactly as it had
been in the earlier one, and he interweaves within a
wavering, restless, fluid and fleeting natural scene a
variety of paradoxical speculations involving sexuality,

love, fidelity, infidelity, integrity and social deceit. Once or twice he deviates into a voice more reminiscent of 'Old Wigs and Sundries', but otherwise the poem is entirely consistent with his earlier use of the reflective/elegiac nine-line stanza.

In April 1845, W. F. Knight was appointed House Steward at the asylum; he encouraged Clare and began to transcribe his poems; Knight left in February 1850, and the work of transcription passed to others. The bulk of Clare's own manuscripts for this period have disappeared, so that the reader is dependent on texts that derive from transcripts. Unfortunately, for all his magnanimity, Knight tended to punctuate Clare's texts in a very maladroit fashion. In this edition, I have chosen to modify Knight's punctuation in the direction of a plainer text.

In Clare's end was his beginning, as he demonstrates so poignantly in the last poem in this selection, where he reverts to the simple syntax of his early poetry and to the fantastic delights of the chapman's store of traditional tales: 'Jack the jiant-killer's high renown' – Clare had valiantly fought with his 'giants': all those negative pressures of disenchantment, despair, neglect, poverty and exile; and finally, at the age of sixty-seven, came poignantly full circle.

On 13 June 1989, a memorial to Clare was unveiled in Poets' Corner, Westminster Abbey: better late than never . . .

Infants' graves are steps of angels where
Earth's brightest gems of innocence repose,
God is their parent, they need no tear,
He takes them to his bosom from earth's woes;
A bud their life-time and a flower their close
Their spirits are an iris of the skies
Needing no prayers – a sunset's happy close.
Gone are the bright rays of their soft blue eyes,
Dews on flowers mourn them and the gale that sighs.

Their lives were nothing but a sunny shower
Melting on flowers as tears melt from the eye
Their death were dew-drops on heaven's amaranthine
     bower*
'Twas told on flowers as summer gales went by.
They bowed and trembled yet they left no sigh
And the sun smiled to show their end was well.
Infants have nought to weep for ere they die.
All prayers are needless – beads they need not tell,
White flowers their mourners are, nature their passing
     bell.

                                        June 1844.*

                        LOVE

            Love is a secret
            Like a bird in a shell
            Like a rose ere it blossom
            All unseen will it dwell.

            'Tis the kernel of fruits
            The germ of all flowers
            The blaze of the diamond
            The moment of hours.

'Tis the star in night's darkness
The sky in the river
The soul in man's bosom
That wears it for ever.

'Tis a word, and the dearest
Each language has shown
'Tis a thought the sincerest
Any tongue has made known.

'Tis a flower in a basket
All bloom and perfuming
'Tis the gem of the casket
Love, beauty, and woman.

SONG

O wert thou in the storm*
    How I would shield thee:
To keep thee dry and warm
    A camp I would build thee.

Though the clouds pour'd again
    Not a drop should harm thee,
The music of wind and rain
    Rather should charm thee.

O wert thou in the storm
    A shed I would build thee;
To keep thee dry and warm,
    How I would shield thee.

The rain should not wet thee,
    Nor thunder-clap harm thee.
By thy side I would sit me,
    To comfort and warm thee.

I would sit by thy side love,
        While the dread storm was over
And the wings of an angel
        My charmer would cover.
                        July 25th 1844

EVENING

'Tis evening, the black snail has got on his track,
And gone to its nest is the wren;
And the packman-snail too, with his home on his back,
Clings on the bowed bents like a wen.

The shepherd has made a rude mark with his foot
Where his shaddow reached when he first came;
And it just touched the tree where his secret love cut
Two letters that stand for love's name

The evening comes in with the wishes of love
And the shepherd he looks on the flowers
And thinks who would praise the soft song of the dove,
And meet joy in these dewfalling hours

For nature is love, and the wishes of love,
When nothing can hear or intrude;
It hides from the eagle, and joins with the dove
In beautiful green solitude.

A VISION*

I lost the love of heaven above
I spurned the lust of earth below
I felt the sweets of fancied love*
And hell itself my only foe.

I lost earth's joys but felt the glow
Of heaven's flame abound in me
Till loveliness and I did grow
The bard of immortality.

I loved but woman fell away
I hid me from her faded fame
I snatched the sun's eternal ray
And wrote till earth was but a name.

In every language upon earth
On every shore, o'er every sea,
I gave my name immortal birth,
And kept my spirit with the free.

                              August 2nd 1844

MARY

It is the evening hour,
    How silent all doth lie,
The horned moon she shews her face
    In the river with the sky;
Just by the path on which we pass
The flaggy lake lies still as glass.

Spirit of her I love,
    Whispering to me
Stories of sweet visions as I rove,
    Here stop and crop with me
Sweet flowers that in the still hour grew,
We'll take them home nor shake off the bright dew.

Mary, or sweet spirit of thee,
    As the bright sun shines tomorrow,
Thy dark eyes these flowers shall see
    Gathered by me in sorrow
In the still hour when my mind was free
To walk alone – yet wish I walk'd with thee.

TO MARY

I sleep with thee and wake with thee
And yet thou art not there:
I fill my arms with thoughts of thee
And press the common air.
Thy eyes are gazing upon mine
When thou art out of sight;
My lips are always touching thine
At morning noon and night.

I think and speak of other things
To keep my mind at rest
But still to thee my memory clings
Like love in woman's breast;
I hide it from the world's wide eye
And think and speak contrary
But soft the wind comes from the sky
And whispers tales of Mary.

The night wind whispers in my ear
The moon shines in my face,
A burden still of chilling fear
I find in every place.
The breeze is whispering in the bush
And the dew fall from the tree
All sighing on and will not hush
Some pleasant tales of thee.

STANZAS*

Black absence hides upon the past
  I quite forget thy face
And memory like the angry blast
  Will love's last smile erase

I try to think of what has been
    But all is blank to me
And other faces pass between
    My early love and thee

I try to trace thy memory now
    And only find thy name
Those inky lashes on thy brow
    Black hair and eyes the same
Thy round pale face of snowy dyes
    There's nothing paints thee there
A darkness comes before my eyes
    For nothing seems so fair

I knew thy name so sweet and young
    'Twas music to my ears
A silent word upon my tongue
    A hidden thought for years
Dark hair and lashes swarthy too
    Arched on thy forehead pale
All else is vanished from my view
    Like voices on the gale

SONNET

Poets love nature and themselves are love,
The scorn of fools and mock of idle pride
The vile in nature worthless deeds approve
They court the vile and spurn all good beside
Poets love nature like the calm of heaven
Her gifts like heaven's love spread far and wide
In all her works there are no signs of leaven
Sorrow abashes from her simple pride
Her flowers like pleasures have their season's birth
And bloom through regions here below

They are her very scriptures upon earth
And teach us simple mirth where e'er we go
Even in prison they can solace me
For where they bloom God is, and I am free.

SONG

I seek her in the shady grove,
    And by the silent stream
I seek her where my fancies rove
    In many a happy dream
I seek her where I find her not
    In spring and summer weather
My thoughts paint many a happy spot
    But we ne'er meet together.

The trees and bushes speak my choice
    And in the summer shower
I often hear her pleasant voice
    In many a silent hour
I see her in the summer brook
    In blossoms sweet and fair
In every pleasant place I look
    My fancy paints her there.

The wind blows through the forest tree
    And cheers the pleasant day
There her sweet voice is sure to be
    To lull my cares away
The very hedges find a voice
    So does the gurgling rill:
But still the object of my choice
    Is lost and abscent still.

SONNET

The flag-top quivers in the breeze
That sighs among the willow trees
In gentle waves the river heaves
That sways like boats the lily-leaves
The bent-grass trembles as with cold
And crow-flowers nod their cups of gold
Till every dew-drop in them found
Is gently shook upon the ground.
Each wild weed by the river-side
In different motions dignified
Bows to the wind, quakes to the breeze,
And charms sweet summer's harmonies
The very nettle quakes away
To glad the summer's happy day

MORNING

The morning comes – the drops of dew
Hang on the grass and bushes too
The sheep more eager bite the grass
Whose moisture gleams like drops of glass
The hiefer licks in grass and dew
That makes her drink and fodder too
The little bird his morn-song gives
His breast wet with the dripping leaves
Then stops abruptly just to fly
And catch the wakened butterfly
That goes to sleep behind the flowers
Or backs of leaves from dews and showers
The yellowhammer haply blest
Sits by the dyke upon her nest
The long grass hides her from the day

The water keeps the boys away
The morning sun is round and red
As crimson curtains round a bed
The dewdrops hang on barley horns
As beads the necklace thread adorns
The dewdrops hang wheat ears upon
Like golden drops against the sun
Hedge-sparrows in the bush cry 'tweet'
O'er nests larks winnow in the wheat
'Till the sun turns gold and gets more high
And paths are clean, and grass gets dry
And longest shadows pass away
And brightness is the blaze of day

THE DYING CHILD

He could not die when trees were green
    For he loved the time too well
His little hands when flowers were seen
    Was held for the blue-bell
      As he was carried o'er the green

His eye glanced at the white-nosed bee
    He knew those children of the spring
When he was well and on the lea
    He held one in his hands to sing
      Which filled his little heart with glee

Infants the children of the spring
    How can an infant die
When butterflies are on the wing
    Green grass and such a sky
      How can an infant die at spring

He held his hand for daiseys white
   And then for violets blue
And took them all to bed at night
   That in the green fields grew
     As childhood's sweet delight

And then he shut his little eyes
   And flowers would notice not
Birds' nests and eggs made no surprise
   Nor any blossoms got
     They met with plaintive sighs

When winter came and blasts did sigh
   And bare was plain and tree
As he for ease in bed did lie
   His soul seemed with the free
     He died so quietly

THE INVITATION*

Let us go in the fields love and see the green tree
Let's go in the meadows and hear the wild bee
There's plenty of pleasure for you love and me
   In the mirths and the music of nature
We can stand in the path love and hear the birds sing
And see the woodpigeons snap loud on the wing
While you stand beside me a beautiful thing
   Health and beauty in every feature

We can stand by the brig-foot and see the bright things
On the sun-shining water that merrily springs
Like sparkles of fire in their mazes and rings
   While the insects are glancing and twitters
You see naught in shape but hear a deep song
That lasts through the sunshine the whole summer long
That pierces the ear as the heat gathers strong
   And the lake like a burning fire glitters

We can stand in the fields love and gaze o'er the corn
See the lark from her wing shake the dews of the morn
Through the dew-bearded woodbine the gale is just
    born
  And there we can wander my dearie
We can walk by the wood where the rabbits pop in
Where the bushes are few and the hedge gapped and thin
There's a wild-rosy bower and a place to rest in
  So we can walk in and rest when we're weary

The skylark, my love, from the barley is singing
The hare from her seat of wet clover is springing
The crow to its nest on the tall elm swinging
  Bears a mouthful of worms for its young
We'll down the green meadow and up the lone glen
And down the woodside far away from all men
And there we'll talk over our love tales again
  Where last year the nightingale sung

Part of
PRISON AMUSEMENTS, *
or
CHILD HAROLD, *continued*

And in the maple bush there hides the style
And then the gate the awthorn stands before
Till close upon it you cannot see't the while
'Tis like to Ivy creeping o'er a door
All green as spring nor gap is seen before
And still the path leads on – till 'neath your hand
The gate waits to be opened and then claps* – the sower
Scatters the seeds of spring beneath his hand
And then the footpath tracks the elting land . . .

Infants are but cradles for the grave
And death the nurse as soon as life begins
Time keeps accounts books for him and they save
Expences for his funeral out of sins
The stone is not put down – but when death wins
Churchyards are chronicles where all sleep well
The gravestones there as afterlives live in
Go search the Scriptures they will plainly tell
That God made heaven – Man himself the hell

There is a chasm in the heart of man
That nothing fathoms like a gulph at sea
A depth of darkness lines may never span
A shade unsunned in dark eternity
Thoughts without shadows – that eye can't see
Or thought imagine 'tis unknown to fame
Like day at midnight such its youth to me
At ten years old it boyhood's secret* came
Now manhood's forty past 'tis just the same . . .

Temple of Minerva

The ruin of a ruin – man of mirth
Pause o'er the past and meditate decay
The very stones are perishing to earth
Foundations though all's left will waste away
Time's chissel on what's left still writes 'Decay'
Which every season wrecks and wears away

A shadow it was present – but 'tis past
Time sickened and life's nature met decay
Convulsive winds seemed sobbing out their last
When ruin's piecemeal Temple passed away
The very stones like clay dissolving lye
And solitude half-fearing learns to sigh

See'st thou the steps of yesterday
The night before the last
See'st thou when darkness went away
And daylight winnowed past
The present is – and shadows are
What was so very bright and fair

Spring meadow-flowers was suns and joy
Of present happiness
But when the summer filled the sky
All was another dress
They changed to seed among the hay
And dyed when summer went away

———————

Now evening rosey streaks – a ribbond sky
Spreads in the golden light of the far West
And mighty rocks are pillowed dark and high
The image and the prototype of rest
The heavens' prophecy where peace is blest
A stillness soft as fall of silent dews
Is felt around – the very dusk looks blest
As is the maiden while her heart pursues
Her evening walk o'er fields in silent dews

Ave Maria,* 'tis the hour of love
When sighs and pains and tears on beauty's breast
Are whispered into blessings from above
Ave Maria, 'tis the hour of rest
For man and woman and the weary beast
And parents love the minature delights
That blesses all with sleep and quiet rest
Ave Maria, 'tis the hour of night
Like to an Indian Maiden dressed in white

The winter-time is over love
Whitethorns begin to bud
And brown and green of freshness love
Enlivens all the wood

There's white clouds got agen the sun
One daisey open on the green
The primrose shows its sulphur bud
Just where the hazel stulps are seen

And ere the April time is out
Along the riding's gravel walk
The bedlam's primrose blooms about
Wi' twenty blossoms on a stalk

How happy seems the drop of dew
That nestles in the daisey's eye
How blest the cloud seems in the blue
That near the sun appears to lie

How happy does thy shadows seem
That stretches o'er the morning grass
They seems to walk as in a dream
I know their shadows as they pass . . .

Song

I wish I was where I would be
Alone with beauty and the free
I wish I was where I have been
A lover on the village green
Where old pits swell'd and mosses grew
Along with one who loved so true

Hath time made no change* and then love is the same
Through calm and through danger dishonour and fame
Whate'er I encounter whate'er I pursue
Human love may be frail – but man's honour is true

Canst thou feel what I breathed on thy bosom that eve
If thy love was a woman's thou'lt ne'er disbelieve
But walk in thy fancys through meadow and glen
Aye walk and be happy and think it again
There's the hills in thy fancy the Park in thy eye
And in midnight so guiltless that beautiful sky
And the stars looked upon us so lovely and warm
And thy own native star shed its beauty so calm
That said in bright colours love never should part
When I lay on thy bosom the man of thy heart

The prude may rail on love and falsehood declaim
Mock love is their liscence and falshood their fame
In abscence they scandalize wrong and decieve
And laugh at their fondness when women believe
But man never wronged them and Eden I see
Where man ever loved and a woman is free
Then leave me still free with thy love to be blest
On the bosom of woman thy wishes are blest
O'er the hills and the hollows on that happy eve
True love was the welcome that cannot decieve

Spring

The sweet spring now is coming
In beautifull sunshine
Thorns buds and wild flowers blooming
Daisey and Celadine
Somthing so sweet there is about the spring
Silence is music ere the birds will sing

And there's the hedgerow pootys
Blackbirds from mossy cells
Pick them where the last year's shoot is
Hedge-bottoms and wood-dells
Striped, spotted, yellow, red, to spring so true
For which the schoolboy looks with pleasures new

On gates the yellowhammer
As bright as Celadine
Sits – green linnets learn to stammer
And Robins sing divine
On brown land-furrows stalks the crow
And magpies on the moor below

In small-hedged closes lambkins stand
Its cud the heifer chews
Like snow-clumps upon fallow land
They shine among the ewes
Or sheets of water by moonlight
The lambkins shine so very white

The lane the narrow lane
With daisy beds beneath
You scarce can see the light again
Untill you reach the heath
Thorn hedges grow and meet above
For half a mile a green alcove

The nettles by garden walls
Stand angrily and dun
Summer on them like prison falls
And all their blossoms shun
The abby's haunted heaps of stone
Is by their treachery overgrown

There's verdure in the stony street
Decieving earnest eyes
The bare rock has its blossoms sweet
The microscope espies
Flowers leaves and foliage everywhere
That cloaths the animated year

Fields meadows woods and pastures
There's spring in every place
From winter's wild disasters
All wear her happy face
Beasts on their feet and birds upon the wing
The very clouds upon the sky look spring

Sunshine presses by the hedge
And there's the pileworts sure to come
The primrose by the rustling sedge
And largest cowslips first in bloom
All show that spring is everywhere
The flowery herald of the year . . .

Last Day

There is a day a dreadfull day
Still following the past
When sun and moon are passed away
And mingle with the blast
There is a vision in my eye
A vacuum o'er my mind
Sometimes as on the sea I lye
Mid roaring waves and wind

When valleys rise to mountain-waves
And mountains sink to seas
When towns and cities temples graves
All vanish like a breeze
The skys that was are past and o'er
That almanack of days
Year-chronicles are kept no more
Oblivion's ruin pays

Pays in destruction,* shades, and hell
Sin goes in darkness down
And therein sulphur's shadows dwell
Worth wins and wears the crown
The very shore, if shore I see,
All shrivelled to a scroll
The Heavens rend away from me
And thunder's sulphurs roll

Black as the deadly thunder-cloud
The stars shall turn to dun
And heaven by that darkness bowed
Shall make day's light be done
When stars and skys shall all decay
And earth no more shall be
When heaven itself shall pass away
Then thou'lt remember me

The red-bagged bee on never-weary wing
Pipes his small trumpet round the early flowers
And the white nettles by the hedge in spring
Hears his low music all the sunny hours
Till clouds come on and leaves the falling showers
Herald of spring and music of wild blooms
It seems the minstrel of spring's early flowers
On banks where the red nettle flowers, it comes
And there all the long sunny morning hums

When reason and religion goes a-benting
Christianity grows lean as specters – and
Pines off to somthing else – none seem repenting
But each get notions none else understand
Wives from their husbands pare off unrelenting
And like pined pigeons mope about the land
Couples awake go silently and dreaming
And love and faith and madness are but seeming

Summer is on the earth and in the sky
The days all sunny and the fields all green
The woods spread o'er her hills a canopy
Of beauty's harmony in every scene
Like to a map the fields and valleys lie
Winds dash in wildest motions the woods green
And every wave of leaves and every billow
Lies in the sun like Beauty on a pillow

There is a freshness in the leafy sprays
That dashes o'er the forest from the wind
The wild sublimity of windy days
Like the rich thinkings of a master-mind
Or dashes on the canvass none can find
In works inferior – when the woods all blaze
With a wild sunset and the winds unbind
Their foliage to the heavens' wild amaze
Field, meadow, wood, rolling o'er stormy days

The roaring of the woods is like a sea
All thunder and comotion to the shore
The old oaks toss their branches to be free
And urge the fury of the storm the more
Louder then thunder is the sobbing roar
Of leafy billows to their shore, the sky,
Round which the bloodshot clouds like fields of gore
In angry silence did at anchor lie
As if the battle's roar was not yet bye

Anon the wind has ceased the woods are still
The winds are sobbed to sleep and all is rest
The clouds like solid rocks too jagged for hills
Lie quietly ashore upon the West
The cottage ceases rocking – each tired guest
Sleeps sounder for the heavy storm's uproar
– How calm the sunset blazes in the West
As if the waking storms would burst no more
And this still even seems more calmer than before

Bluebells how beautifull and bright they look
Bowed o'er green moss and pearled in morning dew
Shedding a shower of pearls as soon as shook
In every wood hedgegap they're shineing through
Smelling of spring and beautifully blue
– Childhood and Spring how beautifully dwells
Their memories in the woods we now walk through
O balmy days of spring in whitethorn dells
How beautifull are woods and their bluebells

Song

   'Tis spring my love 'tis spring
   And the birds begin to sing
   If 'twas winter left alone with you
   Your happy form and face
   Would make a sunny place
   And prove a finer flower then ever grew

   'Tis spring my love 'tis spring
   On the hazels catkins hing
   And the snowdrop wi' blebs o' dew
   Is not more white within
   Then your bosom's hidden skin
   The sweetest bonny flower that ever grew

The sun's arose from bed
All strewn with roses red
But the brightest crimson place
Is nought so fresh and fair
Or so lovely to compare
As thy blushing bonny face

I love spring's early flowers
And their bloom in her first hours
They never half so bright or lovely seem
They are like the happy grace
Of young woman's blushing face
And the green happiness of love's young dream

———————

The sinking sun sheds through the window-glass
A roseiate light upon the painted walls
Green looks the trees, cornfields, and meadow grass
As golden on the road the low sun falls
Loud at their play the city's childern calls
And happy minds seek green spots in the fields
Ere yet the heavy dew of evening falls
While the lone partridge to their ramble calls . . .

Song

The Lark's in the sky love
The flower's on the lea
The whitethorn's in bloom love
To please thee and me
'Neath its shade we can rest love
And sit on the hill
And as we met last love
Enjoy the spring still

The spring is for lovers
The spring is for joy
O'er the moor where the plovers
Wir hover and cry
We'll seek the whitethorn love
And sit on the hill
On some sunny morn love
And be lovers still

Where the partridge is craiking
From morning to e'en
In the wheatlands awaking
That sprouts young and green
Where the brook dribbles past love
Down the willowy glen
And as we met last love
Be lovers agen

The lark's in the grass love
Abuilding her nest
And the brook runs like glass love
'Neath the carrion crow's nest
There the wild woodbines twine love
And till the day's gone
Sun sets and stars shine love
I'll call thee my own

Song

There's pleasure on the pasture lea
And peace within the cottage
But there's na peace at a' for me
While love is in its dotage

I never have a thought o' gude
But worser thoughts will soil it
When heaven is man's happiest mood
The de'il is sure to spoil it

Man's sweetest choice is woman yet
Scenes where her kiss was granted
The choicest place where first they met
Mid flowers by nature planted

And there they dwell in fancy's flights
In valley field and glen
In pleasant dreams and heart delights
Till neist they meet agen

Song*

The bird cherry's white in the dews o' the morning
The wildings are blushing along the hedgeside
The gold-blossomed furze the wild heaths are adorning
And the brook in the hollow runs light by my side
But where is the charmer the voice of the maiden
Whose presence once charmed me the whole summer's
    day
The bushes wi' gold and wi' silver o'erlaiden
Looks cold i' the morning when Phebe's away

The sun rises bright o'er the oaks in the spinney
Bringing gold unto gold on the winbushes there
Blossoming bright as a new-minted guinea
And moist wi' the mist of the morn's dewy air
The flower is bowed down and I let the tired Bee be
All wet wi' night-dew and unable to flye
Such a kindness in me would be pleasure to Phebe
A poor trampled insect would cause her to sigh

The whitethorn is coming wi' bunches of blossoms
The broad sheets of daiseys spread out on the lea
The bunches of cowslips spread out their gold bosoms
While the oak-balls appear on the old spinney tree
Come forward my Phebe wi' dews of the morning
By the old crooked brook let thy early walk be
Where the bramble's arched stalks – glossy leaves are
    adorning
And bits o' woo' hang on the bark o' the tree

Come forward my Phebe by times in the morning
Come forward my Phebe in blebs o' the dew
They bead the young cowslip like pearls i' the dawning
And we'll mark the young shower where the green
    linnet flew
I'll court thee and woo thee from morning to e'ening
Where the primrose looks bright in the ivy's dark green
And the oak o'er the brook in its white bark is leaning
There let me and Phebe wi' morning be seen

––––––––––––––

Tall grows the nettle by the hedgeway side
And bye the old barn-end they shade the wall
In sunshine nodding to the angry tide
Of winds that winnows bye – these one and all
Makes up the harmony of Spring – and all
That passes feel a sudden love for flowers
They look so green – and when the soft showers fall
They grow so fast – Dock, Burdocks, Henbane – all:
Who loves not wild flowers by the old stone wall? . . .*

To Sorrow

'Sorrow is my joy'

Beautiful Sorrow in thy silence thou
Art more then beautiful – not charms of youth
A rosey skin or lily-painted brow
Can match thy looks thou beautiful in truth
Rebecca's faith warm with the love of Ruth
Leave heaven's sunshine on thy thoughtfull brow
Thou beautifull of sorrow and of truth
Hiding no secret sin no broken vow
While in thy raven hair white snowdrops glow . . .

Song

There is a feeling nought can calm
A passion nought can quell
The mention of a sweetheart's name
That fond thoughts dare not tell
To know thee thus my dearest maid
And then to part in twain
The thunder making earth affraid
Will smile upon the main

The just may fall by thunder-shocks
That never knew a crime
And earthquakes rend the lonely rocks
That upward used to climb
But love fond love that wedlock ties
Each other as their own
Then choked to tears and stifled sighs
And petrified to stone

For thee dear maid I touch the strings
And keep my heart awake

'Tis simple truth the ballad sings
That love will not forsake
And stubborn are the hands that strike
The chords to melody
That loved the many all alike*
With a double love for thee

Thy pedigree and titles high
As shadows pass away
And that fine face and brighter eye
Must also meet decay
But love that warmed us at the first
Can live and love alone
Nor ever die by fate accursed
Though petrified to stone

The thunder mutters louder and more loud
With quicker motion hay-folks ply the rake
Ready to burst, slow sails the pitch-black cloud
And all the gang a bigger haycock make
To sit beneath – the woodland winds awake
The drops so large wet all thro' in an hour
A tiney flood runs down the leaning rake
In the sweet hay yet dry the hay-folks cower
And some beneath the waggon shun the shower . . .

O Woman lovely woman how beguiling
Is thy sweet voice of music and thy smiles
Thy cheeks all roses and thy lips all smiling
And where's the treachery that thy heart beguiles

For thy sweet self man labours, sweats, and toils
Mines the whole earth and raviges the deep
For thee the summer in its glory smiles
Yet 'Man was made to mourn'* and women weep
And briars and thorns as harvests both must reap . . .

Poets and Poesy are aspirations
Of minds superior to the common lot
The light and life and ornament of nations
That leave no writing they could wish to blot
Time mossed in centurys finds them unforgot
Green with the leaves of laurel and the bay
The poet's dwelling is a sacred spot
Where pilgrims love when ages pass away
The low mossed cot – the steeple crack'd and grey . . .

Look through the naked bramble and blackthorn
And see the arum show its vivid green
Glossy and rich and some ink-spotted like the morn-
Ing sky with clouds – in sweetest neuks I've been
And seen the arum sprout its happy green
Full of spring visions and green thoughts
Dead leaves a-litter where its leaves are seen
Broader and brighter green from day to day
Beneath the hedges in their leafless spray

Here is the scenes the rural poet made
So famous in his songs – the very scenes
He painted in his words that warm and shade
In winter's wild waste and spring's young vivid greens
Alcove and shrubbery – and the tree that leans
With its overweight of Ivy – Yardley oak
The pheasant's nest* and fields of blossomed beans
The bridge and avenue of thick-set oak
The wilderness – here Cowper's spirit spoke

The Awthorn

I love the awthorn well
The first green thing
In woods and hedges – blackthorn dell
Dashed with its green first spring
When sallows shine in golden shene
These whitethorn places in the black how green

How beautifully green
Though March has but begun
To tend primroses planted in the sun
The roots that further in
Are not begun to bud or may be just begun

I love the whitethorn bough
Hung over the molehill
Where the spring-feeding cow
Rubs off the dewdrop chill
When on the cowslip pips and glossy thorn
The dews hang shining pearls at early morn

Song

There's a little odd house by the side of the Lane
Where the daisys smiles sweet in the spring
Where the morning sun glitters like gold on the pane
And the hedgesparrow trembles his wing
Where chaffinch, green linnet, and Sparrows have tones
That make the green Lane and the cottage their own
The sparrows they chirp and make nests i' the eaves
The chaffinch sings 'pink' in the hedge o' whitethorn
That fences the garden and there the bird weaves
A nest of grey lichen soon as light i' the morn

And there bonny Susan will sit at the door
And see the green linnet at work at its nest
Where the robin flyes in for a crumb on the floor
And seems as if longing to sit on her breast

Song

Come dwell with me
'Neath the greenwood tree
And nature will teach thee plain
That peace and health is liberty
We nowhere else shall gain
Come dwell with me
'Neath the greenwood tree
Where life is not spent in vain

Come where the wilding blows
Like the hedge-dogrose
With its pale and pinky stain
Where the hugh oak rocks
While the tempest blows
Come dwell with me
'Neath the hugh oak tree
Where nature no ill bestows

Full green is the spring
And thrushes they sing
In the hazle and maple tree
Come to the greenwood
And 'twill set thy heart free
In such a still place to be
With all that's beautiful and good

I love the little pond to mark at spring
When frogs and toads are croaking round its brink
When blackbirds' yellow bills 'gin first to sing
And green woodpecker rotten trees to clink
I love to see the cattle muse and drink
And water crinkle to the rude March wind
While two ash dotterels flourish on its brink
Bearing key-bunches children run to find
And water-buttercups they're forced to leave behind

Spring

Pale sun beams gleam
That nurture a few flowers
Pilewort and daisey and a sprig o' green
On whitethorn bushes
In the leaf-strewn hedge

These harbingers
Tell spring is coming fast
And these the schoolboy marks
And wastes an hour from school
Agen the old pasture-hedge

Cropping the daisey
And the pilewort flowers
Pleased with the Spring and all he looks upon
He ope's his spelling-book
And hides her blossoms there

Shadows fall dark
Like black in the pale Sun
And lye the bleak day long
Like blackstock under hedges
And bare wind-rocked trees

'Tis dull but pleasant
In the hedge-bottom lined
With brown seer leaves the last
Year littered there and left
Mopes the hedge-sparrow

With trembling wings and cheeps
Its welcome to pale sunbeams
Creeping through and further on
Made of green moss
The nest and green-blue eggs are seen

All token spring and every day
Green and more green hedges and close
And everywhere appears
Still 'tis but March
But still that March is spring

———————

The wind blows happily on everything
The very weeds that shake beside the fold
Bowing they dance – do anything but sing
And all the scene is lovely to behold
Blue mists of morning evenings of gold
How beautiful the wind will play with spring
Flowers beam with every colour light beholds
Showers o'er the landscape flye on wet pearl wings
And winds stir up unnumbered pleasant things

I love the luscious green before the bloom
The leaves and grass and even beds of moss
When leaves 'gin bud and spring prepares to come
The Ivy's evergreen the brown-green gorse
Plots of green weeds that barest roads engross

In fact I love the youth of each green thing
The grass, the trees, the bushes, and the moss
That pleases little birds and makes them sing
I love the green before the blooms of spring

Sorrow is felt not seen – the grief of verse
Is writ by those who share not in our pain
The pall embrodered and the sable hearse
Are symbols not of sorrow but of gain
What of the scutcheoned hearse and pall remain
When all is past – there sorrow is no more
Sorrow's heart aches – and burning scars will stain
As morning dews – as April showers is o'er
Some tears fall on their graves again . . .

False time what is it but a rogue's account
Of books wrong-kept – time's keystone is the sun
True nature's wronged – and what is the amount
But death's diseases – that their circuit run
Through error and through deeds that fate has done
Religion is the health – the sun's bright ray
By which the goal of Love and Freedom's won
The ocean's tide will flow its natural way
And none its speed and none its course will stay

All nature has a feeling: wood, brooks, fields
Are life eternal – and in silence they
Speak happiness – beyond the reach of books
There's nothing mortal in them – their decay
Is the green life of change to pass away
And come again in blooms revifified
Its birth was heaven, eternal is its stay
And with the sun and moon shall still abide
Beneath their night and day and heaven wide

Twilight

Twilight meek nurse of dews
And mother of refreshing births to flowers
Sweet now a walk to chuse
And roam in thy cool hours
To be an hour away unseen of men
In the green lane or whitethorn-studded glen

Sweet twilight, swarth or pale, meek nurse of dews
Mother of sweet sleep to many flowers
The birth of dewwebbed breezes that imbues
Our hearts to meditation in sweet hours
Sweet twilight nurse of sleep
In watchet stole and web of sober grey

Old times forgetfull memories of the past
Are cold and drear as snow upon our graves
In books less then a shadow's doom will last
But fragments there each stranded volume saves
Like some rich gems washed up from ocean-waves
But now no summer dwells upon the spot
Nor flower to blossom – the eternal blast,
Oblivion, leaves the earth in which they rot
Darkness in which the very light's forgot

Where are the citys* Sodom and Gommorrah
The marble pallaces upon the plain
Citys today and a dead sea tomorrow
And what they was they ne'er will be again
That earth is lost and all its city slain
By the o'erwhelming waves entombed and gone
Search for its ruins now is void and vain
And but one witness saw that ruin done
The ever-burning bright eternal Sun . . .

The heaven of earth's visions – boyhood's dreams –
But too much love turns dirty – here we halt
And face about from heaven and extremes
Ale can't be good if they forget the malt
And earth has lost its savour without salt
Love, hate are nearer kindred than life seems
To own to – if her fault I cannot tell
That sweet that turns to sour and never creams
Makes strange reallities the heaviest dreams

Love tickled is by any bents or straws
A lady-likeing whisper in the dark
A rebel doubtfullness unknown to laws
That looks all eyes and greedy as a shark
Swallows the mall the promenade and park
But such is sham love fond of different faces
Not that which hears the ballads of the lark
True love's the inward self in secret places
What's felt by two in love a third but guesses . . .

O for one real imaginary blessing*
Ideal real blessing blasted through
With sin, and yet how rich is the carressing
Of love as mothers' kisses sweet as Hermon dew
A bright grey eye or black, it knocks mine through
And leaves them dim as stars fall'n from above
Electric shocks they come from God knows who
Milkmaids have eyes the pictures of the dove's
That thrill through bones and marrow. Is it Love?

It is the very essence of all pleasure
It is earth's diamond and the ocean's gem
It is of life and soul the dearest treasure
Woman through life is man's own diadem

To love God truly, may we worship them?
Of life in love how various is the scene
Of infant cherubs Love's the parent stem
I wooed a gipsey wench on Sunday e'ens
And worshiped beggar-girls and courted queens

Love is the fire that burns the heart to cinders
Love is the thought that makes the poets sigh
Sweet as Queen's portraits* stuck in London windows
For loyal subjects in their love to buy
Love is of every heart the painted toy
The idol of man's worship – faces fair
Were my enchanted magic from a boy –
The pouting lip, the colour of the hair
Left me in raptures, next of kin to care

I loved and wooed them in the field like gems
Of too much value for the clown who sung
The azure bluebells in their sapphire stems
Among green bushes, low their mute bells hung
These seemed love's modest maidens dew-bestrung
With blebs o' morning's glittering pearls
I loved them in the valleys where I sung
With their green drapery and crispy curls
I loved them as a crowd of blooming girls

With bonny bosom* white as is the may
Sweet milkmaid o' May mornings – Queen Victoria,
The wild brere blushes wi' the break o' day
Sweet as the cowslip fields that spread before thee,
Sweet are the dusky clouds that sprinkle o'er thee
Filling the cowslip pips wi' pearls untold.
Thy crown and scepter fade from nature's glory
Like toys for tyrants or like garments old –
Be nature's Queen and keep her crown of gold

The wild hedge-rose it is a bonny flower
As ever met the sunshine and the sky
Its gold threads beeded with the summer showers
That patter on the glossy leaves and lye
Like pears that glitter 'neath the maiden's eye
Who stands admiring by the burning flowers
That from her own looks takes a deeper dye
Like feathers on the hedges at morn's hours
They look to fancies happier then ours

I could not walk the fields like common men
And have no fancys nourish – nor could I
Pass the wild rose-bush o'er the foxes' den
And not admire its grandeur silently
Nature's own majesty who could pass bye?
Things left all beauty, like those simple scenes –
The wild rose blushing 'neath a summer sky
The summer morning and the rosey e'en
With all the woodland multitudes of green

Song

We never know the sweets o' joy
Untill it goes away
The sweetest flower no notice wakes
Untill it meets decay

The bright sun shines our heads above
Like rich unnoticed dreams
And when the day is lost in clouds
We value the sunbeams

The spring is nothing when it comes
That seemed so bright before
The merry bee neglected hums
Flowers weeds, and nothing more

The present joy we cannot see
The sweetest comes tomorrow
But when it's past, no longer free
Past joys are present sorrow

Song

I long to think of thee in lonely midnight
When thy spirit comes warm as an angel of light
Thy face is before me in rosey and flame
Which my kiss canna reach and I know not thy name
My heart aches to think on't – 'tis long sin' we met
If love is the truth, love, how can I forget
My arms would have clasped thee to pull thy face down
But when I embraced thee the Vision was flown

And was it true luv' and cud I forget
Thy name, when I feel how enraptured we met?
And can love forget thee sae much and keep true?
Thy vision brought daylight before the cock crew
I saw thee above me in roseate hue
Thy cheeks they were red and thy bosom swelled too
My arm couldna reach those pearl shoulders sae white
Nor my lips cud na kiss wi' thy lips to unite

And can it be love to have loved and forget?
To see thee in visions nor know thy name yet?
Thy face is my own that was worshiped in love
And thou comest before me a light from above
'Tis thyself but I canna yet think o' thy name
Though my cell's light at midnight before the day came
Thy face is still beauty, thy breast rosey's hue,
But thy name I can't think of, and yet love is true

God looks on nature with a glorious eye
And blesses all creation with the sun
Its drapery of green and brown, earth, ocean, lie
In morning as Creation just begun
That saffron East fortells the riseing sun
And who can look upon that majesty
Of light brightness and splendour nor feel won
With love of him whose bright all-seeing eye
Feeds the day's light with Immortallity?

March Violet

Where last year's leaves and weeds decay
March violets are in blow
I'd rake the rubbish all away
And give them room to grow

Near neighbour to the Arum proud
Where dew-drops fall and sleep
As purple as a fallen cloud
March violets bloom and creep

Scenting the gales of early morn
They smell before they're seen
Peeping beneath the old whitethorn
That shows its tender green

The lamb will nibble by their bloom
And eat them day by day
Till briars forbid his steps to come
And then he skips away

'Mid nettle-stalks that wither there
And on the greensward lie
All bleaching in the thin March air
The scattered violets lie

I know the place, it is a place
In spring where nettles come
There milk-white violets show their face
And blue ones earlier bloom . . .

———————

O the first days of summer – morning's blush
Is rife with healthy freshness hung with dew
To dip your hand into a wet rose-bush
And crop the fairest flower that ever grew
Pearled with the silver shine of morning dew
How beautifull it looks how sweet it smells
The breath of virgin morning coming new
That from the sweets of flowers her story tells
And voice of song-birds in the ecchoing dells . . .

STANZAS

Would'st thou but know where Nature clings
    That cannot pass away
Stand not to look on human things
    For they shall all decay:
False hearts shall change and rot to dust
    While truth exerts her powers
Love lives with Nature, not with lust.
    Go find her in the flowers

Dost dream o'er faces once so fair,
    Unwilling to forget?
Seek Nature in the fields and there
    The first-loved face is met*
The native gales are lovers' voices
    As nature's self can prove
The wild field-flowers are lovers' choices
    And Nature's self is Love.

I AM

I am – yet what I am, none cares or knows;*
   My friends forsake me like a memory lost:
I am the self-consumer of my woes –
   They rise and vanish in oblivion's host
Like shadows in love-frenzied stifled throes
   And yet I am, and live – like vapours tost

Into the nothingness of scorn and noise,
   Into the living sea of waking dreams,
Where there is neither sense of life or joys,
   But the vast shipwreck of my life's esteems;
Even the dearest that I love the best
   Are strange – nay, rather, stranger than the rest.

I long for scenes where man hath never trod
   A place where woman never smiled or wept
There to abide with my Creator, God,
   And sleep as I in childhood sweetly slept,
Untroubling and untroubled where I lie
   The grass below – above, the vaulted sky.

SONNET

I feel I am, I only know I am
And plod upon the earth as dull and void
Earth's prison chilled my body with its dram
Of dullness, and my soaring thoughts destroyed.
I fled to solitudes from passion's dream
But strife persued – I only know I am.

I was a being created in the race
Of men disdaining bounds of place and time –
A spirit that could travel o'er the space
Of earth and heaven – like a thought sublime,
Tracing creation, like my maker, free –
A soul unshackled like eternity,
Spurning earth's vain and soul-debasing thrall
But now I only know I am – that's all.

———————

Left in the world alone
Where nothing seems my own
   And everything is weariness to me
'Tis a life without an end
'Tis a world without a friend
   And everything is sorrowful I see

There's the crow upon the stack
And other birds all black
   While November's frowning wearily
And the black cloud's dropping rain
'Till the floods hide half the plain
   And everything is weariness to me

The sun shines wan and pale
Chill blows the Northern gale
   And odd leaves shake and shiver on the tree
While I am left alone
Chilled as a mossy stone
   And all the world is frowning over me

Love lives beyond
The tomb, the earth which fades like dew
I love the fond
The faithfull and the true

Love lives in sleep
The happiness of healthy dreams
Eve's dews may weep
But love delightfull seems

'Tis seen in flowers
And in the even's pearly dew
On earth's green hours
And in the heaven's eternal blue

'Tis heard in spring
When light and sunbeams warm and kind
On angel's wing
Bring love and music to the mind

And where is the voice*
So young and beautifully sweet
As nature's choice
When spring and lovers meet?

Love lives beyond
The tomb, the earth, the flowers, and dew.
I love the fond,
The faithfull, young, and true.

HESPERUS*

Hesperus, the day is gone
Soft falls the silent dew
A tear is now on many a flower
And heaven lives in you

Hesperus, the evening mild
Falls round us soft and sweet
'Tis like the breathings of a child
When day and evening meet

Hesperus, the closing flower
Sleeps on the dewy ground
While dews fall in a silent shower
And heaven breathes around

Hesperus, thy twinkling ray
Beams in the blue of heaven
And tells the traveller on his way
That earth shall be forgiven

THE AUTUMN WIND

The Autumn wind on suthering wings
    Plays round the oak-tree strong
And through the hawthorn hedges sings
    The year's departing song
There's every leaf upon the whirl
    Ten thousand times an hour
The grassy meadows crisp and curl
    With here and there a flower
There's nothing in the world I find
That pleases like the Autumn wind

The chaffinch flies from out the bushes
　　The bluecap 'tee hees' on the tree
The wind sues on in merry gushes
　　His murmuring autumn's minstrelsy
The robin sings his autumn song
　　Upon the crabtree overhead
The clouds like smoak slow sail along
　　Leaves rustle from their mossy bed
There's nothing suits my musing mind
So pleasant as the Autumn wind

How many miles it suthers on
　　And stays to dally with the leaves
And when the first broad blast is gone
　　A stronger gust the foliage heaves
The poplar tree it turns to gray
　　As leaves lift up their underside
The birch it dances all the day
　　To rippling billows petrified
There's nothing calms the quiet mind
So welcome as the Autumn wind

Sweet twittering o'er the meadow grass
　　Soft sueing o'er the fallow ground
The lark starts up as on they pass
　　With many a gush and moaning sound
It fans the feathers of the bird
　　And ruffs the robin's ruddy breast
As round the hovel-end it whirled
　　Then sobs and gallops o'er the West
In solitude the musing mind
Must ever love the Autumn wind

Oct 15th/45

TO A LARK SINGING IN WINTER

Wing-winnowing lark with speckled breast
Has just shot up from nightly rest
To sing two minutes up the West
    Then drop again
Here's some small straws about her nest
    All hid from men.

Thou farmer's minstrel ever cheery
Though winter's all about so dreary
I dare say thou sat warm and erie*
    Between the furrows
And now thy song that flows unweary
    Scorns earthly sorrows

The little mouse comes out and nibbles
The small weed in the ground of stubbles
Where thou, lark, sat and slept from troubles
    Amid the storm
The stubble's icicle began to dribble
    In sunshine warm

Sweet minstrel of the farm and plough
When ploughman's fingers' gin to glow
How beautiful and sweet art thou
    Above his head
The stubble-field is in a glow
    All else seems dead

All dead without the stubble-ground
Without a sight without a sound
But music sunshines all around
    Beneath thy song
Winter seems softened at thy sound
    Nor nips to wrong

On all the stubble-blades of grass
The melted drops turn beads of glass
Rime feathers upon all we pass
　　Everywhere hings
And brown and green all hues that was
　　Feathered like wings

It is a morn of ragged rime
The coldest blast of winter time
Is warmth to this Siberian clime
　　Dead winter sere
And yet that clod-brown bird sublime
　　Sings loud and clear

The red round sun looks like a cheat
He only shines blood-freezing heat
And yet this merry bird's night seat
　　Seems warm's a sty
The stubble-woods around it meet
　　And keep it dry

How safe must be this bird's sweet bed
In stubble-fields with storms o'er head
Or skies like bluest curtains spread
　　Lying so lone
With bit of thurrow o'er her head
　　Mayhap a stone

The god of nature guides her well
To choose best dwellings for hersel'
And in the spring her nest we'll tell
　　Her choice at least
For God loves little larks as well
　　As man or beast

Thou little bird thou bonny charm
Of every field and every farm
In every season cold and warm
    Thou sing'st thy song
I wish thy russet self no harm
    Nor any wrong

Free from the snares thy nature shuns
And nets and baits and pointed guns
Dangers thy timid nature shuns
    May thou go free
Sweet bird as summer onward runs
    I'll list to thee

I'd writ one verse, and half another,
When thou dropt down and joined a brother
And o'er the stubble swopt together
    To play 'till dark
Then in thy night nest shun cold weather
    As snug's a Lark

Old russet fern I wish thee well
Till next year's spring comes by itsel'
Then build thy nest and hide it well
    'Tween rig or thurrow
No doubt may be this is the dell
    – Spring comes the morrow

Then blossomed beans will bloom above thee
And bumble bee buz in and love thee
And nothing from thy nest shall move thee
    When May shines warm
And thy first minstrelsy above thee
    Sing o'er the farm

The spring is come forth but no spring is for me
Like the spring of my boyhood on woodland and lea
When flowers brought me heaven and knew me again
In the joy of their blooming o'er mountain and plain
My thoughts are confined and imprisoned – O when
Will freedom find me my own vallies again?

The winds breathe so sweet and the day is so calm
In the woods and the thicket the flowers look so warm
And the grass is so green so delicious and sweet
O when shall my manhood my youth's vallies meet,
The scenes where my children are laughing at play,
The scenes where my memory is fading away

The primrose looks happy in every field
In strange woods the violets their odours will yield
And flowers in the sunshine all brightly arrayed
Will bloom just as fresh and as sweet in the shade
But the wild flowers that bring me most joy and content
Are the blossoms that blow where my childhood was
    spent

Then I played like a flower in the shade and the sun
And slept as in Eden when daylight was done
There I lived with my parents and felt my heart free
And love – that was yet joy or sorrow to be,
Joy and sorrow it has been like sunshine and showers
And their sun is still bright o'er my happiest hours

The trees they are naked the bushes are bare
And the fields they are brown as if winter lay there
But the violets are there by the dykes and the dell
Where I played 'hen and chickens' – and heard the
    church bell

Which called me to prayer-book and sermons in vain
O when shall I see my own vallies again?

The churches look bright as sun at noon-day
There meadows look green ere the winter's away
There the pooty still lies for the schoolboy to find
And a thought often brings these sweet places to mind
Where the trees waved like thunder no music so well
Then nought sounded harsh but the school-calling bell

There are spots where I played there are spots where I
      loved
There are scenes where the tales of my choice were
      approved
As green as at first – and their memory will be
The dearest of life's recollections to me
The objects seen* there in the care of my heart
Are as fair as at first – and will never depart

Though no names are mentioned to sanction my themes
Their hearts beat with mine and make real my dreams
Their memories with mine their diurnal course run,
True as night to the stars and as day to the sun
And as they are now so their memories will be
Long as sense, truth, and reason remaineth with me.

THE ROUND OAK

The apple-top't oak in the old narrow lane
And the hedgerow of bramble and thorn
Will ne'er throw their green on my visions again
As they did on that sweet dewy morn
When I went for spring pooteys and bird's nest to look
Down the border of bushes ayont the fair spring
I gathered the palm-grass close to the brook
And heard the sweet birds in thorn-bushes sing

I gathered flat gravel-stones up in the shallows
To make ducks and drakes when I got to a pond
The reed-sparrow's nest it was close to the sallows
And the wren's in a thorn-bush a little beyond
And there did the stickleback shoot through the pebbles
As the bow shoots the arrow quick-darting unseen
Till it came to the shallows where the water scarce
    drebbles
Then back dart again to the spring-head of green

The nest of the magpie in the low bush of whitethorn
And the carrion-crow's nest on the tree o'er the spring
I saw it in March on many a cold morn
When the arum it bloomed like a beautiful thing
And the apple-top't oak aye as round as a table
That grew just above on the bank by the spring
Where every Saturday noon I was able
To spend half a day and hear the birds sing

But now there's no holidays left to my choice
That can bring time to sit in thy pleasures again
Thy limpid brook flows and thy waters rejoice
And I long for that tree – but my wishes are vain
All that's left to me now I find in my dreams
For fate in my fortune's left nothing the same
Sweet apple-top't oak that grew by the stream
I loved thy shade once, now I love but thy name

June 19/46

TWILIGHT

Sweet twilight nurse of dews
And mother of sweet hours
With thee a walk I choose
Among the hawthorn bowers
That overhang the molehill greenly gray
Made as it were to intercept the way

Beetles are thy trumpeters
And to thy silence play
Where the soft still rustle stirs
O'er dead winds of the day
'Mid marshy sedge, dull aspens, and pasture-rushes
O'er green cornfields and hedge-row bushes

Thy hours have one light place
Streaky and dunly grey
As if the night was giving place
And bringing back the day
The sun seems coming, so the eye believes,
But darkness deepens round and undeceives

O'er brooks the weeping ash
Hangs cool and grimly dark
I hear the water splash
And then, half-fearing, mark
In ivy'd ash a robber near the stream
Till from a nearer view I find it but a dream

Sweet twilight nurse of night
Thy path the milkmaid treads
With nimble step so light
Scarce bends the cowslips' heads
But hastening on ere by thy light forsook
She leaves her cows all resting by the brook

Sweet twilight thy cool dews
Are beautifully spread
Where the nightingale its song renews
Close by the old cow-shed
In that low hazel oft' I've heard her sing
While sombre evening came on downy wing

The playful rabbit too
Its white scut glancing

Amid the silver dew
I've seen them oft advancing
In troops from spinneys where they love to dwell
Dancing on molehills in the open dell

Spring leaves seem old in green
And the dull thorn is lost in the
Dun twilight – but the hazel still is seen
In sleeping beauty by the old oak-tree
Giving the woods a beauty and a power
While earth seems Eden in such an hour

Sweet twilight in thy dews
And silence I rejoice
Thy odd stars bid me muse
And give to silence voice
Now twilight ceases on the verge of even
And darkness like a pall spreads over heaven

WOOD-ANEMONIE

The wood-anemonie through dead oak-leaves
And in the thickest wood now blooms anew
And where the green briar and the bramble weaves
Thick clumps o' green anemonies thicker grew
And weeping flowers in thousands pearled in dew
People the woods and brake's hid hollows there
White, yellow, and purple-hued the wide wood through
What pretty drooping weeping flowers they are
The clipt frilled leaves the slender stalk they bear
On which the drooping flower hangs, weeping dew
How beautiful through April time and May
The woods look filled with wild anemonie
And every little spinney now looks gay
With flowers 'mid brush-wood and the hugh oak-tree

I love thee nature with a boundless love
The calm of earth the storms of roaring woods
The winds breathe happiness where e'er I rove
There's life's own music in the swelling floods
My harp is in the thunder-melting clouds
The snow-capt mountain and the rolling sea
And hear ye not the voice where darkness shrouds
The heavens? There lives happiness for me

Death breathes its pleasures when it speaks of him
My pulse beats calmer while its lightnings play
My eye with earth's delusions waxing dim
Clears with the brightness of eternal day
The elements crash round me – it is he
And do I hear his voice and never start
From Eve's posterity I stand quite free
Nor feel her curses rankle round my heart

Love is not here – hope is – and in his voice
The rolling thunder and the roaring sea
My pulse they leap and with the hills rejoice
Then strife and turmoil is a peace to me
No matter where life's ocean leads me on
For nature is my mother and I rest
When tempests trouble, and the sun is gone,
Like to a weary child upon her breast

Flowers shall hang upon the palls
Brighter than patterns upon shawls
And blossoms shall be in the coffin-lids
Sadder than tears on grief's eyelids
Garlands shall hide pale corpses' faces
When beauty shall rot in charnel places
Spring flowers shall come in dews of sorrow
For the maiden goes down to her grave tomorrow

Last week she went walking and stepping along
Gay as first flowers of spring or the tune of a song
Her eye was as bright as the sun in its calm
Her lips they were rubies her bosom was warm
And white as the snowdrop that lies on her breast
Now death like a dream is her bedfellow-guest
And white as the sheets – aye and paler than they
Now her face in its beauty has perished to clay

Spring flowers they shall hang on her pall
More bright than the pattern that bloomed on her shawl
And blooms shall be strewn where the corpse lies hid
More sad than the tears upon grief's eyelid
And ere the return of another sweet May
Shall be rotting to dust in the coffined clay
And the grave whereon the bright snowdrops grow
Shall be the same soil as the beauty below

                                     Feby 11th/47

———————

   How hot the sun rushes
   Like fire in the bushes
The wild flowers look sick at the foot of the tree
   Birds' nests are left lonely
   The pewit sings only
And all seems disheartened and lonely like me

   Baked earth and burnt furrows
   Where the rabbit he burrows
And yet it looks pleasant beneath the green tree
   The crow's nest look darkly
   O'er fallows dried starkly
And the sheep all look restless as nature and me

Yet I love a meadow, dwelling
Where nature is telling
A tale to the clear stream – it's dearest to me
To sit in green shadows
While the herd turns to gadders
And runs from the hums of the fly and the bee

This spot is the fairest
The sweetest and rarest
This sweet sombre shade of the bright green tree
Where the morehen's flag-nest
On the water's calm breast
Lies near to this sweet spot that's been mother to me

MARY: A BALLAD

The skylark mounts up with the morn
The vallies are green with the spring
The linnets sit in the whitethorn
To build mossy dwellings and sing
I see the thorn-bush getting green
I see the woods dance in the spring
But Mary can never be seen
Though the all-cheering spring doth begin

I see the grey bark of the oak
Look bright thro' the underwood now
To the plough-plodding horses they joke
But Mary is not with her cow
The birds almost whistle her name
Say where can my Mary be gone
The spring brightly smiles – and 'tis shame
That she should be absent alone

The cowslips are out on the grass
Increasing like crowds at a fair
The river runs smoothly as glass
And the barges float heavily there
The milkmaid she sings to her cow
But Mary is not to be seen
Can Nature such absence allow
At milking on pasture and green?

When Sabbath it comes to the green
The maidens are there in their best
But Mary is not to be seen
Though I walk till the sun's in the West
I fancy still each wood and plain
Where I and my Mary have strayed
When I was a country swain
And she was the happiest maid

But woods they are all lovely now
And the wild flowers blow all unseen
The birds sing alone on the bough
Where Mary and I once have been
But for months she now keeps away
And I am a lonely hind
Trees tell me so from day to day
When waving in the wind

Birds tell me so upon the bough
That I'm threadbare and old
The very sun looks on me now
A being dead and cold
Once I'd a place where I could rest
And love and quiet be
That quiet place was Mary's breast
And still a hope to me –

The spring comes brighter by day
And brighter flowers appear
And though she long has kept away
Her name is ever dear
Then leave me still the meadow-flowers
Where daffies blaze and shine
Give but the spring's young hawthorn-bower
For then sweet Mary's mine

SONG

How silent comes this gentle wind
And fans the grass and corn
It leaves a thousand thoughts behind
Of happiness forlorn
The memory of my happier days
When I was hale and young
Where still my boyish fancy strays
Corn-fields and woods among

It fans among the lazy weeds
And stirs the wild flowers' leaves
Sweet is the playful noise it breeds
While the heart its joys receives
While listening to the gentle sounds
That murmur thro' the grass
And must I love the airy sounds
Of crows that o'er me pass

And larks that fly above the corn
Frit by a jilted stone
A few yards high at eve or morn
Then drop and hide alone
I love to see the breeze at eve
Go winnowing o'er the land
And partridges their dwellings leave
And call on either hand

I love the all that nature loves
The water, earth, and sky
The greenness of the leafy groves
Brown fallows rising high
The breezes of the early morn
The early evening breeze
The Brown Lark's mattins in the corn
The rook's song in the trees

I love the haunts of solitude
The coverts of the free
Where man ne'er ventures to intrude
And God gives peace to me
Where all I hear and all I see
In peace of freedom roam
Here shall my heart's own dwelling be
And find itself at home

AUTUMN

I love the fitfull gusts that shakes
    The casement all the day
And from the mossy elm-tree takes
    The faded leaf away
Twirling it by the window pane
With thousand others down the lane

I love to see the shaking twig
    Dance till the shut of eve
The sparrow on the cottage-rig
    Whose chirp would make believe
That spring was just now flirting by
In summer's lap with flowers to lie

I love to see the cottage-smoke
    Curl upwards through the naked trees
The pigeons nestled round the cote*
    On dull November days like these
The cock upon the dunghill crowing
The mill-sails on the heath agoing

The feather from the raven's breast
    Falls on the stubble-lea
The acorns near the old crow's nest
    Fall pattering down the tree
The grunting pigs that wait for all
Scramble and hurry where they fall

SONG

Where the ash-tree weaves
Shadows over the river
And the willow's grey leaves
Shake and quiver –
Meet me and talk, love,
Down the grasshopper's baulk, love,
And then love for ever.

There meet me and talk, love,
Of love's inward feelings
Where the clouds look like chalk, love,
And the huts and the shielings
Lie like love o'er the river
Here talk of love's feelings
And love on for ever.

Where the bee hums his ballads
By the river so near it
Round docks and wild salads
While all love to hear it,

We'll meet by the river
And by old willow-pollards
Bid love live for ever.

Jan^ry 13th 1848

THE WIND

The frolicksome wind through the trees and the bushes
Keeps sueing and sobbing and waiving all day
Frighting magpies from trees and from whitethorns the
    thrushes
And waveing the river in wrinkles and spray
The unresting wind is a frolicksome thing
O'er hedges in floods and green fields of the spring

It plays in the smoke of the chimney at morn
Curling this way and that i' the morn's dewy light
It curls from the twitch-heap among the green corn
Like the smoke from the cannon i' th' midst of a fight
But report there is none to create any alarm
From the smoke on the ground hiding meadow and
    farm

How sweet curls the smoke o'er the green o' the field
How majestic it rolls o'er the face o' the grass
And from the low cottage the elm-timbers shield
In the calm o' the evening how sweet the curls pass
I' the sunset how sweet to behold the cot smoke
From the low red-brick chimney beneath the dark oak

How sweet the wind whispers o' midsummer's eves
And fans the winged elder-leaves o'er the old pales
While the cottage smoke o'er them a bright pillar leaves
Rising up and turns clouds by the strength of the gales
O' sweet is the cot 'neath its colums of smoke
While dewy eve brings home the labouring folk

The fly or beetle on their track
Are things that know no sin
And when they whemble on their back
What terror they seem in
The shepherd boy wi' bits o' bents
Will turn them up again
And start them where they nimbly went
Along the grassy plain
And such the shepherd boy is found
While lying on the sun-crackt ground

The lady-bird that seldom stops
From climbing all the day
Climbs up the rushes' tassle-tops
Spreads wings and flies away
He sees them – lying on the grass
Musing the whole day long
And clears the way to let them pass
And sings a nameless song
He watches pismires on the hill
Always busy never still

He sees the traveller-beetle run
Where thick the grass-wood weaves
To hide the black-snail from the sun
He props up plantain leaves
The lady-cows have got a house
Within the cowslip pip
The spider weaving for his spouse
On threads will often slip
So looks and lyes the shepherd boy
The summer long his whole employ

O could I be as I have been
  And ne'er can be no more
A harmless thing in meadows green
  Or on the wild seashore

O could I be what once I was
  In heaths and valleys green
A dweller in the summer grass
  Green fields and places green

A tennant of the happy fields
  By grounds of wheat and beans
By gipsey's camps and milking-bield
  Where lussious woodbine leans

To sit on the deserted plough
  Left when the corn was sown
In corn and wild weeds buried now
  In quiet peace unknown

The harrow's resting by the hedge
  The roll within the dyke
Hid in the ariff and the sedge
  Are things I used to like

I used to tread through fallow lands
  And wade through paths of grain
When wheat-ears pattered on the hands
  And headaches left a stain

I wish I was what I have been
  And what I was could be
As when I roved in shadows green
  And loved my willow-tree

To gaze upon the starry sky
And higher fancies build
And make in solitary joy
Love's temple in the field

AN INVITE TO ETERNITY

Wilt thou go with me sweet maid
Say maiden wilt thou go with me
Through the valley-depths of shade
Of night and dark obscurity
Where the path hath lost its way
Where the sun forgets the day
Where there's nor life nor light to see
Sweet maiden wilt thou go with me

Where stones will turn to flooding streams
Where plains will rise like ocean-waves
Where life will fade like visioned dreams
And mountains darken into caves
Say maiden wilt thou go with me
Through this sad non-identity*
Where parents live and are forgot
And sisters live and know us not

Say maiden wilt thou go with me
In this strange death of life-to-be
To live in death and be the same
Without this life or home or name
At once to be and not to be
That was and is not – yet to see
Things pass like shadows – and the sky
Above, below, around us lie.

The land of shadows wilt thou trace
And look nor know each other's face
The present mixed with seasons gone
And past and present all as one
Say maiden can thy life be led
To join the living with the dead
Then trace thy footsteps on with me
We're wed to one eternity

CHILDHOOD

O dear to us ever the scenes of our childhood
The green spots we played in, the school where we met
The heavy old desk where we thought of the wildwood
Where we pored o'er the sums which the master had set
I loved the old church-school both inside and outside
I loved the dear ash-trees and sycamore too
The graves where the buttercups burning gold outvied
And the spire where pelitory dangled and grew

The bees i' the wall that were flying about
The thistles the henbane and mallows all day
And crept in their holes when the sun had gone out
And the butterfly ceased on the blossoms to play
O dear is the round stone upon the green hill
The pinfold hoof-printed with oxen – and bare
The old princess-feather-tree growing there still
And the swallows and martins wheeling round in the air

Where the chaff whipping outwards lodges round the
    barn-door
And the dunghill-cock struts with his hens in the rear
And sings 'Cockadoodle' full twenty times o'er
And then claps his wings as he'd fly in the air

And there's the old cross with its roundabout steps
And the weathercock creaking quite round in the wind
And there's the old hedge with its glossy red heps
Where the green-linnet's nest I have hurried to find

– To be in time for the school or before the bell rung.
Here's the odd martin's nest o'er the shoemaker's door
On the shoemaker's chimney the old swallows sung
That had built and sung there in the seasons before
Then we went to seek pootys among the old furze
On the heaths, in the meadows, beside the deep lake
And returned with torn cloathes all covered wi' burrs
And oh what a row my fond mother would make

Then to play boiling kettles just by the yard-door
Seeking out for short sticks and a bundle of straw
Bits of pots stand for teacups after sweeping the floor
And the children are placed under school-mistress's awe
There's one set for pussy, another for doll
And for butter and bread they'll each nibble an awe
And on a great stone as a table they loll
The finest small teaparty ever you saw

The stiles we rode upon 'all a cock-horse'
The mile-a-minute swee
On creaking gates – the stools o' moss
What happy seats had we
There's nought can compare to the days of our
    childhood
The mole-hills like sheep in a pen
Where the clodhopper sings like the bird in the
    wild-wood
All forget us before we are men

Oct. 15th/48

336

The girl I love is flesh and blood
   With face and form of fairest clay
Straight as the firdale in the wood
   And lovely as a first spring day

The girl I love's a lovely girl
   Bonny and young in every feature
Richer than flowers and strings o' pearl
   A handsome and delightful creature

She's born to grace the realms above
   Where we shall both be seen together
And sweet and fair the maid I love
   As rose trees are in summer weather

O bonny straight and fair is she
   I wish we both lived close together
Like as the acorns on the tree
   Or foxglove-bell in summer weather

Come to me love and let us dwell
   Where oak-trees cluster all together
I'll gaze upon thy bosom's swell*
   And love yes love thee then forever

Her face is like another's face
   As white another's skin may prove
But no one else could fill her place
   If banished from the maid I love

When life's tempests blow high
In seclusion I tread
Where the primroses lie
And the green mosses spread
Where the bottle-tit hangs
At the end of a twig
Where the humble bee bangs
That is almost as big

Where I feel my heart lonely
I am solitude's own
Talking to myself only
And walking woods lone
In the wood-briars and brambles
Hazel-stools and oak-trees
I enjoy such wood-rambles
And hear the wood-bees

That sing their wood-journey
And stop at wood-blooms
Where the primroses burn ye
And the violet perfumes
There to myself talking
I rub through the bushes
And the boughs where I'm walking
Like a sudden wind rushes

The wood-gate keeps creaking
Opened ever so slow
And from boughs bent to breaking
Often starts the odd crow
Right down the green riding
Gladly winds the wild bee
Then through the woodsiding
He sucks flowers in glee

He flies through the stovens
Brown, hazel, and grey
Through fern-leaves like ovens
Still singing his way
He rests on a moss-bed
And perks up his heels
And strokes o'er his small head
Then hies to the fields

I enjoy these wood-rambles
And the juicey wheat-fields
Where the woodrose and brambles
A shower's covert yields
I love the wood-journey
Where the violets melt blue
And primroses burn ye
With flames the day through

THE EVENING IS FOR LOVE

The evening is for love As the morning is for toil
Though the fire is from above The pot is got to boil
A hard day's work is mine And I'll live wi' care no more
So I'll see dew come to the woodbine At Isabella's door

Wi' hairy leaves and droping flowers The
    canterberry-bell
Grows underneath the hazle-bower By most folks
    favoured well
Up the bean-stalks creeps the snail The moth sleeps
    down below
The grey mist creep along And I'll a courting go

I'll gang and Isabella see Nor more i' love repine
By her yard gate's the elder-tree By her door the
    streaked woodbine

And red pink-bunches on the bed And pansies blue and
yellow
The West is glowering gold and red And I'll gang to
Isabella

I'll court her a' the lee-lang night And tomorrow being
Sunday
I'll wrap her in my heart's delight And uggle her till
Monday
Her bosom is so fair and white she never had a fellow
I'll gang and stay till broad daylight Wi' my handsome
Isabella

HER LOVE IS ALL TO ME

O cold is the winter day And iron is the ground
And winter's snow has found his way For fifty miles
around
I turn a look to every way And nothing to be seen
The frozen clouds shuts out the day And snow hides all
the green

The hedges all of leaves are bare My heart beats cold and
chill
O once I loved a pretty girl And love her dearly still
Though love is but a frozen pearl As you may plainly
see
My lovely girl is handsome As any maid can be

Freeze on the bitter biteing sky Snows shade the naked
tree
All desolate alone am I Yet I'll love none but thee
No tears I shed my love to show To freeze before they
fall
No sighs I send along the snow But she's my all in all

The footpath leaves the ruts and carts O'er furrow and
    o'er rig
And my love lives at the 'White Hart'* A stone throw
    from the brig
She's like a ballad sung in tune And deep in love to be
Her face is like the rose in June And her love is all to me

THE DAISY–BUTTON TIPP'D WI' DEW

The daisy–button tipped wi' dew Green like the grass
    was sleeping
On every thing 'neath heaven blue In moonlight dew
    was weeping
In dark wood sung the Nightingale The moon shone
    round above me
My arms were clasped round Mary Gale My dearest do
    you love me?

Her head a woodbine wet wi' dew Held in the
    moonlight sleeping
And two in one together grew Wi' daisy-buds a
    weeping
O' Mary Gale sweet Mary Gale How round and bright
    above thee
The moon looks down on grassy vale My dearest can
    you love me?

How sweet the moonlight sleeps and still Firdale and
    hedge-row brere
The molewarp's mound and distant hill Is moonlight
    everywhere
The totter-grasses' pendalums Are still as night above
    me
The bees are gone and nothing hums My dearest do you
    love me?

The moonlight sleeps o'er wood and wall Sweet Mary
  while you're nigh me
Can any charm o' courtship fail And any joy pass by me?
The gossamer all wet wi' dew Hung on the brere above
  me
She leaned her cheek and said 'I do, And ever mean to
  love thee'

NOW IS PAST

Now is past, the happy now,
When we together roved
Beneath the wild woods' oak-tree bough
And nature said we loved
          Winter's blast
The now since then has crept between
And left us both apart
Winters that withered all the green
Hath froze the beating heart
          Now is past

Now is past since last we met
Beneath the hazle-bough
Before the evening sun was set
Her shadow stretched below
          Autumn's blast
Has stained and blighted every bough
Wild strawberrys like her lips
Have left the mosses green below
Her bloom's upon the hips
          Now is past

Now is past is changed agen
The woods and fields has painted new
Wild strawberrys which both gathered then
None knows now where they grew
          The sky's o'er cast

Wood-strawberrys faded from woodsides
Green leaves have all turned yellow
No Adelaide walks the woodsides
True love has no bedfellow
Now is past

LITTLE TROTTY WAGTAIL

Little trotty wagtail he went in the rain
And tittering tottering sideways he ne'er got straight
again
He stooped to get a worm and looked up to catch a fly
And then he flew away ere his feathers they were dry

Little trotty wagtail he waddled in the mud
And left his little foot marks trample where he would
He waddled in the water-pudge and waggle went his tail
And chirrup up his wings to dry upon the garden rail

Little trotty wagtail you nimble all about
And in the dimpling water-pudge you waddle in and
out
Your home is nigh at hand and in the warm pigsty
So little Master Wagtail I'll bid you a 'Good bye'
Augst 9th/49

CLOCK-A-CLAY

In the cowslip's peeps I lye
Hidden from the buzzing fly
While green grass beneath me lies
Pearled wi' dew like fishes' eyes
Here I lie a Clock-a-clay
Waiting for the time o' day

While grassy forests quake surprise
And the wild wind sobs and sighs
My gold home rocks as like to fall
On its pillar green and tall
When the pattering rain drives by
Clock-a-Clay keeps warm and dry

Day by day and night by night
All the week I hide from sight
In the cowslip's peeps I lie
In rain and dew still warm and dry
Day and night and night and day
Red black-spotted Clock-a-clay

My home it shakes in wind and showers
Pale green pillar topt wi' flowers
Bending at the wild wind's breath
Till I touch the grass beneath
Here still I live lone Clock-a-clay
Watching for the time of day

THE SWEETEST WOMAN THERE

From bank to bank the water roars Like thunder in a storm
A Sea in sight of both the shores Creating no alarm
The water-birds above the flood Fly o'er the foam and
    spray
And nature wears a gloomy hood On this October day

And there I saw a bonny maid That proved my heart's
    delight
All day she was a Goddess made An angel fair at night
We loved and in each other's power Felt nothing to
    condemn
I was the leaf and she the flower And both grew on one
    stem

I loved her lip her cheek her eye She cheered my
    midnight gloom
A bonny rose 'neath God's own sky In one perrenial
    bloom
She lives 'mid pastures evergreen And meadows ever
    fair
Each winter spring and summer scene The sweetest
    woman there

She lives among the meadow floods That foams and
    roars away
While fading hedgerows distant woods Fade off to
    naked spray
She lives to cherish and delight All nature with her face
She brought me joy morn noon and night In that low
    lonely place

AUTUMN

The thistledown's flying Though the winds are all still
On the green grass now lying Now mounting the hill
The spring from the fountain Now boils like a pot
Through stones past the counting It bubbles red-hot

The ground parched and cracked is Like overbaked
    bread
The greensward all wrecked is Bents dried up and dead
The fallow fields glitter Like water indeed
And gossamers twitter Flung from weed unto weed

Hill-tops like hot iron Glitter hot i' the sun
And the Rivers we're eyeing Burn to gold as they run
Burning hot is the ground Liquid gold is the air
Whoever looks round Sees Eternity there

And must we part that once so close
And fond were knit together
Love's buds betorn by wonton force
The flowers for summer weather
And must my happy thoughts decay
And summer blossoms wither
The hope that cheered me many a day
Must now belong to neither

Yet still the cottage-chimney smokes
Beneath the spreading walnut
Though heeded not by other folks
There evil can no gall put
Green grass there looks never cold
'Sward daisies none looks whiter
The willow-leaves fall off like gold
In autumn and look brighter

To Bessey I'll not say farewell
Nor trouble feel at parting
I'll love the Cottage where ye dwell
And feel one truth as certain
For nature's self will dwell wi' me
To charm all sorts o' weather
And love and truth will still agree
And leave us both together

THE CROW SAT ON THE WILLOW

The Crow sat on the willow tree
A-lifting up his wings
And glossy was his coat to see
And loud the ploughman sings

I love my love because I know
The milkmaid she loves me
And hoarsely croaked the glossy crow
Upon the willow tree
I love my love, the ploughman sung
And all the field wi' music rung

I love my love a bonny lass
She keeps her pails so bright
And blythe she trips the dewy grass
At morning and at night
A cotton drab her morning-gown
Her face was rosey health
She traced the pastures up and down
And nature was her wealth
He sung and turned each furrow down
His sweetheart's love in cotton gown

My love is young and handsome
As any in the town
She's worth a ploughman's ransom
In the drab cotton gown
He sung and turned his furrows o'er
And urged his team along
While on the willow as before
The old crow croaked his song
The ploughman sung his rustic lay
And sung of Phebe all the day

The crow was in love no doubt
And wi' a many things
The ploughman finished many a bout
And lustily he sings
My love she is a milking-maid
Wi' red and rosey cheek

O' cotton drab her gown was made
I loved her many a week
His milking-maid the ploughman sung
Till all the fields around him rung

THE PEASANT POET

He loved the brook's soft sound
The swallow swimming by
He loved the daisy-covered ground
The cloud-bedappled sky
To him the dismal storm appeared
The very voice of God
And where the Evening rock was reared
Stood Moses with his rod
And every thing his eyes surveyed
The insects i' the brake
Were creatures God almighty made
He loved them for his sake
A silent man in life's affairs
A thinker from a Boy
A Peasant in his daily cares –
The Poet in his joy

SONG

The wind waves o'er the meadows green
And shakes my own wild flowers
And shifts about the moving scene
Like the life o' summer hours
The little bents with reedy head
The scarce-seen shapes o' flowers
All kink about like skeins o' thread
In these wind-shaken hours

All stir and strife and life and bustle
In every thing around we see
The rushes whistle, sedges rustle,
The grass is buzzing round like Bees
The butterflyes are tossed about
Like skiffs upon a stormy sea
The bees are lost amid the rout
And drop in green perplexity

Wilt thou be mine thou bonny lass
Thy drapery floats so gracefully
We'll walk along the meadow-grass
We'll stand beneath the willow-tree
We'll mark the little reeling bee
Along the grassy ocean rove
Tossed like a little boat at sea
And interchange our vows of love

OH COME TO MY ARMS

O' come to my arms i' the cool o' the day
When the veil o' the evening falls dewy and grey
O' come to me under the awthorn green
When eventide falls i' the bushes serene

O' come to me under the awthorn tree
When the lark's on his nest and gone bed is the bee
When the veil of the evening falls dark on the scene
And we'll kiss love and court i' the bushes so green

O' come to me dear wi' thy own maiden head
Where the wild flowers and rushes shall make thee a bed
We will lie down together in each other's arms
Where the white moth flirts by and gives us alarms

349

Where the rush-bushes bend and are silvered wi' dew
Ere the sunbeam the red cloud O' morning breaks
    through
Thy face is so sweet and thy neck is so fair
O' come at eve dearest and live with me there

REMEMBER DEAR MARY

Remember dear Mary love cannot decieve
Love's truth cannot vary dear Mary believe
You may hear and believe it believe it and hear
Love could not deceive those features so dear
Believe me, dear Mary, to press thy soft hand
Is sweeter than riches in houses and land

Where I pressed thy soft hand at the dewfall o' eve
I felt the sweet tremble that cannot deceive
If love you believe in Belief is my love
As it lived once in Eden ere we fell from above
To this heartless this friendless this desolate earth
And kept in first love Immortality's birth

'Tis there we last met I adore thee and love thee
There's nothing beneath thee around thee above thee
I feel it and know it I know so and feel
If your love cannot shew it mine cannot conceal
But knowing I love I feel and adore
And the more I behold – only loves thee the more

SONG

I wish I was where I would be
With love alone to dwell
Was I but her or she but me
Then love would all be well
I wish to send my thoughts to her
As quick as thoughts can fly
But as the wind the waters stir
The mirrors change and flye

SONG

She tied up her few things*
And laced up her shoe-strings
And put on her bonnet worn through at the crown
Her apron tied tighter
Than snow her cap's whiter
She lapt up her earnings and left our old town

The Dog barked again
All the length o' his chain
And licked her hand kindly and huffed her good bye
Old hens prated loudly
The Cock strutted proudly
And the horse at the gate turned to let her go bye

The Thrasher-man stopping
The old barn-floor wopping
Wished o'er the door-cloth her luck and no harm
Bees hummed round the thistle
While the red Robins whistle
And she just cast one look on the old mossy farm

'Twas Michaelmas season
They'd got corn and pears in
And all the Fields cleared save some rakings and tythes
Cote-pigeon-flocks muster
Round beans-shelling cluster
And done are the whettings o' reap-hooks and scythes

Next year's flowers a-springing
Will miss Jinney's singing
She opened her Bible and turned a leaf down
In her bosom's forewarnings
She lapt up her earnings
And ere the sun's set'll be in her own town

SONG

I hid my love when young while I
Coudn't bear the buzzing of a flye
I hid my love to my despite
Till I could not bear to look at light
I dare not gaze upon her face
But left her memory in each place
Where e'er I saw a wild flower lye
I kissed and bade my love goodbye

I met her in the greenest dells
Where dew-drops pearl the wood bluebells
The lost breeze kissed her bright blue eye
The bee kissed and went singing bye
A sunbeam found a passage there
A gold chain round her neck so fair
As secret as the wild bee's song
She lay there all the summer long

I hid my love in field and town
Till e'en the breeze would knock me down
The bees seemed singing ballads o'er
The flye's buzz turned a lion's roar
And even silence found a tongue
To haunt me all the summer long
The riddle nature could not prove
Was nothing else but secret love

SONG

I peeled bits o' straws and I got switches too
From the grey peeling Willow as Idlers do
And I switched at the flyes as I sat all alone
Till my flesh, blood, and marrow wasted to dry bone
My illness was love though I knew not the smart
But the beauty o' love was the blood o' my heart

Crowded places, I shunned them as noises too rude
And flew to the silence of sweet solitude
Where the flower in green darkness buds, blossoms, and
    fades
Unseen of a shepherd and flower-loving maids
The hermit-bees find them but once and away
There I'll bury alive and in silence decay

I looked on the eyes o' fair woman too long
Till silence and shame stole the use o' my tongue
When I tried to speak to her I'd nothing to say
So I turned myself round and she wandered away
When she got too far off – why I'd something to tell
So I sent sighs behind her and talked to mysel'

Willow-switches I broke and I peeled bits o' straws
Ever lonely in crowds in nature's own laws
My ball-room the pasture, my music the bees'
My drink was the fountain, my church the tall trees.
Whoever would love or be tied to a wife
When it makes a man mad a' the days o' his life?

THE RAWK O' THE AUTUMN

The rawk o' the Autumn hangs over the woodlands
Like smoke from a city dismembered and pale
The sun without beams burns dim o'er the floodlands
Where white cawdymaws slow swiver and sail
The flood froths away like a fathomless ocean
The wind winnows chill like a breeze from the sea
And thoughts of my Susan give the heart an emotion
To think, does she e'er waste a thought upon me?

Full oft I think so on the banks of the meadows
While the pale cawdymawdy flies swooping all day
I think of our true love where grass and flowers hid us
As by the dyke-side o' the meadows we lay
The seasons have changed since I sat wi' my true love
Now the flood roars and raves o'er the bed where we lay
There the bees kissed the flowers – Has she got a new love?
I feel like a wreck of the flood cast away

The rawk of the Autumn hangs over the woodlands
Like smoke from a city sulphurously grey
The heronshaw lonely hangs over the floodland
And cranks its lone story throughout the dull day
There's no green on the hedges, no leaves on the darkwood
No cows on the pasture or sheep on the lea
The linnets cheep still and how happy the lark would
Sing songs to sweet Susan to remind her of me

Woman had we never met
I nor thou had felt regret
Never had a cause to sigh
Never had a wish to die
 To part and cease to love thee

Had I shared the smallest part
Of friendship from a woman's heart
Never had I felt the pains
Of these ever-galling chains
 Or ever ceased to love thee

And never on my burning brow
Felt the Cain-curses I do now
That withers up the anxious brain
Blighting what never blooms again
 When woman ceased to love me

The Spring may come, the sun may shine
The earth may send forth sweets divine
What pain I've felt, have still to know,
The nought in Nature e'er to show
 Since woman ceased to love me

Woman had we never met
Love had witnessed no regret
Never left us cause to sigh
Or me a vainer wish to die
 To part and cease to love thee

I envy e'en the fly its gleams of joy
In the green woods from being but a boy
Among the vulgar and the lowly bred
I envied e'en the hare her grassy bed
Innured to strife and hardship from a child
I traced with lonely step the desert wild
Sighed o'er bird-pleasures but no nest destroyed
With pleasure felt the singing they enjoyed
Saw nature smile on all and shed no tears
A slave through ages though a child in years
The mockery and scorn of those more old
An Esop in the world's extended fold
The fly I envy settling in the sun
On the green leaf and wish my goal was won

SONG

My old lover left me I knew not for why
He left me wi' kisses I parted in tears
After painting my cheeks i' the rosey bloom's dye
And swearing my eyes were the gems o' the spheres
My lover has left me I knew not for why
Two years and three months he has wandered afar
The things that were hisn I've put them all by
And from the fire corner removed the armchair
I once had a sweetheart I knew not for why
But I think I could love all the days o' my life
But he left me one morning like a bird i' the sky
And the cloud-wracks o' heaven seemed boiling in strife
My sweetheart he left me I knew not for why
He's left me alone for two desolate years
The swallows on holliday-wings chitter bye
And my eyes looking silent keep filling wi' tears

I can't be myself let me do as I will
I think till I'm blind and feel willing to die
But my true love has left me and there remains still
He kissed me and left me nor do I know why

SONG

I'll come to thee at eventide
When the West is streaked wi' grey
I'll wish the night thy charms to hide
And daylight all away

I'll come to thee at set o' sun
Where whitethorn's i' the may
I'll come to thee when work is done
And love thee till the day

When daisey-stars are all turned green
And all is meadow-grass
I'll wander down the bank at e'en
And court the bonny lass

The green banks and the rustleing sedge
I'll wander down at e'en
All slopeing to the water's edge
And in the water green

And there's the luscious meadowsweet
Beside the meadow-drain
My lassie there I once did meet
Who I wish to meet again

The water-lilies were in flower
The yellow and the white
I met her there at even's hour
And stood for half the night

We stood and loved in that green place
When Sunday's sun got low
Its beams reflected in her face
The fairest thing below

My sweet Ann Foot my bonny Ann
The meadow-banks are green
Meet me at even when you can
Be mine as you have been

THE WINTER'S COME*

Sweet chesnuts brown like soleing-leather turn,
The larch trees, like the colour of the sun
That paled sky in the Autumn seem'd to burn.
What a strange scene before us now does run
Red, brown, and yellow, russet, black, and dun,
Whitethorn, wild cherry, and the poplar bare,
The sycamore all withered in the sun,
No leaves are now upon the birch-tree there,
All now is stript to the cold wintry air.

See, not one tree but what has lost its leaves,
And yet the landscape wears a pleasing hue,
The winter chill on his cold bed receives
Foliage which once hung o'er the waters blue,
Naked, and bare, the leafless trees repose,
Blue-headed titmouse now seeks maggots rare,
Sluggish and dull the leaf-strewn river flows,
That is not green, which was so through the year,
Dark chill November draweth to a close.

'Tis winter and I love to read in-doors,
When the moon hangs her crescent up on high
While on the window-shutters the wind roars
And storms like furies pass remorseless by,
How pleasant on a feather-bed to lie,
Or sitting by the fire in fancy soar,
With Milton or with Dante to regions high,
Or read fresh volumes we've not seen before,
Or o'er old Burton's 'Melancholy' pore.

Spring comes and it is May – white as are sheets
Each orchard shines beside its little town
Childern at every bush a poesy meets
Bluebells and primroses – wandering up and down
To hunt birds' nests and flowers a stone's-throw from
     town
And hear the blackbird in the coppice sing
Green spots appear like doubling a book down
To find the place again and strange birds sing
We have no name for in the burst of spring

The sparrow comes and chelps about the slates
And pops in to her hole beneath the eaves
While the cock-pigeon amourously awaits
The hen on barn-ridge, crows and then leaves
With crop all ruffled – where the sower heaves
The hopper at his side his beans to sow
There he with timid courage harmless thieves
And whirls around the teams and then drops low –
While plops the sudden gun and great the overthrow

And only o'er the heaths to ramble
Mary thou my partner be
Down the cool lanes lined wi' bramble
Mary wind the brook wi' me
Tho' before wi' glooms surrounded
When encircled in thy arms
Beating heart wi' troubles crowded
Throbs to rest on Mary's charms.

Mary when life's shadow reaches
Stalkingly across the lane
When thine and mine the even stretches
Like two giants o'er the plain
Then's the time the pleasure stealeth
Which I often wish to see
Then's the time my bosom feeleth
All its joy belong to thee.

Then may Fortune shower her treasures
On her highly favored few
Little shall we miss the pleasures,
Mary, which we never knew.
Fate and Fortune, long contrary,
Grant but one request to me
Bless me in the charms of Mary
Nothing more I ask of thee.

I look on the past and I dread the tomorrow
My life grows a burthen I wish to lay down
Times meet one wi' naught but new tidings of sorrow
And cares tan the bloom of my summer-leaf brown
If life owns a joy it ne'er fell to my portion
If pleasure's a substance the shadow was mine
A skiff on the waves of a wild-tossing ocean
Where no rocks befriend me such life to resign.

Spring's done wi' me and my summer is waning
Time's out of call wi' my best younger days
Hope's only prop of support now remaining
Is autumn attired in her mourning-array
Autumn haste on and come winter encroaching
As on my bare head the leaves part from the tree
I'll feel consolation of slumbers approaching
When death does the same to my sorrows and me.

TO JOHN CLARE*

Well, honest John, how fare you now at home?
The spring is come and birds are building nests
The old cock-robin to the stye is come
With olive feathers and its ruddy breast
And the old cock with wattles and red comb
Struts with the hens and seems to like some best
Then crows and looks about for little crumbs
Swept out by little folks an hour ago
The pigs sleep in the sty the bookman comes
The little boy lets home-close-nesting go
And pockets tops and tawes where daiseys bloom
To look at the new number just laid down*
With lots of pictures and good stories too
And Jack the jiant-killer's high renown

NOTES

Introduction

p. 15 Cf. Russell Brain: *Some Reflections on Genius*, 1960. Lord Brain concluded that Clare was *not* schizophrenic, but suffering from a manic-depressive (circular) psychosis: this would be consistent with the 'sanity' of his poetry and the alienations of his conversations and letters.

p. 20 These quotations are from William James: 'On a Certain Blindness in Human Beings'.

p. 22 Seamus Heaney's observations are from his essay 'In the Country of Convention', *Preoccupations*, Faber, 1980.

The Poems
Sources of Texts

Days and Seasons: all texts newly transcribed from Peterborough MSS A40, A41, A43, A45 and A54, collated with *The Midsummer Cushion*, ed. Anne Tibble and R. K. R. Thornton (MidNag/Carcanet), 1979 (in these notes, *M C*), and with *The Rural Muse*, ed. R. K. R. Thornton (MidNag/Carcanet), 1982 (*R M*); except for 'Summer Evening' and 'Crows in Spring', which come from Eric Robinson and Geoffrey Summerfield, eds., *Selected Poems and Prose of John Clare*, Oxford University Press, 1967 (*R S*), a transcript of texts from various Northampton and Peterborough MSS. In the case of a few words, I have preferred the *R S* variant to that in MS A54.

Landscapes with Figures: all texts newly transcribed from MSS as above, except for 'A Sunday with Shepherds and Herd-boys', and 'Snow Storm', which come from *R S*.

Birds and Beasts: all texts transcribed from MSS as above, except for 'To the Snipe', 'The Martin', 'The Hedgehog', 'The Fox' and 'The Badger', from *R S*.

Loves: all texts from MSS as above, except for 'Dedication to Mary' and 'I've ran the furlongs . . .' (*RS*).

Changes and Contradictions: all texts transcribed from MSS as above, except for 'The Mores' (*RS*) and 'The Lament of Swordy Well', from E. Robinson and D. Powell, *John Clare*, Oxford University Press, 1984 (*RP*).

Madhouses . . . : all texts transcribed from Northampton MSS 6, 8, 9, 10, 19 and 20, Peterborough MS A 62, and Bodleian MS Don. A 64, except for the first three poems, which appeared in the *English Journal*, May 1841.

The English Bastille: all texts transcribed from Knight's transcripts, Peterborough MS D 24, and from MSS 6, 9, 10 and 19, as above; except for 'And only o'er the heaths . . .' and 'I look on the past . . .' which were published in the USA in June 1937.

p. 31 Clare used the sonnet-form throughout his life. In his early sonnets he is an invisible spectator, watching and listening; in the prospect, he blends both near and far, animating the landscape with movements of birds, animals and representative humans. Many of these sonnets end with a brief evaluation, an affirmation of positive satisfactions.

p. 32 *The Wheat Ripening*: Clare's models for his earlier poetry derive from eighteenth-century topographical poetry: the marks of 'literariness' can be detected in 'What time the . . .', 'maiden', 'list' the clown', 'lark's ditty': this is clearly not the language of his village neighbours.

p. 33 *A Morning Walk*: throughout 1831 and 1832 Clare wrote out a fair copy of the poems that he wished to include in a projected volume, *The Midsummer Cushion*: his proposal to publish this by subscription failed, and some of the contents of the manuscript were selected, modified, edited and cleaned up by other hands to form *The Rural Muse*, 1835. Since the poems in the *Midsummer Cushion* manuscript (Peterborough, MS A 54) comprise much of Clare's own presentation of his early maturity (poems written through the 1820s and early 1830s, his age being twenty-seven to thirty-nine), I have chosen most of the poems of the pre-asylum years from this source.

p. 34 *All nightly things are on the run*: *MC* reads 'on the rout', but the rhyme-scheme requires 'run'.

p. 38 *some wild mysterious book*: many chapbooks offered ways of telling fortunes.

p. 39 *Or list' the church-clock's humming sound*: *MC* reads 'Or watch . . .'

p. 40 *Strength to ferry*: at the beginning of this line, the preposition, *for*, is understood.

p. 45 *Evening Pastime*: Clare was a voracious reader throughout his life. Here he instances two poets who influenced his early work: Thomson, whose *Seasons* was the most popular and influential poem of the eighteenth century, and Cowper, whose quiet voice Clare loved. Bloomfield's case was specially interesting to Clare, for the older poet also came out of the lower strata of English society: his poetry sold very well for a time, and many genteel readers took a patronizing interest in him; he turned his back on his own culture, dismissing it as vulgar, and died after suffering severe melancholy and poverty.

p. 52 *Sport in the Meadows*: working to establish a poetic language, Clare sometimes went astray: here he has become infatuated with the -en ending, which for late eighteenth- and early nineteenth-century readers offered a sense of the antique: Chatterton used dozens of such devices in his forgeries, and the strongest model for such tricks was probably Spenser.

p. 55 *Tuteling*: i.e. Tootling. *MC* reads 'Tutting'.

p. 65 *To see the startled frog his rout pursue*: 'rout' is used by Clare to signify either 'route' or 'path', or 'lively activity', or both.

p. 66 *And swallows heed*: i.e., and I heed swallows . . . as is their custom, rising first.

p. 67 *And wind-enarmourd aspin*: the best appreciation and analysis of Clare's language is Barbara M. H. Strang's essay, 'John Clare's Language', published as an appendix to *RM*. Of 'enarmourd' she writes, '*Enarmoured* surely "contains" *enamoured*, but . . . appears in contexts in which the image of *armour* is also appropriate . . .' Cf. p. 51, first line.

   As wonting: 'wonting' *or* 'wanting'? Either/or? Or both/ and? As Barbara Strang remarks, 'It is not the editor's business to preclude the reader from perceiving these double images.'

p. 72 *but where is pleasure gone?*: sporadically, even in relatively early poems, Clare surprises his reader with a sudden and unexpected inrush of bleakness, melancholy or disenchantment.

p. 74 *While hasty hare*: *MC* reads 'tasty'.

Emmonsails Heath: otherwise known as Ailsworth Heath, and now a nature-reserve. This is the heath that Clare crossed when, as a boy, he went off in search of the edge of the world.

p. 75 *Lolham Brigs*: or Bridges. A splendid series of stone arches carries the old Roman road across the flood-plain on either side of the River Welland.

p. 80 *Waving the sketching pencil*: *MC* reads 'sketchy'.

p. 82 *Displaying . . . at all*: this runs fairly close to the kinds of 'proper' sentiments that his patrons, especially Admiral Lord Radstock, urged him to express.

Stray Walks: the affirmation of the value of 'wandering', and of the serendipitously educative powers of nature that accrue to the wanderer – this occurs frequently in Clare, as in Wordsworth. The contrary values of constraint and calculation were neatly satirized by both Wordsworth (*Prelude*, Book 5) and Byron (*Don Juan*, Canto 1, stanzas XVI and L). Clare's commitment to wandering also appears in the next poem in this selection.

p. 93 *A Sunday with Shepherds and Herdboys*: the oral culture of the shepherds was for Clare a great treasure; in this poem he establishes a contrast between the claims of the Bible and those of traditional romances. At this juncture Clare himself is ambivalent: on the one hand he characterizes the tellers of tales as 'ignorant'; on the other, he invests such tales with the accolade of 'Natural'. On Clare's relationship with oral traditions, see George Deacon's remarkable book, *John Clare and the Folk Tradition* (Sinclair Browne), 1983.

p. 97 *A Cromwell-trench*: a landmark-remnant of the Civil War.

p. 104 *Where boys unheeding passed*: *MC* reads 'past'. Clare tended to use 'past' for both 'passed' and 'past'. Where this seems likely to create uncertainty in the modern reader, I have distinguished them.

p. 111 *Thriving on seams*: here 'seam' is used in its older, now obsolete, sense of an intervening strip of land, i.e. with water on both sides. In the next line, the manuscript reads 'island', but the sense requires the plural; 'swell' is used transitively.

p. 119 *But they who hunt the field*: i.e. gypsies, Clare was on close terms with the gypsies of his area: it was from them that he learned to play the fiddle; and when he came to escape from his first asylum, it was to gypsies that Clare typically turned for guidance.

p. 120 *The shepherd threw*: the manuscript reads 'through', but there seems to be nothing gained from keeping such errors in transcription. We all make such mistakes, especially when tired or momentarily inattentive, and they have no linguistic/stylistic significance whatsoever. This stanza offers an extreme case of Clare's parataxis, each line comprising a simple sentence. The disjointedness seems to express the rhythm of the action.

p. 121 *The Badger*: in this sonnet-sequence, I have chosen to place the 'Some keep a baited badger . . .' sonnet after the first, rather than last, since in the terminal position it is gratingly anti-climactic.

p. 125 *To violets I compare*: in *MC*, the second word reads 'voilets'. In an equally good manuscript source, it reads 'violets'. The case for the former is that it offers a clue to Clare's phonetics. The case for 'violets' is that it is free of quaintness and does not draw attention to itself as odd. The presentation of Clare's poetry raises many such questions: my present purpose is to minimize distractions or obstacles, while respecting the peculiar integrity of Clare's text.

p. 126 *Dedication to Mary*: in the manuscripts, 'Mary' appears in the title as four asterisks and in line 1 as M * * *. Clare's conduct as a lyrical poet was fraught with circumstantial problems, since he was paying explicit homage to Mary whilst living with Martha (Patty).

p. 130 *Scarce nine days passed us ere we met*: *MC* omits 'us', but the metre requires it.

Now nine years' suns: Clare's relationship with Mary ended in 1816; this poem was published in the *Souvenir* in 1826.

p. 131 *Ballad*: the last stanza encapsulates Clare's dilemma: 'another (Patty) claims [to be] akin' but Mary must recognize her own right also to claim a bond. This is a foreshadowing of Clare's later obsessive efforts to resolve the contradictions of his emotions, which finally gave rise to his belief that he had committed bigamy.

p. 135 *The Enthusiast*: this is one of Clare's most ambitious attempts to achieve psychological sense or coherence *à propos* Mary's place in his mind, her continuing and virtually continuous 'presence'. He achieves only a partial resolution in the paradox of 'aching joy'. So it was to be, for the rest of his life.

White: Henry Kirke White, the son of a butcher, was encouraged by Southey and published a volume of precocious verse. He died at the age of twenty-one in 1806.

p. 138 *That blue of thirteen summers bye*: if Clare had last met Mary in 1816, this would suggest an 1829 dating for the poem.

p. 143 *Ballad*: the last stanza offers Clare's alternative resolution of his contradictions: 'woman's cold perverted will/ And soon-estranged opinion': not merely disenchantment but also a dismissive bitterness. Clare returned to this view in his 'Old Wigs and Sundries' under the influence of Byron's *Don Juan*, but it was not by any means his most characteristic determination.

p. 145 *Ere sun*: the MS reads 'suns', but the sense requires 'sun'.

p. 152 *The Robin's Nest*: Clare's withdrawal into the more remote or 'private' retreats of nature is both negative and positive. It derives in part from the '*De contemptu mundi*' theme in late-eighteenth-century poetry; it is also a matter of a personal liking for solitude and of social disenchantment; it is probably most emphatically rooted in an almost pre-conscious affinity with the less compromised reaches of natural life.

p. 156 *Wild heaths to trace – and note their broken tree*: *MC* reads 'not', but the sense requires 'note'.

p. 164 *Yet to all minds*: *MC* reads 'mind'.

p. 165 *The morn with saffron stripes*: *MC* reads 'saffron strips', but Clare elsewhere writes 'stript' for 'striped', and was familiar with Byron's liking for 'saffron'.

p. 171 *The hated sign by vulgar taste is hung*: here Clare transfers the term 'vulgar' from the poor to the landowners. Cf. E. P. Thompson's comment on a similar turn in Wordsworth: *Education and Experience*, Leeds University Press, 1963.

p. 172 *Nor carry round some names to win*: in their edition of Clare (Oxford University Press, 1984), *RP* omit 'to win', producing an incomplete line.

p. 190 *On the twenty-ninth of May*: Oak-apple Day, officially the celebration of Charles II's escape, probably derived from an earlier rural festival.

p. 193 *The Old Man's Song*: Clare was not yet forty when he wrote this. It has clear affinities with the poetry of Cowper's melancholia, but rehearses the themes of Clare's own circumstances, prior to and following the move or flitting to Northborough. He enclosed this and other poems in a letter to L. T. Ventouillac, 9 May 1830, who had asked Clare for some 'short, lyrical, *spirited* compositions' (*Letters*, ed.

M. Storey, Oxford University Press, 1985, p. 507). In the version enclosed with the letter, 'Joy once reflected brightly of prospects overcast' reads, 'of prospects that are past', and 'Is overspread with glooms' reads, 'Is overcast with . . .'

'Joy once reflected brightly of prospects overcast . . .': 'reflected' may signify 'mirrored' or 'thought of'; 'of' may therefore be intended as 'off'.

p. 195 *Remembrances*: the names refer to some of Clare's favourite walks around Helpstone; the two named oak trees were both felled to make way for the new boundaries, hedgerows and ditches of enclosure.

p. 196 *While I see the little mouldiwarps*: the mole-catcher hung dead moles on the tree, to display the fact that he had done his job. Nowadays, the moles are stuck on the barbs of barbed-wire.

p. 198 *The Flitting*: this and the following poem, 'Decay', were written after Clare's removal to Northborough. There is a draft of part of 'Decay' on a letter written to Clare at Northborough. Surprisingly, Clare manages to turn the conclusion of 'The Flitting' to a positive note: whatever time and change do to us, nature will survive.

Molehills and rabbit-tracks: *MC* reads 'tracts'.

p. 207 *A make-believe on April-day*: i.e. April Fools' Day.

p. 208 *in Clare's memory*: in the 1820s Clare had idolized Byron; in 1824, he wrote an eloquent account of Byron's funeral, which he witnessed during a visit to London that also included some exposure to the city's low-life: the French Playhouse, with its 'smoke, smocks, smirks, smells and smutty doings'; displays of pugilism at the Fives Court; and The Hole in the Wall, in Chancery Lane, run by the most celebrated ex-pugilist, Jack Randall.

Clare's library contained J. H. Reynolds's *The Fancy* (1820), a spoof-memoir of a poet apparently modelled on Clare, in which Byron and the dubious world of pugilism were closely associated: 'Of all the great men of this age, in poetry, philosophy, or pugilism, there is no one of such transcendant talent as Randall . . . Lord Byron is a wonderful poet, with a mind weighing fourteen stone; but he is too sombre a hitter, and is apt to lose his temper. Randall has no defect . . .'

In the same year, Taylor's *London Magazine* published a review of Thomas Medwin's *Journal of the Conversations of Lord Byron*, which featured Byron's promiscuity, his contempt for women and a simple tribute that must have caught Clare's fancy: 'Of all my schoolfellows, I know no one for whom I have retained so much friendship as for Lord Clare'; and it was Byron who had written: 'I have a passion for the name of "Mary"' (*Don Juan*, Canto 5, stanza IV); who had treated of bigamy (stanza XX); who had written of 'hopes which will not deceive' (*Childe Harold's Pilgrimage*, Canto 3, stanza CXIV); and even of 'bedlamites broke loose' (*Don Juan*, Canto 6, stanza XXXIV). Again in 1820, in his second *Letter to John Murray*, Byron had come to John Clare's defence.

p. 211   *Maid of Walkherd*: clearly modelled on Byron's 'Maid of Athens, ere we part'.

p. 212   *The Gipsy Camp*: it was the local gypsies who showed Clare the road leading north out of Epping Forest, prior to his escape in July 1841.

   Nigh Leopard's Hill: in 1837, John Taylor, who had published Clare's first three volumes, sought the advice of Dr George Darling, who had treated Clare's ailments during his visits to London. Darling recommended that Clare be placed in the care of Dr Matthew Allen, at his private asylum, Fairmead House, High Beech, in Epping Forest, north of London. In 1830, Taylor had published Dr John Conolly's *Inquiry Concerning the Indications of Insanity*, and, like Conolly, Allen was committed to the humane treatment of the insane. His *Cases of Insanity, with Medical, Moral and Philosophical Observations* had been published in 1831, and Taylor published his *Essay on the Classification of the Insane* in 1838. Allen's mental science was an odd mixture of good sense, animal magnetism, phrenology and the influences of weather. Clare was admitted in June 1837, and Allen found his mind 'not so much lost and deranged as suspended in its movements by the oppressive and permanent state of anxiety, and fear, and vexation, produced by the excitement of excessive flattery at one time, and neglect at another, his extreme poverty and over-exertion of mind, and no wonder that his feeble bodily frame . . . was overcome.'

p. 214   *Ballad*: the capitalization of every word occurs in Clare's manuscripts sporadically, and is seemingly an attempt to achieve emphasis so as to be attended to.

   Don Juan: after Byron's death in 1824, a fashionable literary game was to write 'continuations' of his *Don Juan*: one of them, published in 1825, was in Clare's library. Clare

369

himself drafted an advertisement for *his* poem, thus: 'Speedily will be published / The sale of Old Wigs and Sundries/ A Poem by Lord Byron' (M S S 6 and 8).

The central theme of Clare's 'Old Wigs . . .' is the pervasiveness of deceit: in a remarkable letter to his wife, he remarks: 'I am in Prison because I won't leave my family and tell a falsehood . . . Truth is the best companion for it levels all distinctions in pretentions . . . Truth, wether it enters the Ring or the Hall of Justice, shows a plain Man that is not to be scared at shadows or big words . . .'

Clare's targets are marital deceit, political deceit, social deceit: Wigs offered him both a pun on Whigs and also an emblem of the deceitful disguise of the powerful. His *pugilistic* challenge was issued on 1 May 1841:

Jack Randall's Challange to All the World Jack Randall The Champion Of The Prize Ring Begs Leave To Inform the Sporting World That He Is Ready To Meet Any Customer In The Ring Or On The Stage To Fight For The Sum Of £500 Or £1000 A Side A Fair Stand Up Fight half Minute Time Win Or Loose he Is Not Particular As to Weight Colour Or Country All He Wishes Is To Meet With a Customer Who Has Pluck Enough To Come To The Scratch

Jack Randall

May 1st 1841

His *Byronic* challenge was 'Old Wigs and Sundries'.

p. 216 *And I of blunt*: money.

p. 217 *beaten hollow*: in the election, July 1841.

Noble Lord John: in June and July 1841, the newspapers announced the forthcoming marriage of Lord John Russell and Lady Fanny Elliot. Victoria and Albert were married in February 1840, and Albert first left her to visit the Continent in March 1844. Clare, it seems, was revising this poem in that year.

p. 218 *And so resign*: Melbourne resigned in August 1841.

the young princess: Victoria Adelaide, born November 1841.

p. 219 *I've never seen*: i.e. animals, unlike humans, cannot practise deceit or disguise.

Ponders End: three miles from High Beech.

'Cease your funning': from Gay's *Beggar's Opera*.

Eliza Phillips: the text of the poem in MS 8 is followed by this letter:

My dear Eliza Phillips

Having been cooped up in this Hell of a Madhouse till I seem to be disowned by my friends and even forgot by my enemies for there is none to accept my challanges which I have from time to time given to the public I am almost mad in waiting for a better place and better company and all to no purpose It is well known that I am a prize fighter by profession and a man that never feared anybody in my life either in the ring or out of it – I do not much like to write love letters but this which I am now writing to you is a true one – you know that we have met before and the first oppertunity that offers we will meet again – I am now writing a New Canto of Don Juan which I have taken the liberty to dedicate to you in remembrance of Days gone bye and when I have finished it I would send you the vol if I knew how in which is a new Canto of Child Harold also – I am my dear Elize

yours sincerely
John Clare

p. 220 *Doctor Bottle*: Allen would collect urine samples from the patients for analysis, especially for signs of VD: cf. 'Some p-x-d . . .'

To see red hell, and further on, the white one: there were three separate houses at High Beech asylum: Fairmead, Springfield and Leopard's (or Leppit's) Hill. If Fairmead was Allen's residence, then the two 'hells' would be Springfield and Leopard's Hill, where the patients lived, women in the first and men in the second: the colours may simply be a reference to the colours of brick and stucco.

p. 221 *Next Tuesday*: Clare's birthday was 13 July.

Lord Byron? Poh: this seems to be intended as the voice of an intrusive Cockney interlocutor, dismissing Byron; Clare's response to this dismissal seems to begin at line 3. The choice of a Cockney dialect is entirely appropriate, since most of Allen's patients would be from London and the home counties.

Who wed two wives: Byron's sexual adventures here connect with Clare's delusion that he himself was 'imprisoned' for 'bigamy'.

371

And buy the book: Clare ends with his abiding preoccupation – how to sustain his vocation as poet *and* make a living by it.

p. 222 *Prison Amusements, or Child Harold*: in about 1848, Clare wrote to Mary Howitt: 'I have poetical sweethearts too, which my fancy dwells on as it did when I was single. So, in writing of these as my fancy dictates, they grow imperceptibly into a Vol. and then I call it "Child Harold", of which I wrote much both in Essex and here, which I did and do merely to kill time, and whose more proper title might be "Prison Amusements".' He used the title again in a letter to Knight in July 1850.

Many are poets: cf. Byron: 'Many are poets who have never penn'd . . .' ('The Prophecy of Dante').

No zeal: Clare explicitly turns away from the political matters of 'Old Wigs and Sundries'.

Great little minds: i.e. small-minded people who are economically or socially powerful. Cf. 'The Mores' and 'The Elm Tree'.

p. 224 *She in the Lowlands*: a reference to Mary Joyce, in the Fens, and Clare, separated in the relative elevation of Epping Forest. The terms echo those of Burns.

p. 225 *Keeps off the tempest*: images of shipwreck persist throughout the poetry of Clare's asylum years; a debt, perhaps, to Byron. Cf. *Don Juan*, Canto 5, stanza IV.

I've wandered: this and the next Song were written immediately after Clare's arrival at Northborough, 23 July 1841, after his escape from High Beech.

p. 226 *Falsehood is here*: in 'Old Wigs and Sundries', falsehood involved the whole social/political fabric. Here it is construed in personal terms: he cannot believe those who tell him that Mary died in 1838.

The church-spire: the spire of Glinton church. Glinton was Mary's village, and the spire was visible for miles around.

p. 227 *Here let the Muse*: again, Clare is aware that it is not this poem's business to deal with matters that appear in 'Old Wigs . . .'

Mere painted beauty: Clare sporadically contrasts the 'truth' of the rural ingenuousness of such women as Mary and the deceitful pretensions of women of sophistication, worldliness or fame.

p. 228 *Sweet Susan . . . And Bessey*: women's names occur frequently in the poems, letters and jottings of the asylum years. Many of them have been identified, from directories, as actual people – shopkeepers' daughters, publicans' wives and so on. Clare's susceptibility to women persisted virtually undiminished in his later years.

p. 229 *Written in a Thunderstorm*: written on Thursday, 15 July, five days before Clare made his escape. The writing of the rest of the poem seems to follow his escape. Even though he *has* escaped, '. . . shades are still my prison where I lie'.

p. 230 *Mary how oft*: these stanzas seem to have been provoked by the fact that Mary was not there to receive him on his return: since he cannot accept her death, he can only assume that she has betrayed him.

p. 231 *God's decree*: i.e. monogamy.

p. 232 *'To be beloved'*: Coleridge: 'The Pains of Sleep'.

p. 233 *Now melancholly autumn*: Clare returns to his native scene in his favourite season.

p. 234 *And freeze like Niobe*: cf. Byron, *Childe Harold's Pilgrimage*, Canto 4, stanza LXXIX.

p. 236 *lives*: MS reads 'lifes'.

p. 238 *No moment-hand*: i.e. the minute-hand of the clock.

p. 239 *Peace-plenty*: harvest celebrations.

This life: here the 'Old Wigs . . .' tone and matter intrude briefly.

p. 242 *Then he the tennant*: in this stanza Clare writes of himself in the third person, a sign that he is simultaneously writing of Byron, hence the 'princely palace'.

p. 243 *O Mary dear, three springs*: this seems to be some kind of recognition that his crucial severance from Mary occurred three years ago, i.e. in 1838, the year of her death.

E'en round her home I seek her there: the manuscript reads 'I seek her here'.

p. 246 *From bank to bank*: cf. 'The Flood', and 'Lolham Brigs'.

And there the ivy: MS omits 'the'.

p. 247 *Here's a health*: Burns's voice.

p. 251 *'Tis solitude in citys*: since it is Clare's practice to incorporate immediate current experience into his poem, this may be support for the view that Clare continued to write this sequence in Northampton, after 29 December 1841.

p. 255 *The Paigles Bloom* and *On the retireing solitudes of May* (next stanza): probably late spring/early summer, 1842.

p. 258 *The Happy Milk Maid . . . E'en Queens Might Sigh*: Clare later develops this distinction. See p. 305.

p. 261 *Mary would be in the mind*: in the manuscript, there is a blank before 'Mary'.

p. 263 *Mary and Martha*: emblems of two complementary aspects of woman as mate: romantic and domestic.

p. 266 *I hear the clapping gate*: this image is taken up again, offering a linking motif, in the first stanza of the continuation of 'Prison Amusements': see p. 282.

p. 267 *I am their like, a desert man*: cf. Byron: 'Oh! that the desert were my dwelling-place/With one fair spirit for my minister' (*Childe Harold's Pilgrimage*, Canto 4, stanza CLXXVII).

p. 268 *Martinmass*: November 1841.

p. 269 *Bastille*: a recurring motif in Clare's letters from Northampton.

p. 270 *Royce wood and Tenters Nook*: near Helpstone.

p. 272 *amaranthine bower*: the 'amarant' was a mythical everlasting flower; 'amaranths' were decorative flowers, e.g. love-lies-bleeding. The two terms were elided long ago.

June 1844: the Knight transcripts are in two or more hands; the punctuation is variable and often misguided; some poems are dated.

p. 273 *O wert thou in the storm*: modelled on Burns's 'O, wert thou in the cauld blast . . .'

p. 274 *A Vision*: in Clare's Northampton poetry, the poetry of seeing with the physical eye is gradually complemented, but never displaced, by a poetry of visionary seeing, beyond time and place.

fancied love: cf. his letter to Matthew Allen, in which he distinguishes between 'one of my fancys', i.e. Patty, and 'my poetical fancy', i.e. Mary (*Letters*, ed. Storey, p. 650).

p. 276 *Stanzas*: the title probably derives from Byron's 'Stanzas for Music'.

p. 281 *The Invitation*: the natural world is apprehended more and more through the ear as Clare ages; his eyes register a variety of vibrant movements that will not be still (this observation I owe to Tim Chilcott).

p. 282 *Prison Amusements*: I have supplied the title; MS 19 contains none, but the evidence of Clare's letters strongly supports the view that this is of a piece with the earlier sequence. Clare's text is preceded by a quotation from Cowper's 'The Task': 'O for a Lodge in some vast wilderness/Some boundless contiguity of shade/Where rumour of oppression and deceit/Of unsuccessful or successful war/

Might never reach me more'. There is a strong affinity between this and the last stanza of the previous sequence.

    The gate . . . then claps: see note to p. 266.

p. 283 *boyhood's secret*: a reference to Clare's first experience of terror or vastation: secret, because he had kept it to himself.

p. 284 *Ave Maria*: cf. Byron, *Don Juan*, Canto 3, stanza CII.

p. 286 *Hath time made no change*: the stanza pattern here breaks down and Clare shifts to rhyming couplets.

p. 289 *Pays in destruction*: cf. Byron, 'pays off moments in an endless shower/Of hell-fire . . .' (*Don Juan*, Canto 2, stanza CXCII).

p. 294 *Song*: most of the songs in this sequence are unsuccessfully rendered in the language of Burns, but there was not enough iron in Clare's soul to maintain a Burnsian tone.

p. 295 *the old stone wall*: this stanza is followed by this quatrain: 'Verses on Olney: A charm is thrown o'er Olney plains/By Cowper's rural muse/While sunshine gilds the river Ouse/In morning's meadow dews.'

p. 297 *That loved the many all alike*: Clare acknowledges that many young women have attracted his affections/aroused his desires. He rushes to redeem himself in the last line of the stanza.

p. 298 *Yet 'Man was made to mourn'*: cf. Burns, 'Man was made to Mourn'.

    The pheasant's nest: the manuscript reads 'peasants'. 'Yardley Oak' was one of Cowper's most celebrated poems; it included a recognition of the claims of Fancy over Reason that Clare would himself endorse.

p. 304 *Where are the citys*: cf. the reference to Sodom, p. 249. Clare's interest in the fate of Sodom is not merely a case of his growing fascination with the vision of some apocalyptic destruction, but also derives specifically from the fascinated revulsion which the perverse sexuality of some of the inmates at High Beech seems to have aroused in him.

    Following this stanza is a song which I omit from this selection. It is dated 15 February 1845.

p. 305 *O for one real . . . blessing*: in this stanza and those that follow, Clare explores the various types of women that had aroused his feelings and desires; starting with the paradox of 'real imaginary' and 'Ideal real', he lays bare his own erotic susceptibility. As on p. 258, the thought of milkmaids – pastoralized innocence or a tumble in the hay – is associated with the converse type, the queen, via gypsy wench and beggar girls.

p. 306 *Sweet as Queen's portraits*: these would have appeared in all the shop-windows of Northampton, in November 1844, when Queen Victoria made a progress through the town on her way to Burghley House. Triumphal arches were erected, and Clare was allocated a seat near one.

With bonny bosom: this stanza vividly demonstrates the peculiar vulnerability of Clare's unedited texts. Without punctuation, it seems to be incoherent nonsense; but when we recognize that toward the end of the second line Clare turns away from the milkmaid, to apostrophize the Queen, as if addressing her from his seat in the stands, his lines begin to make good rhetorical sense. What, then, does he tell the Queen? That the 'jewels' of nature's dew and showers are to be preferred to the lavish worldly jewels of courtly display: 'from nature's glory' = from comparison with . . . The last line of the stanza can be construed as addressed to the Queen, or as Clare's return to the milkmaid, or even as both.

p. 310 *The first-loved face is met*: the transcript reads: 'The first love face . . .'

p. 311 *none cares or knows*: it seems that no member of his family ever visited him in Northampton.

p. 313 *And where is the voice*: the transcript reads: '& where is voice'.

p. 314 *Hesperus*: cf. Byron, *Don Juan*, Canto 4, stanza CVII.

p. 316 *warm and erie*: i.e. eerie in its first meaning, of fearful or timid.

p. 320 *The objects seen*: the MS reads 'seem', but the syntax and sense require 'seen'.

p. 330 *round the cote*: the MS reads 'coat'.

p. 334 *Through this sad non-identity*: identity is a recurring subject of Clare's reflections. Here he recognizes that a secure sense of one's own identity rests on being recognized by others, and that the breakdown of relationships can render one's own sense of identity insecure. Cf. Mrs Gaskell: 'A solitary life cherishes mere fancies until they become manias.'

p. 337 *I'll gaze upon thy bosom's swell*: the transcript offers 'thy blossom's well'; the feebleness of the image and of the adverb can serve to alert us to an act of bowdlerizing. I have taken the liberty of offering a conjectural restoration of Clare's most probable words.

p. 341 *And my love lives at the 'White Hart'*: Clare addressed some of his Northampton poems, like letters, to specific young women; in this case, Mary Ludgate, to whom he wrote a loving letter in code, addressing her as his 'dear daughter'. She lived at the White Hart Inn, Cotton End, and had conceivably drawn a pint for him.

p. 351 *She tied up her few things*: Clare recalls an important part of the traditional agricultural year: young people went to hiring fairs or statutes, in search of employment. Here the girl has reached the term of her contract and is returning home, for a short break, before hiring herself out again.

p. 358 *The Winter's Come*: the first line contains the only figure of speech that Clare derived from Northampton's staple industry – the manufacture of boots and shoes. Clare would have read Dante in the translation by his friend, H. F. Cary: Clare wrote to Cary in October 1832, after Cary had offered him philosophical consolation following the move to Northborough. Burton's *Anatomy of Melancholy* enjoyed an enthusiastic revival in the early nineteenth century, largely owing to the advocacy of Charles Lamb.

These stanzas appear in a manuscript of 1850; Clare was still extending, albeit more sporadically, his 'Prison Amusements' sequence.

p. 361 *To John Clare*: this poem is dated 10 February 1860, and raises the question: to *which* John Clare? His son, John, was born 16 June 1826, and would be thirty-three, but Clare no longer reckoned the years.

the new number just laid down: chapmen – men who bought a stock of chapbooks, ballads, broadsides from provincial publishers – hawked them from village to village. One of Clare's manuscripts was entitled 'Halfpenny Ballads'. The stock-in-trade of the chapmen was a variety of traditional romances and truncated versions of popular novels. See Geoffrey Summerfield, *Fantasy and Reason*, Chapter 2, Methuen/Georgia University Press, 1985, and George Deacon, *op. cit.*, pp. 34ff.

GLOSSARY

a	at, in, or on; as in a bed, a row, a church
agen	against; variant spelling of again
ariff	goosegrass
aw(e)	haw
ayont	beyond
Ball	traditional name for a plough-ox or a cart-horse
bate	to harass
batter	to wear, trample
baulk	grass strip separating ploughed fields
bedight	decorated
bee-fly	a fly that resembles a bee
bee-spell	the pattern in a glass marble, which resembled a swarm of bees, more clearly seen when it was wetted by licking
bent	grass-stalk
a-benting	running to seed
besprent	to sprinkle, to make to glitter
bevering	taking refreshment, time out from work to take food and drink

bield	shelter
blea	bleak
bleb	drop, blob, bubble
bottle	bottle-shaped blossom
bottly	bottle-shaped
brake	fern
brawl	to bawl, shout
brawn	boar; male prostitute
brere	briar
brig	bridge
brunt	to burst through, push
brustle	to rustle; bustle
bumbarrel	long-tailed tit
by times	betimes
carlock	charlock
cat-gallows	home-made hurdle made of sticks
cawdymawdy	gull
checkering	patterned like a chequer-board
chelp	to chirp; chatter
chicker	to chirp
chitter	to chirp
chock	to pitch marbles
chock-hole	a hole in the ground into which to pitch marbles
cirging	surging
clack	chatter
clam	to be enfeebled from hunger

clamm	clamp
clap	to set on
clink	a sharp blow
clink and bandy-chock	a game of marbles
clock-a-clay	a ladybird
clodhopper	wheatear or whinchat
clomb, clumb	climbed
closen	small enclosed fields (an old plural ending)
clout	to clothe, to clog; to stud, patch, repair
clown	a rustic
clutter	to make a clatter, to bustle
cowslap	cowslip
cowslap-peeps	cowslip blossoms
crab	crab apple
crank	twisted; croaking
crankle	to twist
creepy	narrow, constricting
crim. con.	adultery (criminal conversation)
crimple	to wrinkle or ruffle
crizzle	to begin to freeze
croodle	to shrink from cold
crook	to wander
crow-flower	buttercup or ragged robin
crumble	small crumb

crump	to crunch, as crisp snow underfoot
cuck	to throw for someone to catch
cuck a ball	May-game ball, made of flowers
cuckoo	cuckoo-flower, an orchis
curdle	to ripple or bubble
cuts	woodcut illustrations
dab	to strike
daffies	daffodils
dimute	diminutive
dizen	adorned
dock	common dock, antidote for nettle-stings
Doll	conventional milkmaid's name
dotterel	pollarded tree
dowie	dreary
drabble	to trail in the wet; to soak
drowk	to droop
duck and drake	children's game, in which flat stones or pieces of slate are made to skim and bounce on water
ducking stone	the stone to be knocked off the top of a pile, in a children's game
elting	soft and damp, as when freshly turned by the plough
enarmourd	enamoured and/or armoured

enew	enough
erie	fearful, nervous
fernowl	nightjar
finweed	rest-harrow
firdale	fir-tree
firetail	redstart
flag	wild iris
flaze	flare, smoking flame
flirt	to flutter, flit
flit	to move house
flusker	to fly off suddenly
fodder/fother	to feed stock
fountain	spring
frail	flail
frit	frightened
gadders	agitation of animals provoked by the gad-fly
gale	breeze
gang	to go
gelid	jelly-like
gen	against
gin	trap
glabber	to chatter, gabble
gleans (noun)	gleanings
glib	smooth, slippery
goss	gorse
grain	large branch

grub	to uproot, dig out
grubble	to grasp greedily
gulled	hollowed
headache	poppy
hen and chickens	children's game of pursuit
hep	hip
hing	to hang
hirkle	to crouch down against cold winds
hirple	to limp, to crouch
hisn	his
hist (noun)	hissing
home-close	enclosed pasture near the house
hugh	huge
hurd	to hoard
huzz	to rush noisily
jetty	jet-black
jilt	to throw fast
jockolate	phonetic version of chocolate
joll	to lurch
keck	hollow dried stalk of umbelliferous plant
kink about	to shake, as with laughter
knap	to nibble, browse
knarl	to nibble
knewt	newt
ladysmock	cuckooflower

lambtoe	bird's-foot trefoil
land	a division of arable ground
lap	to curl into a bundle
lare	to rest in hiding or shelter
ling	heather
link	measure
list'	to listen to
loose	to lose
lunge	to lurch
majoram	marjoram
massy	massive
mealy	dappled; as clouds, or lichen on bark
mere mark	boundary marker, especially for edge of fen
mizled	wet with rain
molewarp/mouldiwarp	mole (earth-thrower)
mortared	lined with mud
morts of	many
mun	must
nine peg morris	traditional country game played with pegs
oddling	odd one; solitary
paigle	cowslip
peep	see cowslap
pelitory	masterwort or sneezewort
perk	to sit up, stretch, come to attention

pettichap	chiffchaff
pill	to peel, strip bark
pindar, pinder	one who collects and impounds stray animals
pinfold	pound
pink	chaffinch
pismire	ant
plat(t)	smooth level surface, as a lawn
pleachy	bleached
poesy	both posy (of flowers) and poetry
pooty	snail; its shell
popple	poplar
pranking	lively, restless
prevade	to pervade
princess feather tree	lilac
prog	to poke or prod
protentious	portentous
prove	to solve
prune	to preen
puddock	kite or buzzard
pudge	puddle
pudgy	soaked in puddles
quaking	cawing raucously
ramp	to grow rampantly; to make a commotion; to rush
rawky	misty

reak	to hang or rise like steam
reciept	recipe
ride	open grassy track in woodland
rig	ridge
rock	to sway
roil	to seethe, to make angry, to agitate
roll	roller for making soil level
rosey	rose-coloured (*adj.*); rose (*noun*)
rotten	rotten timber
rout	route; lively activity
sawn	to saunter
scrat	to scratch
scrawl	to scramble, clamber
screed	strip of land
scrip	bag, wallet, satchel
scrowed	marked with lines
seam	strip of land with water on both sides
seemly	seemingly
shepherd's purse	a common cruciferous weed
shieling	rough wooden building
shill	shrill
shoaf	sheaf
shool	to shuffle, saunter
shoon	shoes

sinkfoil	cinquefoil, potentilla
skewish	shying
sluther	to slither
snuff/snuffbox	nose; vagina
snuft	to sniff
soodle	to saunter, dawdle
sooth (adj.)	true, genuine
sprent	sprinkled
sprotes	twigs, firewood
sputter	to move fast, causing a commotion
startle	to start suddenly, shoot out
steamer	steam-boat
stoven	tree-stump
stowk	stook, shock, of wheat
streak	to stretch
strinkle	to sprinkle
strown	strewn
struttle	sticklebacks or similar small fry
stuffing-thorns	bunch of hawthorn twigs used to stuff a hole in a hedge
stulp	tree-stump
stunt	stunted
sturt	to start suddenly
sue	to sigh
suther	to make rushing sounds
swail	shade

swaily	shady
swath	row of scythed hay, left to dry out
swathed	covered, clothed
swathy	dry, as of swath; or swarthy
swea, swee	to swing, sway
swift	lizard
swiver	to hover, flutter
swop	to swoop
taw	marble, as in children's game; often of clay
teem	to pour
then	than
thorn	thornbush
throstle	song-thrush
thurrow	furrow
totter-grass	quaking-grass
touchwood tree	a tree diseased by fungus
trace	to walk along or through
trap	guardian, warder
tray	hurdle
trepid	trembling, nervous
turk	a sadist
tutle	to tootle
twank	to twang
twitch	couch grass
tyke	churl
uggle	to cuddle

varified	variegated
watchet	sky-blue
water-blab	marsh marigold
wew, whew	to rush through the air; to call (bird)
whemble	to turn topsy-turvy
while	until
wift	whiff, puff
wildered	wild, uncultivated
wilding	wild flower, esp. rose
wop	to thrash, beat
yaum	a length of thatch-straw
yclad	clothed
yoe	ewe
younker	youngster

INDEX OF FIRST LINES

I envy e'en the fly its gleams of joy 356
I feel I am, I only know I am 311
I hid my love when young while I 352
I long to think of thee in lonely midnight 308
I lost the love of heaven above 274
I love at eventide to walk alone 62
I love it well, o'ercanopied in leaves 57
I love the fitfull gust that shakes 329
I love the awthorn well 299
I love to see the old heath's withered brake 74
I never pass a venerable tree 179
I peeled bits o' straws and I got switches too 353
I saw her in my spring's young choice 264
I seek her in the shady grove, 278
I sleep with thee and wake with thee 276
I think of thee at early day 251
I went in the fields with the leisure I got, 211
I wish I was where I would be 285
I wish I was where I would be 351
I'll come to thee at eventide 357
In the cowslip's peeps I lye 343
In this cold world without a home 254
In thy wild garb of other times 83
Infants' graves are steps of angels where 272
It is the evening hour, 275
I've left mine own old home of homes 198
I've loved thee Swordy Well and love thee still 82
I've wandered many a weary mile 225
Just by the wooden brig a bird flew up 104
Leaves from eternity are simple things 158
Let us go in the fields love and see the green tree 281
Little trotty wagtail he went in the rain 343
Love is a secret 272
Love lies beyond 313
Lovely Mary when we parted 233
Lover of swamps 111
Maid of Walkherd, meet again, 211
Many are May time is to the meadows coming in 52
Many are poets – though they use no pen 222
Midsummer's breath gives ripeness to the year 148
Musing beside the crackling fire at night, 45
My old lover left me I knew not for why 356
No single hour can stand for nought 238

INDEX OF TITLES

398